the films of
Alan

THE CITADEL PRESS

Ladd

by Marilyn Henry and Ron DeSourdis

SECAUCUS · N.J.

For Lou Valentino, a dear friend and a friend to all movie buffs, whose aid, counsel, and encouragement were not only invaluable, but also absolutely necessary to the success of this venture; and to Bob Harman, whose enthusiasm, generosity, and kindness kept the project underway.

ACKNOWLEDGMENTS

Lou Valentino, Bob Harman, Eric Benson, John Cocchi, Beverly Linet, Ernie Shepherd, Art Dodge, Bob Harrington, Bob Johnson, Art Mc-Clure, Richard Bojarski, Loraine Burdick, Tony Matthews, Don Pellow, Gene Maiden, Marge Meisinger, Fred McFadden, Richard Hayes, Ray Pence, George Ulrich, Dale Manesis, Greg Revak, Ed Agustus, Gary Punswick, Arthur Tonna, Joe and Betty Gomes, Lloyd Nolan, Teet Carle, Howard da Silva, Virginia Mayo, Gordon Douglas, Lizabeth Scott, Noah Beery, Jr., Robert Preston, Richard Webb, Wanda Hendrix, Sue Carol Ladd, the American Film Institute, the Memory Shop, Eddie Brandt's Saturday Matinee, Movie Star News, Film Favorites, Paramount Pictures, Modern Sound Pictures, Telewide Systems, Boston Public Library, Worchester Public Library, Evansville Public Library, the University of Wisconsin Film Archives, and friends Howard Schweig, Skip Bawell, Marilyn Durham, Ewing Dupont, Mac MacGregor, and George Zeno.

DESIGNED BY LESTER GLASSNER

First edition

Copyright © 1981 by Marilyn Henry and Ron DeSourdis
All rights reserved
Published by Citadel Press
A division of Lyle Stuart Inc.
120 Enterprise Ave., Secaucus, N.J. 07094

In Canada: Musson Book Company
A division of General Publishing Co. Limited
Don Mills, Ontario

Manufactured in the United States of America by
Halliday Lithograph, West Hanover, Mass.

Library of Congress Cataloging in Publication Data

Henry, Marilyn.
    The films of Alan Ladd.
    I. Ladd, Alan.   I. DeSourdis, Ron.   II. Title.
PN2287.L13H4   791.43′028′0924   81 4997
ISBN 0-8065-0736-5
                                    AACR 2

CONTENTS

Introduction

I first met Alan Ladd at Paramount studios in the cast of *Wild Harvest* in August 1947. The cast was a good group: Dorothy Lamour, Robert Preston, Allen Jenkins, Tony Caruso; and the director was that wonderful ex-newspaperman Tay Garnett.

The picture was shot under not-so-usual circumstances—a studio strike was threatened by one of the branches of studio workers, and if a picket line were thrown up around the studio, our picture would have to close down. To eliminate this possibility, the chief members of the cast were asked to live at the studio. Spending five or six days glued together on a hot set, having three meals a day at the same long table in the commissary, yakking over drinks until bedtime— you either became close friends or you collected some new enemies. Alan and I became friends— and stayed that way.

Alan's home was just about the halfway point between Hollywood and my home, and hardly a week went by that I didn't drop in for a quick one. I never had any fear of intruding, for Alan loved company, friends—though he was shy of strangers and avoided crowds. His dislike of crowds was well founded. The impression that Alan stood at least six-feet-plus was so successfully imprinted on the public mind that when someone met him for the first time it came as a shock and prompted involuntary exclamations that, understandably, wounded Alan's pride.

And this leads to a story. Alan was extremely sentimental. In September 1956, my wife, Mell, and I flew from Rome to Athens. We heard that Alan and Sue were staying at the Grand Bretagne Hotel, and we decided to run over and surprise them. When Alan opened the door we expected whoops, laughter—instead, he took one look at us, burst into tears, threw his arms around my neck, and sobbed. It took a minute before I could unpeel him with the plea that we were exhausted (we had just got in and hadn't even been to our own hotel room yet) and could he pour us a drink? He calmed down and poured the drinks, and we had a heartwarming reunion.

Later, back at the Palace Athenae, makeup man Henry Villardo brought us up to date on the cause of Alan's emotional outburst. Hating to travel, Alan had been coaxed away from his fortress, his home in Holmby Hills, to go to Athens to star in *Boy on a Dolphin* with some little-known Italian actress named Sophia Loren and to be guided by a director he didn't know. When he arrived he found that the actress was several inches taller than he was and so bountifully equipped in features and figure that she was certain to make fifty percent of any two-shot a waste of film. Added to that, the director, Jean Negulesco, had already become quite interested in her. They had been shooting for six weeks under these unpromising conditions, with one more week to go, and Alan was miserable.

Mell and I departed Athens to tour Greece and met the Ladds several weeks later in Naples. Alan wasn't feeling good. He loved highly spiced food; his stomach did not. (He had had ulcers for years.) The result was many sleepless nights in pain. I don't doubt that his delicate digestion contributed to his early death.

Alan possessed to a high degree a quality that I've seen equaled by only two other stars: Rita Hayworth and Gary Cooper. None of the three were superb actors or technicians, but all had the ability to make a quite ordinary scene become—when projected on a screen—a thing of sensitive beauty and strength. I believe that this gift was what made Alan the sensational screen star he was.

He was a good friend, and I valued that friendship. I miss him very much.

LLOYD NOLAN

ALAN LADD
The Legend and the Life

His features, unlike Bogart's or Raft's, were nearly perfect. His eyes, in their heavy-lidded insolence, could pick up on a dame's curves or the furtive movements of a thug's hands with equal ease. His body moved with an animal grace that gave the impression that he knew exactly what he was doing and never wasted any motion doing it.

His deep, smooth voice could go steel hard and make grown men tremble or turn husky-warm and make grown women quiver. His romantic technique ran from wry cockiness to a calculated indifference, with never a hint of promises given or kept.

He was aloof, self-sufficient, occasionally lonely, and sometimes outside the law.

His aura was one of great cool, of a forceful, masculine presence with a strong undercurrent of violence and heavy sex appeal. He was one of the last of an almost extinct species: the genuine, full-blown, one hundred percent born-to-it *movie star*.

That's how the fans who went to the movies in the 1940s saw Alan Ladd.

On first look Ladd would seem to be an unlikely candidate for superstardom. Little of his sexy, hard-edged, loner quality seemed to be part of his real-life self. He was quite small and blond in an era when neither quality could be considered an asset to a leading man. Away from the camera, he had an eager, boyish sort of grin and a reserved, courteous manner that was in direct contrast to everything he was on screen. He did not carouse, play the horses, or chase starlets. He was, in fact, something of a square. None of this mattered to his fans, however, for on screen he was one of a kind, an electric personality.

The camera can sometimes perform strange feats, can take a perfectly nice, harmless, hardworking guy and turn him into a rugged, explosive, he-man star. (It can even achieve the opposite effect, as witness the letdown of Richard Burton's first rushes in Hollywood.) What comes through on camera may be something scarcely there in person, but in the world of Hollywood stardom, only the camera counts.

In a May 1970 *Show* magazine article, Dirk Bogarde, discussing his own long love affair with the camera, relates a story about Ladd that seems to say it all: Ladd, coming into the studio commissary after a morning on the set, is greeted by his drinking buddies, who try to send him up with a mocking, "And what did you do on the set this morning, Alan?"

Ladd picks up his drink, takes a swallow, gives it the proper pause, and answers straight-faced, "I did a great look."

Ladd, Bogarde insists, knew all about a great look and how to use one.

his Christmas party in November. From the whole world, letters poured in and presents by the carload, but it was Alan Ladd who visited that bedside and joked and sang and tried to make a little boy's last Christmas his merriest. That's the side of Laddie people so rarely seek or expect. The Laddie who gets all tangled up trying to explain how beautiful and warm and unbelievable his and Sue's love is. Who candidly admits he has no other interest save the movies and that he loves "double bills and the stinkers, too." "Pictures can help the whole world get closer together," he frowns. "Love is love wherever you put it, with simple stories that every nation understands." So even though he won't admit it ("I was a dummy in school!"), Laddie's a brain boy. It takes careful planning to do those ruthless, dead-pan killers of his, do them so well he gets five secretaries' worth or three-fifths of all of Paramount's fan mail. But still he won't push. Has a 7-year contract with no concessions which means he can't refuse to do a picture "like some of the big stars—guess Paramount wants to keep me on the hard side." Ever since that first-time-ever-to-see-a-movie, Alana's a trifle confused over her reel and real Daddies. Caught a glimpse of him slugging it out on the screen, reached out one uncertain hand to stroke his cheek and finally triumphantly crowed, "Daddy here!" Laddie's local board can't decide whether to let him fight the war by toting a gun again or by moving-making, but however, we've a champ on our side who knows what he's talking about when he says, "What we need is breaks for good people."

Alan Ladd

A movie camera is a monstrous thing, picking up on the most intimate detail with a ruthless eye. Ladd knew how to give the camera exactly what was needed, those telling nuances of expression which would be completely lost to a theater's first row of seats. The lift of a brow, the play of muscle in a jaw, the curl of a lip, and most of all, the eyes—these are a movie actor's tools, and Ladd knew how to make the most of them.

This is not to say that his range was particularly versatile. Ladd was incapable of exaggerated gestures or emotions. After he became a star he was nearly always the taciturn tough guy. To see him in an early film such as *Joan of Paris*, in which he had a near-maudlin death scene, is rather startling if one is familiar only with the later Ladd. He was good in *Joan of Paris*, but without the tough guy buildup he might very well have wound up playing nice, pal-to-the-hero parts and never caused a breath of excitement. In fact, he played many brief

As Raven, his most famous early role.

nice-guy roles before he landed the part that turned his life around.

One critic, after seeing Ladd's first hit, *This Gun for Hire*, wondered how such a "spectacular personality as Alan Ladd could have gone unnoticed for so long." The explanation would seem simple. Ladd was incredibly handsome, and when he played juveniles, nice college boys, and spoiled heirs, he simply looked the part and nothing much happened. But cast that clean-cut boy against type, glaze those expressive eyes with a crazed, unblinking stare, flatten the boyish grin to a humorless quirk of the lips, draw the vital, athletic energy into a coiled tension, and something unexpected happens—a blazing screen miracle. He couldnt' miss.

Though the critics were seldom long on praise for Ladd's acting abilities, one must consider: For a small, shy, self-effacing, moody young man to come across on screen as a hard, cynical, sexy, self-contained tough guy—isn't that some acting job? The movies might be routine, the scripts short on characterization and motivation; yet Ladd was always in character. When he was on screen you didn't look at anyone else. He had the natural actor's gift for make-believe, and he could catch you up in it.

Young film buffs who are discovering Ladd for the first time will find an odd kinship between his early portrayals and the sort of antihero that has become popular in the last twenty-five years. Rebellious youths, men who make their own rules, loners who face impossible odds and win—such types are familiar to any fan who followed Ladd's career.

The critics—and our parents—worried about the effect Ladd's violent movies had on American youth. Bosley Crowther, who had written a glowing review of Ladd's performance in *This Gun for Hire*, followed the review with some carefully worded doubts: "It is no gross exaggeration to say that Mr. Ladd has been the hottest new actor to hit pictures since Clark Gable or, maybe, Tyrone Power. . . . And it is apparently his tight-lipped violence his fans love—especially the kids—his neo-Chicago-gangster toughness combined with a touch of pathos. Is it that youngsters see in him some vague implication of themselves? . . . Do they see imaged in him their own insecurities, s sympathetic rebel against the problems and confusions of modern youth? And do they find vicarious pleasure in his recourse to violence? The old-fashioned gangster in movies has been passé for quite some time. But Mr. Ladd is a new sort of gangster—a moral gangster. There is despair in him."

Those words of Crowther's appeared in the *New York Times* in 1943. Throughout the 1940s Ladd played that semi-moral gangster type, unable to break away from the typecasting that had catapulted him to fame. The critics, who had gathered to proclaim him the screen's most promising new actor after the success of *This Gun for Hire*, began to be concerned about his antiestablishment attitude and to make cracks about his "stone face" and side-of-the-mouth delivery. Crowther led the pack, never writing another flattering review of a Ladd film until *Shane*, and even then he didn't like to give Ladd too much credit.

Possibly the critics' lukewarm appraisal had more to do with Ladd's publicity than with any assessment of his acting. Bogart seemed to revel in living the tough, hard-drinking, nonconforming cynic he played on the screen, and rebels such as Robert Mitchum and Marlon Brando have made a game out of being *persona non grata* to the press. The press has liked them better for it. To treat acting as if it were a silly profession and embarrassing to a real man—that's the way the other tough guys managed to gain respectability.

It also helped if they got into brawls or tangled with the police now and then. There was always that possibility that Bogart or Mitchum actually was as tough as he seemed on screen—but there was never any doubt in Ladd's case. He was acting at being tough, and it was a role he left behind on the sound stage. He was a rebel only on film.

Ladd was thoroughly pleased at being a big movie star, and he made no secret of it, telling anyone who would listen how grateful he was to his wife, his fans, his studio, his friends. Hard-working and ambitious, he seemed also to be a faithful husband and a model father. In fact, there was practically nothing for the gossips to chew over—no secrets, no vices, no temperament, nothing even slightly scandalous.

He might be tame; yet a star of his magnitude had

to have publicity, so Ladd and his wife, Sue Carol, encouraged the fan magazines. It is easy to say that this was a mistake, that it cooled Ladd's mysterious screen quality, but Sue had been his agent before becoming his wife, and she had worked so hard at promoting Ladd to stardom that she may have felt any publicity was good publicity. It seemed to work—the fans loved him no matter what the magazines wrote.

What they wrote was cloying fluff about the Ladds' perfect marriage and ideal family life, printed along with dozens of photos of Ladd hugging his wife and kids and beaming that boyish grin—none of which had anything to do with the virile, tough-guy façade his studio was building for him. All through his career, Ladd's reel self was at war with his real self. One had only to read articles with such titles as "The Alan Ladds' Million-dollar Recipe for Marriage" or "Her Heart Belongs to Laddie" (Sue's, that is), to wonder whether one should take him seriously at all.

Nevertheless, the fans took him seriously enough at the box office. Not one of his Paramount pictures ever lost money, and many of them finished in their given year's list of top moneymakers. He was a goldmine for Paramount and so popular that a week's fan mail could amount to twenty thousand letters.

That kind of success can be off-putting to those critics who do not care to use the words *art* and *money* in a common breath. To these skeptics Ladd was merely a parody of violence and toughness, a case of mass bad taste. Even after he gave what director George Stevens described as "one of the classic performances on the screen" in *Shane*, some critics were unwilling to revise their opinions. This lack of prestige in his chosen profession, along with the cruel jokes about his size, became the bane of his existence.

For some reason Alan Ladd's name seems to have become synonymous with short. Mention Ronald Colman, George Raft, Charles Boyer, John Garfield, James Cagney, Edward G. Robinson, Bing Crosby, Claude Rains, Mario Lanza, Humphrey Bogart, and there is no similar reaction, though all were below the five-foot-nine inch mark—some well below.

Lack of height seems to be of little interest where today's leading men are concerned. Dustin Hoffman, Richard Dreyfuss, Robert Blake and Jack Nicholson are all well under average stature; yet they do not bother to cover their size in any way that might suggest they consider it a detriment.

Perhaps in Ladd's case it was his studio's secrecy and anxiety about his height that exaggerated it once it became known. Paramount disguised Ladd's lack of inches with all sorts of manipulation, from scaling down the sets to laying planks around the set for him to walk and stand upon.

Ladd did what he had to do because the studio said it was necessary, but it isn't hard to imagine what it cost him in pride and self-esteem. He developed an excessive sensitivity concerning his height and disliked making personal appearances because of it.

Most small men compensate, often by developing aggressive personality traits. With Ladd it was an iron will and a determination to *be* somebody. He tackled every new challenge with a competitive thoroughness that bordered on obsession, whether it was learning to dive, dance, act, or play golf. Ladd was quoted as saying, "I have to get ninety percent of my work down to reflexes." This was a technique left over from Ladd's days as a swimming and diving competitor. His coach would have him spend hours just bouncing on the diving board without going into the water, sometimes until his feet would be bleeding from the rough coconut matting. But when he had the approach down perfectly he found he could soar into the pool, giving all his concentration to what happened in the air, to what was most important.

Able to laugh at himself, Ladd could not bear to have others laugh at him—which is true of most of us, but in the acting profession that fear can swell to the proportions of neurosis. Shyness stems from self-awareness, from the nervous idea that everyone is watching you. Actors are often shy and hope to hide behind make-believe.

The need to prove himself, to make himself more acceptable to the world, was a compulsion even in Ladd's youth. He was a simple man made complex by childhood poverty, thwarted boyhood dreams, adult rejection, family tragedy. Later this was turned upside-down by the mobs of fans, the interviews and picture posing, and the sudden wealth. With such shifts in fortune, it would be difficult for anyone to get a secure grasp on one's identity.

Ladd seemed to have everything—fame, money, luck, looks, loving fans, and a supportive family—yet these were not enough to save him from himself. In his middle years, when his looks began to go and the jokes about his size and his stone face turned more vicious, all his old insecurities and fears returned to haunt him, hastening his decline into alcoholism in the late 1950s. What we sensed all along, even in the lackluster films, was brought to fruition. There was tragedy in the man.

Ladd was the only tough guy who was also a matinee idol. The critics were usually men, and men apparently saw him as a Johnny-one-note, a personality whose pictures were mainly actioners with plenty of fights and side-of-the-mouth dialogue. But there was much more to Ladd than that. They should have asked a woman.

It wasn't just that he was handsome; it was the *way* he was handsome. Ladies who were used to the tall, dark, suave charmers found in Ladd a very different sort of dream man.

To begin with there was that remarkable coloring— dark, heavy brows and tanned skin making a startling contrast with the sun-streaked blond hair. He had a well-shaped head, save for a tendency to jowliness, and his sensitive features were dominated by gray-green eyes that photographed darker than they were. Because the pupils

were nearly half covered by the upper lids, he had a sultry, disquieting gaze, at once aloof and insinuating.

Ladd's good looks didn't stop at the neck. He was a superb athlete with an impressive array of sleek, tanned muscles, which Paramount took every opportunity to expose. The insertion of one scene in which Ladd stripped to the waist became almost obligatory in a Ladd film. Tay Garnett, who directed him in several action films, once described Ladd as "an Atlas in miniature." James Mason, who co-starred with Ladd in *Botany Bay*, was quoted as commenting that Ladd "had the exquisite co-ordination and rhythm of an athlete, which made it a pleasure to watch him when he was being at all physical."*

Even Ladd's hands were attractive. Never hurried, never awkward, those lean fingers could reach up, snag a cigarette from a pocket, flash out a lighter, snap it into flame, and light up—all in one neat, controlled motion. He always wore the same jewelry—an ID bracelet and a chain ring—which became as closely identified with Ladd as the silver whistle was with Lauren Bacall.

Beyond these elements, the looks, the voice, the physical grace, the most significant facet of his appeal was an attitude he projected. On screen his manners—or lack

The Films of James Mason, Clive Hirschhorn, Citadel, 1977.

of them—were designed to inspire awe, even fear. When he seemed most withdrawn, females found him most sexually attractive. He appeared to be the sort of man a woman could never take for granted. He didn't trust most people, and he particularly didn't trust women. He could give a woman a look that said loud and clear, "I can't be kidded, baby, so don't try." Like Bob Mitchum, he seemed impervious to a woman's less subtle machinations.

This was infinitely fascinating to the millions of women watching that shadow on the screen, aching for the chance to break through that tough shell and assuage his loneliness, to show him how true love could warm his heart and, incidentally, rechannel his ruthlessness. What he required was the *right* woman—and every woman in the audience secretly imagined she was it. Men saw only his cool facade. Women glimpsed the fire beneath—or thought they did!

There was also a hint of something deeper and less defined—a melancholy, a sensitivity, a vulnerability. If any of his 1940s scripts had allowed this other side to show to any real degree, Ladd might have developed as a stronger actor and attained the stature of a true immortal of the screen. Without it, his tough-guy image has little dimension.

There were hints of Ladd's other side in *This Gun for Hire*, where he played the kind of killer who "succeeded in reducing murder to an act as irrelevant as crossing the street," as Richard Schickel described it. Raven might be cold, but he is reached by the pity of the pretty blond girl, and it is clear that her sympathy both confuses and frightens him, even while it softens him. There was a touch of this quality in *Whispering Smith*, more than a hint in *The Great Gatsby*, and finally, with the gentle gunman of *Shane*, we see it come to full flower.

It is easy to blame Paramount for the one-dimensional Ladd image, but Paramount was, after all, in business, and Ladd was the only he-man type they had out of a studio full of bland leading men. So they spiked his films with plenty of fights, chases, and tough talk and allowed very little screen time for developing in-depth characterizations. Even his lovemaking was perfunctory. Ladd usually got the girl (though you didn't automatically assume he was altar-bound), but the pairing often occurred at the end, without much preliminary courtship.

In the old star system, scripts were tailored to a star's screen image, and in Ladd's case, quality was often sacrificed to that end. It was a matter of giving the fans what they expected—and Paramount gaining big profits without too much investment. Top leading ladies, first-rate production people, expensive literary properties—who needed such extravagances, when all you really had to do to make big money was put the name *Ladd* on the marquees?

"The indestructible man," Darryl Zanuck once dubbed Ladd. "He stays on top in mediocre films. Imagine where he would be if he were cast in worthwhile and important ones."

Regardless of this, there are, to any true Ladd fan, many memorable screen moments in the career that spanned some thirty-odd years. . . .

Ladd, blond, boyish, eyes full of pain, struggling to hang on as his buddies in *Joan of Paris* watch him die. "Baby . . . ?" someone whispers, but it is too late . . . his boy's body slumps in their arms.

Dawn outlining a stark railroad bridge . . . the chatter of gunfire . . . a lone figure in a dark suit zigzagging across the planks, then finally making a wild leap onto the bed of a railroad car passing underneath and disappearing into a cloud of gritty smoke. That unforgettable chase in *This Gun for Hire*.

Blackness . . . the glitter of moonlight touching ripples in the river . . . a silent movement, then a glistening shoulder cutting the water cautiously and a blond head emerging with knife held firmly between teeth. A splash—and another of the enemy drifts to the bottom of the river in *China*.

Ladd, dapper, sleek, sitting in a New Orleans restaurant reading a racing tip sheet while his partner babbles on about a mobster who is on his way over to do them bodily harm. . . . Ladd's languid eyes sliding sideways to glance at the worried man, then calmly sliding back to the paper with an unconcern that amounts to dismissal. The quintessential Ladd, knowing, fearless, facing the odds with great style in *Salty O'Rourke*.

Rain falling on dark streets, puddles reflecting garish neon . . . a lone figure in a sodden trench coat trudging along until a small coupe pulls up alongside and a girl's voice calls, "You could get a lot wetter if you laid in the gutter. . . ." Ladd meets Lake in *The Blue Dahlia*.

A hand reaching up, taking the cigarette from the girl's numbed fingers . . . a husky voice speaking through a trail of smoke . . . "If I live long enough, I might get too crazy about you. . . ." Ladd mesmerizing a velvet-eyed Gail Russell in *Calcutta*.

The sounds of a wild party drifting on the night . . . a man alone, wearing a dinner jacket and a cloak of mystery, leaning on a terrace wall, staring out across the moonlit lake to the other shore where a green beacon winks on and off. . . . Gatsby, alive and just as Fitzgerald conceived him.

The buckskin-clad gunman, wounded arm held slack, guiding his horse inexorably into the distant meadow as a small boy's tear-stricken cry echoes off the mountains around him . . . "Shane . . . Shane, come back! . . ."

If the images grow a little dim after *Shane*, it is because the Ladd mystique began to fade after that.

Ladd left Paramount to seek a better deal with Warner Bros. For the first time he enjoyed script and cast approval. Weary of his perennial tough-guy act, he longed to let the world know he could do something besides pull down his hat and shoot straight. It would be too much to expect fans to accept an entirely different Ladd, but he hoped to soften and expand the old image. The familiar good-bad Ladd went noble and put his might firmly on the side of right. He traded in his old .32

ALAN LADD
IN PARAMOUNT PICTURES

Roscoe on a big Colt .45 and his snap-brimmed beaver or a neat Stetson. Alas, he was still pulling down his hat and shooting straight, but the claustrophobic alleyways and gray cityscapes had given way to open spaces and mountain vistas.

Once, his face had the smooth perfection of a diamond. Once, he had tremendous presence, a power, a vitality he generated even when motionless. With middle age came lines of character in the face, a softening of expression. Gone was the tension, the charismatic power. Oh, he could still call it up on occasion, but he was no longer able to demonstrate it simply by his presence. He remained tough and heroic but without those fascinating shades of gray in his image, he was just another good guy.

Perhaps it was the natural progression of things—and there are those fans who find his cowboy character most satisfying. And yet one remembers best the enigmatic Ladd of the 1940s, the trench-coated menace, the quiet, unemotional man of action who moved fast and deadly—and always alone.

In the fan magazines, Alan Ladd's life was most often compared to the Horatio Alger theme. Behind the scenes there were a few who wondered if perhaps it resembled instead the Faust legend.

Ladd was born in Hot Springs, Arkansas, on September 3, 1913, and his start in life was humble in the extreme. His mother had immigrated from England at the age of nineteen. His father, Alan Ladd, Sr., was an accountant who traveled a great deal and Alan could remember little about him except that he died when Alan was four. That left Ina Raleigh Ladd to deal with life and a small son the best way she could. She had no relatives in this country, and if her husband's relatives were around, there is no evidence that they gave her either aid or comfort. Alan could not recall any aunts or cousins or, in fact, any kinfolk at all.

At the age of five, Alan and a playmate were playing with matches one day and set fire to the apartment where he lived with his mother. Alan was unhurt, but all their belongings were destroyed. Ina took what money she had left and moved with her son to Oklahoma City. In later life, Alan would sometimes refer to himself as a dumb Okie kid. Oklahoma City was probably the first place he remembered clearly.

There was never much money, and Alan was already undernourished and undersized. He was miserable at school and related only to his mother. Then he had to learn to share her when she married a house painter named Jim Beavers.

Beavers decided to pack up his new family and set off for California, where he was sure he could find plenty of house-painting jobs. It took months in their beat-up

ALAN LADD
IN PARAMOUNT PICTURES

old Ford to travel the distance from Oklahoma to California. As Alan later described it, it was a journey straight out of *The Grapes of Wrath*, with everything they owned tied onto the top, sides, and back of the car. At night they pitched tents to sleep, and sometimes they had to pause several days while Beavers worked for enough money to buy gas. It was a very hand-to-mouth existence, one that left its mark on the young boy.

In Flagstaff, Arizona, the family ran out of money again and had to stop. Ina got a job in the kitchen of a large farm, and Alan and his stepfather went into the fields to work as hands. Alan was eight, and that was the first of a great many mean jobs he would have to take in order to live.

When they finally reached Pasadena, California, Alan had missed a good chunk of school and was old for his class, though still undersized. School continued to be an off-and-on prospect through the hard times; therefore, Alan eventually graduated from high school at the advanced age of twenty.

If California was the Promised Land, the promise was very modest. The family lived in a tent first, then a shack, and even shared a rented house, until Beavers finally got a job in Hollywood painting movie sets at the studios. By then the years of meager food and care caught up with Alan. A doctor advised the Beaverses to move the sickly boy to a place where there was fresh air and home-grown food. So once again they moved, this time to the San Fernando Valley, which was then scarcely settled. Alan had room to run and fresh oranges right off the trees, and his health improved, though he did not grow much.

Alan admitted in later years that he was a kid with a chip on his shoulder, ready to read insults into almost anything that was said to him. Small wonder—he had so little experience in playing with children his own age. His classmates dubbed him Tiny, a name he detested, though it stuck throughout the rest of his school days. By the time he reached high school, however, *Tiny* had become a term of friendly affection.

The odd jobs continued, paper-delivery routes, candy-store sweeping—"The guy used to count the candy when I'd leave, and I hated him for it"—fruit-picking jobs. At fourteen he worked in a grocery, washing vegetables and sacking. The only place he didn't work was at school; his marks were low. He stayed close to his folks and had few friends.

Then came high school, and a whole new world opened up to him. He discovered he had the makings of a first-rate athlete. Small he might be, but his wiry body was sleek with muscle, probably because of all those years of youthful labor. He went out for the track team, and he did the hundred-yard dash in 9.8 seconds and the two hundred in 20.2. When he took up swimming he was like a fish who had found a natural home. He spent hours every day practicing form and diving. He was president of the swim team and, by his junior year, president of his class. His accomplishments brought him a certain amount of admiration and acclaim. Young Ladd was developing into a friendly, personable charmer. His marks improved also.

He won medals and ribbons for swim meets and then

The high school swim team. Ladd is at far left. Even in those days he was small but mighty, with plenty of muscle power.

eft) With his
r, Ina Ladd
Beavers

A rare shot of young Ladd behind the counter of Tiny's Patio. Menu features "Tiny's special . . . 20¢."

Ladd at about seventeen or eighteen

became Southern California Diving Champion and established a new record for the fifty-yard interscholastic meet. By 1931, he had a top coach, Clyde Swenson, and was busy preparing for the 1932 Olympics with every good hope of making the team.

The coach insisted that Ladd stick to diving and forget other high school team sports. Alan was popular at Hollywood High, and it was a big temptation for him to be a hero for his school, so while the swim team was away on tour, Alan, who had to stay behind because he could not afford to travel, spent much of his time working out with the football team. When the coach returned and wanted Alan to show his ability, Alan was so out of practice that he hit his head on the board while trying an intricate dive. He lost his nerve, and Coach Swenson let him go—a heartbreak for a youngster who had come that close to the Olympics.

Alan discovered girls, and girls discovered him. "Tiny" Ladd took up a whirling social life, dating all the pretty girls and winning dance cups at local ballrooms. During his senior year, Alan joined the drama class and began to get a few parts in school productions. He had a fine voice and a poised manner on stage, and he was chosen to play KoKo in Gilbert and Sullivan's *The Mikado*. He was such a hit that he was singled out for special praise by critics on the local papers.

As KoKo in a high school Mikado.

Showing his diving prowess during a high school swim meet.

This led him to rush out and enroll when he hear
that Universal Studios was putting together a trainin
program for young actors and actresses in an effort t
cultivate new stars. Theoretically, it was a fine idea, bu
in practice the program didn't pan out, though they kep
Ladd four months—longer than many of his college
trained classmates (including Tyrone Power).

The Depression was keeping the Beavers at the povert
level, and Alan continued to work part-time, doing life
guard duty at the North Hollywood pool. Finally, i
1934, he graduated from high school. There wasn't mucl
question of college—he was needed at home to hel
support the family.

He found work as an ad salesman for a local throwaway
newspaper, the *Sun-Record*, and worked up to ad man
ager. While still at the paper he borrowed enough money
to open a small hamburger stand across the street fron
the pool at which he had been a lifeguard. He called th
place Tiny's Patio and brought his mother in to help ru
it. Ina had gone steadily downhill through the years o
hardship and had given up dreams of a better life. Sh
depended on liquor more and more to make life bearable
and her growing mental instability worried Alan.

Tiny's Patio did a fair business for a while, and Ala
quit the paper to run the café full time. It wasn't a ver
glamorous way to make a living, but he kept at it fo
a year until it became clear the place would never mak
much profit. He then sold out and went looking fo
other work.

During this time, he was courting a pretty youn
neighborhood woman Marjorie Jane Harrold, callec
Midge by her family and friends. Midge was a petit
blond from a well-off, respectable family. Although he
folks liked Alan well enough, they were not anxious fo
Midge to marry anyone with such a shaky financial fu
ture.

Alan got a job as a grip and general maintenance mar
at Warner Bros., at a salary that did not compensate fo
the dangers of working on high scaffolds over the sound
stages. Being that close to the movies started Ladd
dreaming again, and he soon quit Warners and took his
savings and enrolled in the Ben Bard School of Acting,
which did a lot of advertising. Studio talent scouts were
supposed to look in on the students there, but no one
noticed young Alan Ladd.

From time to time, Alan would get a bit role or some
work as a film extra. He and Midge eloped in October
1936 without telling their families, and after the ceremony they returned to their own homes, because Alan
had no way to support a wife. When Alan's stepfather
died of a heart attack that year, Alan moved into an
apartment shared by an old school chum.

How Alan survived during this period is virtually
unknown. He was evidently hanging around the studios,
occasionally getting small parts and also doing some
radio spots. Like a boy with his nose pressed to the
candy-store window, he saw the life of a movie actor as
something worth almost any sacrifice to attain. The
movie work was sporadic, and the radio jobs kept him

ting, though more often than not his diet consisted
of coffee and jelly donuts. Alan never did develop much
of a taste for big meals or gourmet dishes.

When Midge became pregnant, she and Alan had to
tell their families and hope for understanding. Alan's
mother was too buried in her own grief and alcoholic
despair to show much interest. Midge moved into the
shared apartment, and they made the best of things.

On October 22, 1937, Alan Ladd, Jr., was born. Alan
had a small apartment ready for them when Midge
brought the baby home from the hospital, but they had
little chance to be a family together before Ina Beavers
moved in with them, having no other place to go and
no income. It was an unhappy arrangement, and Alan
resented the money Ina spent on liquor.

That November, after a bitter quarrel, Ina killed herself by swallowing ant paste. Alan witnessed her ago-
nizing death and never fully recovered from the shock.
Suicide often generates guilt in those left behind over
the insidious question of where the blame lies.

Doors continued to be slammed in Alan's face. Tact-
less casting directors would tell him he was too small,
too blond, too thin, too something. He was never the
right type. *Tenacious* best describes Ladd at this point.
Alan had always exercised an inflexible will when pursuing a goal. Since height and coloring didn't matter in
radio, Alan concentrated on getting jobs at KFWB and
other stations in the Los Angeles area. He worked on
developing his voice, reading aloud to Midge at home,
trying to get the proper modulation. This stint working
in radio taught him the value of a rich, deep voice. Soon
he was doing a few network shows—supporting roles in
such dramas as *Texaco Star Theater* and *Lux Radio Theater*.
When Lux broadcast *Only Angels Have Wings* with Cary
Grant and Jean Arthur, for example, Ladd played a two-
line part, one of many such roles.

Early in 1939 Alan signed with an agent, Sue Carol
of the Sue Carol–Bruce Shedd Agency. The story has
frequently been told how Sue heard Alan doing two roles
on the same radio show, an old man and a boy, and was
so impressed that she called the station and invited the
actor to come to her office for an interview. Considering
how good his voice was, it may really have happened
that way. In any case, Alan was later quoted as saying,
"She thought I'd be sixty years old. We were both glad
I wasn't."

Sue has often described their first meeting and her
first impression of him. "He was wearing a long white
trenchcoat. His eyebrows and eyelashes were pitch-black
over level green eyes which were deep and unfathomable—an actor's eyes. He was for me."

If these quotes sound a bit too enthusiastic coming
from two people who were already married, it should be
remembered that by the time the statements were made,
former entanglements had been covered over or rear-
ranged.

Sue Carol came from an upper-middle-class Jewish
family and was born and raised in Chicago. She was
married briefly in the mid-twenties to Allan Keefer. In

*Evelyn Lederer turns into Sue Carol, movie flapper and the delight
of the early talkie musicals.*

Typical Sue Carol sheet-music cover.

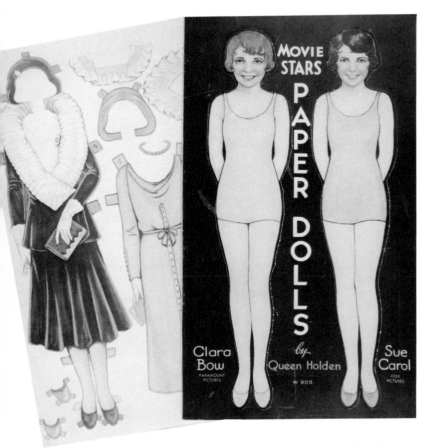

Sue Carol appeared in the first commercial paper-doll book, sold in stores in 1931.

1927 Sue (real name, Evelyn Lederer) went to the West Coast with her mother for what was intended as a short visit.

A chance meeting with a young actor named Nick Stuart led to an interview with a casting director at the old Fox Studios, and before long Evelyn had become Sue Carol and was doing parts in silent movies. Sue Carol the starlet was pretty, with dark bobbed hair, big, happy brown eyes, and a great deal of charm and personality. When talkies came in, she starred in a number of jazz musicals and flapper films. The song "Sweet Sue" was written for her, and her face graced a number of sheet music covers.

Sue married Nick Stuart in 1930, and two years later she gave birth to a baby girl, Carol Lee, named after herself and her best friend, Dixie Lee, Bing Crosby's first wife. By 1934, she and Stuart were divorced.

In 1936 Sue was married for the third time, to a writer named Howard Wilson. She had given up her film career and was energetic and restless. She also had a good business head. She soon decided to open a talent agency and formed a partnership with another agent, Bruce Shedd.

When Alan met Sue, he was hoping for a contract from the Columbia radio network, but Sue persuaded him he was movie material. She was certain he could make it big if he cooperated with her plans to get him parts.

As soon as he signed with Sue, she approached every studio in town trying to get Alan into the offices of casting directors. During this time, Alan practically lived in Sue's car, keeping an extra suit of clothes there in case he had to make a fast change for an audition. In an interview given to S. R. Mook just after his big break, Alan was quoted as saying, "I'd fallen head over heels in love with Sue by that time, but she was married. . . . I used to chauffeur her around the studios and wait while she called on casting directors. Everyone knew she was plugging me, and if anyone saw me they thought I was with her on an interview. And I used to coach her other clients when they were going out for tests—kids who had no experience. Anything to be with her." Published in a 1942 fan magazine, this interview was obviously given before the official Ladd biography was tidied up.

Sue landed Alan a brief but impressive role in a Douglas Fairbanks, Jr., seagoing adventure called *Rulers of the Sea*, and he did well enough for critics to designate his role as best incidental performance of the month. When his parts were bigger, the pictures were smaller—he had near leads in such B movies as *Her First Romance*, a Monogram musical, *The Black Cat*, with Basil Rathbone, and *Hitler, Beast of Berlin*, the first PRC release. He also did a Soundie, a jukebox record with visual. And there were several commercial films used to advertise or inform, often sent to clients and schools.

Alan was never as sure of the future as Sue was. Smart, aggressive, and ten years older than Alan, she fed his

Soundie: I Look at You. *Ladd sang and took over the baton for a moment for Rita Rio and her all-girl orchestra. Rita later became actress Dona Drake.*

dreams and minimized his fears—not an easy task, because Alan had a habit of wanting the best and expecting the worst. Alerted to a tryout for the coveted lead in *Golden Boy*, a part for an Italian, Alan darkened his blond hair with cake mascara and hurried to the audition, only to have the mascara run down his neck owing to the heat and his own nervous perspiration. Ironically, another blond "Italian" got the part: William Holden. Holden would seem to be a step ahead of Ladd during the rest of his career. In fact, a year after the release of *Golden Boy*, which made Holden a star, Ladd was to play a bit role in *Those Were the Days*, a film in which Holden starred.

During this time of struggle, Ladd's personal life was in turmoil. He had become emotionally, as well as professionally, dependent on Sue Carol, and though his wife had tried to be understanding of his ambitions, she also had the practical business of raising a child to deal with.

No one had encouraged Alan or believed in him as Sue had. She was good at mapping out strategy, and she had friends all over town who alerted her of possible parts for Alan. With every part he played, Ladd was gaining confidence. He finally broke with Midge and moved out. Their divorce became final in 1941.

Things began to pick up for Alan. He landed a small but pivotal role in an RKO drama about the French underground called *Joan of Paris*. Alan played Baby, the young flier who dies in a touching scene near the end of the picture. The scene was focused on Ladd, and he was very good. Executives at RKO were ready to offer a five-hundred-dollar-a-week contract.

However, at that moment Sue was on the trail of bigger and better things for the actor. The career-turning role of Raven in *This Gun for Hire* was less than a year away.

Trying to look dark and debonair, Ladd had not yet found his image in this early studio portrait.

THE EARLY FILMS
1932-41

Between 1932 and 1941 Alan Ladd worked around or in movies as a student, extra, bit player, supporting player, and grip. He was involved in at least twenty-eight films, probably more. Even the most dedicated Ladd fan has missed spotting him in some of the titles credited to him, and Ladd himself could not remember them all. It is possible that he was at times too far in the background of a scene, or he was in a scene that was shot but cut from the final print, or he was signed for a picture and never used. In any case, the following are the films most often listed as Ladd's early credits. Where the roles are known and Ladd can be recognized, his roles are described.

ONCE IN A LIFETIME
Universal   (1932)

CREDITS

Director, Russell Mack. *Producer*, Carl Laemmle, Jr. *From the play by* Moss Hart *and* George S. Kaufman. *Adaptation*, Seton I. Miller. *Running time, 75 minutes.*

CAST

JACK OAKIE, SIDNEY FOX, ALINE MacMAHON, RUSSELL HOPTON, ZASU PITTS

A comedy of Hollywood's early talkie days. Ladd was enrolled in a class Universal had organized to develop new talent, and he supposedly made his debut, as a projectionist, in this film. Close scrutiny has not turned up a face that looks like Ladd's.

SATURDAY'S MILLIONS
Universal   (1933)

CREDITS

Director, Edward Sedgwick. *Producer*, Carl Laemmle, Jr. *Screenplay*, Dale Van Every. *From a* Saturday Evening Post *serial by* Lucian Cary. *Photography*, Charles Stumar. *Running time, 77 minutes.*

Grady Sutton, Arline Judge, Ladd behind in second row in Pigskin Parade.

CAST

ROBERT YOUNG, JOHNNY MACK BROWN, ANDY DEVINE, LEILA HYAMS, MARY CARLISLE, GRANT MITCHELL, RICHARD TUCKER, JOE SAWYER

This film about the ups and downs of college football gave Ladd a tiny bit as a student on campus.

PIGSKIN PARADE
20th Century-Fox   (1936)

CREDITS

Director, David Butler. *Associate producer*, Bogart Rogers. *Screenplay*, Harry Tugend, Jack Yellen, William Conselman. *From a story by* Arthur Sheekman, Nat Perrin, Mark Kelly. *Photography*, Arthur Miller. *Music director*, David Buttolph. *Running time, 93 minutes.*

CAST

STUART ERWIN, PATSY KELLY, JACK HALEY,
JOHNNY DOWNS, BETTY GRABLE, ARLINE
JUDGE, DIXIE DUNBAR, JUDY GARLAND, TONY
MARTIN, GRADY SUTTON

Ladd played another student role in this musical college
romp and sang "Down with Everything" with the Yacht
Club Boys.

HOLD 'EM NAVY
Paramount   (1937)

CREDITS

Director, Kurt Neumann. *Screenplay*, Erwin Gelsey, Lloyd
Corrigan. *From a story by* Albert Shelby LeVino. *Photography*, Henry Sharp. *Running time, 67 minutes.*

Ladd as a nightclub waiter in Come On Leathernecks. *Marsha
Hunt and Leon Ames are at the far right.*

CAST

LEW AYRES, MARY CARLISLE, JOHN HOWARD,
ELIZABETH PATTERSON, BENNY BAKER, AR-
CHIE TWITCHELL, TULLY MARSHALL, BILL
DANIELS

A U.S. Naval Academy film, with football and mid-
shipmen's rivalries. Ladd had a bit as a CQ.

ALL OVER TOWN
Republic   (1937)

CREDITS

Director, James Horne. *Associate producer*, Leonard Fields.
Screenplay, Jack Townley. *From a story by* Richard English.
Photography, Ernest Miller. *Music director*, Alberto Col-
ombo. *Running time, 61 minutes.*

E OLSEN, CHIC JOHNSON, MARY HOWARD,
RRY STOCKWELL, FRANKLIN PANGBORN,
MES FINLAYSON, EDDIE KANE, STANLEY
LDS

other tiny bit for Ladd in a typical Olsen and Johnson
nedy.

ST TRAIN FROM MADRID

ramount   (1937)

REDITS

rector, James Hogan. Producer, George M. Arthur.
enplay, Louis Stevens, Robert Wyler. Based on a story
Paul Hervey Fox, Elsie Fox. Photography, Harry Fish-
k. Running time, 77 minutes.

AST

ROTHY LAMOUR, LEW AYRES, GILBERT RO-
ND, LEE BOWMAN, KAREN MORLEY, AN-
ONY QUINN, HELEN MACK, EVELYN BRENT,
BERT CUMMINGS, LIONEL ATWILL, OLYMPE
ADNA

d was an extra, a soldier in this film concerning
nish refugees.

ULS AT SEA

amount   (1937)

EDITS

ctor, Henry Hathaway. Producers, Henry Hathaway,
ver Jones. Screenplay, Grover Jones, Dale Van Every.
d on story by Ted Lesser. Photography, Charles Lang,
Costumes, Edith Head. Song, "Susie Sapple," by Leo
in, Ralph Rainger. Running time, 92 minutes.

CAST

GARY COOPER, GEORGE RAFT, FRANCES DEE,
HENRY WILCOXON, HARRY CAREY, OLYMPE
BRADNA, ROBERT CUMMINGS, PORTER HALL,
GEORGE ZUCCO, VIRGINIA WEIDLER, JOSEPH
SCHILDKRAUT, PAUL FIX, TULLY MARSHALL

There is some doubt that Ladd was in this tale about the
1842 slave trade on the high seas. Sometimes he is listed
as one of the sailors.

THE GOLDWYN FOLLIES

United Artists-Sam Goldwyn   Technicolor
(1938)

CREDITS

Director, George Marshall. Producer, Sam Goldwyn.
Screenplay, Ben Hecht. Associate producer, George Haight.
Photography, Gregg Toland. Music director, Arthur New-
man. Ballets, George Balanchine. Songs, George and Ira
Gershwin, Kurt Weill, Ray Golden. Running time, 115
minutes.

CAST

ADOLPHE MENJOU, ZORINA, ANDREA LEEDS,
KENNY BAKER, HELEN JEPSON, PHIL BAKER,
ELLA LOGAN, JEROME COWAN, CHARLES KULL-
MAN, EDGAR BERGEN and CHARLIE Mc-
CARTHY, THE RITZ BROTHERS

In this Technicolor extravaganza, Ladd had a bit as an
auditioning singer.

FRESHMAN YEAR
Universal   (1938)

CREDITS

Director, Frank McDonald. *Producer*, George Bilson. *Screenplay*, Charles Grayson. *From a story by* Thomas Ahearn, F. Maury Grossman. *Photography*, Elwood Bredell. *Running time, 65 minutes.*

CAST

DIXIE DUNBAR, STANLEY HUGHES (MARK DANIELS), CONSTANCE MOORE, WILLIAM LUNDIGAN, TOMMY WONDER, ERNEST TRUEX, FRANK MELTON, ALDEN (STEPHEN) CHASE, RAYMOND PARKER, FAY McKENZIE

In this campus story, Ladd had a bit as a student.

Frederick Giermann, Roland Drew, Ladd, and unknown player in Hitler, Beast of Berlin.

COME ON LEATHERNECKS
Republic   (1938)

CREDITS

Director, James Cruze. *Associate producer*, Herman Schlom. *Screenplay*, Sidney Salkow, Dorrell, Stuart McGowan. *Original story* Sidney Salkow. *Running time, 65 minutes.*

CAST

RICHARD CROMWELL, MARSHA HUNT, LEON AMES, EDWARD BROPHY, BRUCE MacFARLANE, ROBERT WARWICK, HOWARD HICKMAN, JAMES BUSH

Annapolis football star has conflict with father, who wants son to follow family tradition and join marines. Ladd had a bit as a club waiter.

RULERS OF THE SEA

Paramount (1939)

CREDITS

Director, Frank Lloyd. *Producer*, Frank Lloyd. *Associate producer*, Lou Smith. *Screenplay*, Talbot Jennings, Frank Cavett, Richard Collins. *Photography*, Theodor Sparkuhl. *Special effects*, Gordon Jennings. *Running time, 96 minutes.*

CAST

DOUGLAS FAIRBANKS, JR., MARGARET LOCK-WOOD, WILL FYFFE, GEORGE BANCROFT, MONTAGU LOVE, DAVID TORRENCE, VAUGHAN GLASER, ALAN LADD

Ladd got billing as a young seaman in this story of the beginnings of the steam-powered engine. His brief performance was cited as "Best incidental performance of the month" by critics.

A bit role in Ruler of the Sea. *Margaret Lockwood and Douglas Fairbanks, Jr., are the smiling couple.*

With Tom Tyler, Victor Jory, Earl Askam, and Esther Estrella in an early Zane Grey western, Light of Western Stars, *1940.*

HITLER, BEAST OF BERLIN
(LATER RELEASED AS BEASTS OF BERLIN, AND LATER HELL'S DEVILS)
Producers Distributing Corp. (Later known as PRC) (1939)

CREDITS

Director, Sherman Scott (Sam Newfield, aka Peter Stewart). *Associate producer*, Sigmund Neufeld. *Based on story "The Goose Step"* by Shepard Traube. *Photography*, Jack Greenhalgh. *Musical director*, Dave Chudnow. *Running time, 87 minutes.*

CAST

ROLAND DREW, STEFFI DUNA, GRETA GRANSTEDT, ALLAN (ALAN) LADD, LUCIEN PRIVAL, VERNON DENT, JOHN ELLIS, GEORGE ROSENER

This was the first feature released by PRC. and it was immediately banned in New York as too inflammatory to the sensitive political climate of 1939. After a little cutting and softening of the title to *Beasts of Berlin*, this B film played around the country and continued to be the object of controversy, if not critical praise. This film is a curiosity today. Though cheaply made, it was quite outspoken at a time when that was not considered appropriate. It did well at the box office because of the publicity. Years later it made still more money as a release "starring" Alan Ladd and retitled *Hell's Devils*.

THE GREEN HORNET
Universal (1940)

CREDITS

Directors, Ford Beebe, Ray Taylor. *Associate producer*, George Plympton. *Screenplay*, George Plympton, Basil Dickey, Morrison Wood, Lyonel Margolies. *Based on the radio show* The Green Hornet. *Photography*, William Sicker, Jerry Ash. *Running time, serial in 13 episodes.*

CAST

GORDON JONES, KEYE LUKE, WADE BOTELER, PHILIP TRENT, ANNE NAGEL, WALTER McGRAIL, GENE RIZZI, JOHN KELLY, RALPH DUNN

Ladd had a tiny bit as Gilpin in this action filled crime serial.

CROSS COUNTRY ROMANCE
RKO Radio (1940)

CREDITS

Director, Frank Woodruff. *Producer*, Cliff Reid. *Executive producer*, Lee Marcus. *Screenplay*, Jerry Cady, Bert Grane. *From the novel* Highway to Romance, *by* E. Brown. *Music director*, Roy Webb. *Photographer*, J. Roy Hunt. *Running time, 68 minutes.*

CAST

GENE RAYMOND, WENDY BARRIE, HEDDA HOPPER, BILLY GILBERT, GEORGE P. HUNTLE (JR.), BERTON CHURCHILL, TOM DUGAN, EDGAR DEARING

One of the popular chase-across-country romance stories with Ladd in a tiny bit as First Mate Williams.

LIGHT OF WESTERN STARS
Paramount (1940)

CREDITS

Director, Lesley Selander. *Producer*, Harry Sherman. *Screenplay*, Norman Houston. *From the novel by* Zane Grey. *Photography*, Russell Harlan. *Running time, 64 minutes.*

CAST

VICTOR JORY, JOANN SAYERS, RUSSELL HAYDEN, NOAH BEERY, JR., ALAN LADD, J. FARRELL MacDONALD, TOM TYLER, RUTH ROGERS, ESTHER ESTRELLA, EDDIE DEAN, RAD ROBINSON

There were three previous film versions of this popular Zane Grey novel, made in 1918, 1925, and 1930. Jor

Ladd with Thurston Hall in In Old Missouri, *1940.*

...vas the hero this time, and Ladd's part was small, a ...owhand who hangs around the saloon, dances with a ...antina girl (Estrella), then is involved in the shooting ...f Sheriff Tyler.

In this Conrad tale of a man who is a recluse on an island that is invaded by cutthroats, Ladd played March as an eighteen-year-old—a bit that may have been cut from the final print.

VICTORY
Paramount   (1940)

CREDITS

Director, John Cromwell. *Producer*, Anthony Veiller. *Screenplay*, John L. Balderston. *Based on the novel by* Joseph Conrad. *Photography*, Leo Tover. *Running time, 79 minutes.*

CAST

FREDRIC MARCH, BETTY FIELD, SIR CEDRIC HARDWICKE, JEROME COWAN, SIG RUMANN, MARGARET WYCHERLY, FRITZ FELD, LIONEL ROYCE

IN OLD MISSOURI
Republic   (1940)

CREDITS

Director, Frank McDonald. *Producer*, Armand Schaefer. *Screenplay*, Dorrell and Stuart McGowan. *Photography*, Ernest Miller. *Music director*, Cy Feuer. *Songs sung by* the Hall Johnson Choir. *Running time, 68 minutes.*

As a sailor in Captain Caution.

CAST

LEON WEAVER, FRANK WEAVER, JUNE WEAVER, JUNE STOREY, MARJORIE GATESON, THURSTON HALL, ALAN LADD, LORETTA WEAVER, MILDRED SHAY

The Weaver family in a tale of sharecroppers who confront their landlord, only to find he is in terrible financial difficulties too. He also has a wastrel son (Ladd) and a society wife who wants a divorce. He begs the Weavers to change places with him, and they straighten out his affairs and his family in a happy ending.

GANGS OF CHICAGO
Republic   (1940)

CREDITS

Director, Arthur Lubin. *Associate producer*, Robert North. *Original screenplay*, Karl Brown. *Photography*, Elwood Bredell. *Music director*, Cy Feuer. *Running time, 66 minutes.*

CAST

LLOYD NOLAN, BARTON MacLANE, LOLA LANE, RAY MIDDLETON, ASTRID ALLWYN, HORACE McMAHON, HOWARD HICKMAN, LEONA ROBERTS, DWIGHT FRYE

Lloyd Nolan plays a criminal who uses his knowledge of law for his own nefarious purposes, betraying friends and finally facing justice. Ladd had a tiny bit part.

BROTHER RAT AND A BABY
Warner Bros. (1940)

CREDITS

Director, Ray Enright. *Producers*, Jack L. Warner, Hal B. Wallis. *Associate producer*, Robert Lord. *Screenplay*, John Monks, Jr., Fred Finklehoffe. *Photography*, Charles Rosher. *Sequel to Brother Rat, 1938, Warner Bros. Running time, 87 minutes.*

CAST

WAYNE MORRIS, PRISCILLA LANE, EDDIE ALBERT, JANE BRYAN, RONALD REAGAN, JANE WYMAN, PETER B. GOOD, LARRY WILLIAMS, ARTHUR TREACHER, MORONI OLSEN, JESSIE BUSLEY, PAUL HARVEY

The comedy was strained in this sequel, which featured the same setting, Virginia Military Institute, and the same three cadets. Ladd was one of the many cadets in the background.

CAPTAIN CAUTION
Hal Roach–United Artists (1940)

CREDITS

Director, Richard Wallace. *Producers*, Richard Wallace, Grover Jones. *Screenplay*, Grover Jones. *Based on novel by* Kenneth Roberts. *Photography*, Norbert Brodine. *Music*, Phil Ohman. *Lyrics*, Foster Carling. *Running time, 85 minutes.*

CAST

VICTOR MATURE, LOUISE PLATT, LEO CARRILLO, BRUCE CABOT, ROBERT BARRAT, VIVIENNE OSBORNE, MILES MANDER, ANDREW TOMBES

In this fair adaptation of the Roberts seafaring novel about privateers during the War of 1812, Ladd was far down in the cast as Newton, a mutinous young sailor/prisoner.

THOSE WERE THE DAYS
Paramount (1940)

CREDITS

Director, J. Theodore Reed. *Producer*, J. Theodore Reed.

With Roscoe Karns, Ruth Donnelly, and Lois Ranson in Meet the Missus.

Screenplay, Don Hartman. *Based on* Siwash Stories, *by* George Fitch. *Photography*, William Shea. *Assistant director*, George Hippard. *Running time, 74 minutes.*

CAST

WILLIAM HOLDEN, BONITA GRANVILLE, EZRA STONE, JUDITH BARRETT, TOM RUTHERFURD

In this lighthearted romantic film, a middle-aged couple reminisce about their courtship days at college. Ladd was Keg, one of the students.

MEET THE MISSUS
Republic   (1940)

CREDITS

Director, Mal St. Clair. *Producer*, Robert North. *Screenplay*, Val Burton, Ewart Adamson, Taylor Cavan. *Photography*, Ernest Miller. *Running time, 68 minutes.*

CAST

ROSCOE KARNS, RUTH DONNELLY, SPENCER CHARTERS, GEORGE ERNEST, LOIS RANSON, POLLY MORAN, ASTRID ALLWYN, ALAN LADD,

Here Ladd had the role of the legal-minded boyfriend of Lois Ranson, the pretty daughter of the Higgins family. Gran Higgins falls into the clutches of a love-starved widow. Another in the Higgins Family series.

HER FIRST ROMANCE
Monogram   (1940)

CREDITS

Director, Edward Dmytryk. *Producer*, I.E. Chadwick.

Screenplay, Adele Comandini. *Photography*, John Mesca[.] *Running time, 77 minutes.*

CAST

EDITH FELLOWS, WILBUR EVANS, JUDITH LIN[N]DEN, JACQUELINE WELLS (JULIE BISHOP), ALA[N] LADD, MARION KIRBY, ROGER DANIEL

A Yuletime release, *Her First Romance* was a more th[an] ordinarily ambitious picture for Monogram. Featur[ed] was little Edith Fellows, once a child actress in su[ch] films as *Pennies from Heaven* with Bing Crosby, now grow[-] ing up and ready for musical romance. This Cinderell[a] type script was written by the same writer who had do[ne] *Three Smart Girls* for Deanna Durbin a few years befor[e.] Wilbur Evans, Fellows's co-star, had a big, robust voic[e] and the film features several duets.

The story concerned a plain-jane co-ed, Fellows, an[d] her beautiful, conniving sister, Wells. Complication[s] were provided by an attractive cousin, Linden, and h[er] on-again, off-again fiancé, Ladd. When the sisters com[-] pete for the same man, Evans, Ladd gets caught in th[e] middle as a red herring. When he believes Evans [is] making a play for Linden, Ladd knocks Evans down. A[ll] ends well, however, with Ladd marrying Linden an[d] Evans confessing love for Fellows.

Certainly this was not the Ladd who dominated th[e] Paramount lot throughout the 1940s, but the part wa[s] his largest to date, and he got to use his fists. Monogra[m] got more mileage out of *Her First Romance* by re-issuin[g] it later as *The Right Man* and billing both Ladd an[d] Wells (who had moved to Warners and changed h[er] name to Julie Bishop) over the title.

THEY MET IN BOMBAY
Metro-Goldwyn-Mayer   (1941)

CREDITS

Director, Clarence Brown. *Producer*, Hunt Stromberg[.] *Screenplay*, Edwin Justus Mayer, Anita Loos, Leon Go[r]don. *Based on a story by* John Kafka. *Photography*, Willia[m] Daniels. *Running time, 86 minutes.*

CAST

CLARK GABLE, ROSALIND RUSSELL, PETE[R]

With Jacqueline Wells (later Julie Bishop) in Her First Romance.

ORRE, JESSIE RALPH, REGINALD OWEN, MAT-
HEW BOULTON, EDWARD CIANNELLI, LUIS
LBERNI

dd had a tiny role, as a British soldier, and one line,
es, sir," in this drama concerning a suave jewel thief
able) and a sleek lady crook (Russell) whose schemes
awry when the thief inadvertently becomes a hero
ile posing as a British officer. Ladd was one of those
der Gable's command.

ADET GIRL
)th Century-Fox   (1941)

REDITS

rector, Ray McCarey. *Producer,* Sol M. Wurtzel. *Screen-
y,* Stanley Rauh, H. W. Hanemann. *From a story by
k Andrews, Richard English. Photography,* Charles
arke. *Running time, 68 minutes.*

AST

AROLE LANDIS, GEORGE MONTGOMERY, JOHN

SHEPPERD (SHEPPERD STRUDWICK), WILLIAM
TRACY, JANIS CARTER, ROBERT LOWERY, BASIL
WALKER, CHARLES TANNEN, CHICK CHAN-
DLER, OTTO HAN, JAYNE HAZARD

Ladd again had an unbilled bit in this patriotic comedy
in which Cadet Montgomery has to decide whether to
carry on family tradition and study for a West Point
commission or marry Landis.

GREAT GUNS
20th Century-Fox   (1941)

CREDITS

Director, Monty Banks. *Producer,* Sol. M. Wurtzel. *Screenplay,* Lou Breslow. *Photographer,* Glen MacWilliams.
Music director, Emil Newman. *Running time, 74 minutes.*

Citizen Kane, 1941. *Ladd is at far left with pipe. Paul Stewart in foreground.*

CAST

STAN LAUREL, OLIVER HARDY, SHEILA RYAN, DICK NELSON, EDMUND MacDONALD, CHARLES TROWBRIDGE, LUDWIG STOSSEL, KANE RICHMOND, MAE MARSH, PAUL HARVEY, ETHEL GRIFFIES, CHARLES ARNT

Laurel and Hardy in the army and saddled with the usual tough-sergeant problems. Ladd had a one-sentence bit as a soldier in a photo shop.

CITIZEN KANE
RKO Radio   (1941)

CREDITS

Director, Orson Welles. *Producer,* Orson Welles. *Screenplay,* Orson Welles, Herman J. Mankiewicz. *Camera,* Gregg Toland. *Production Company,* Mercury Productions. *Associate producer,* Richard Barr. *Art director,* Van Nest Polglase. *Music director,* Bernard Herrman. *Running time, 119 minutes.*

CAST

RSON WELLES, JOSEPH COTTEN, EVERETT LOANE, DOROTHY COMINGORE, GEORGE OULOURIS, RAY COLLINS, RUTH WARRICK, RSKINE SANFORD, WILLIAM ALLAND, AGNES OOREHEAD, RICHARD BAER, PAUL STEW-RT, FORTUNIO BONA-NOVA, JOAN BLAIR, UDDY SWAN, HARRY SHANNON

dd was recognizable by his voice in the famous scene which the reporters are at Xanadu to go over the life d possessions of the late, great Kane. Hat pushed back, pipe between his teeth, Ladd had three lines and a oment when his face was illuminated enough to be entified, in this much-lauded first Orson Welles fea-re film which focused intimately on a Hearst-like, all-owerful newspaper tycoon.

HE RELUCTANT DRAGON
alt Disney/RKO Radio   Technicolor   (1941)

REDITS

ve-action director, Alfred Werker. Cartoon directors, amilton Luske, Jim Handley, Ford Beebe, Edwin Ver-, Jasper Blystone. Screenplay, Ted Sears, Al Perkins, rry Clemmons, Bill Cottrell. Live-action photography, rt Glennon, Winton Hoch. Songs, Larry Morey, Frank urchill, Charles Wolcott. Running time, 72 minutes.

AST

OBERT BENCHLEY, WALT DISNEY, NANA RYANT, FRANCES GIFFORD, BUDDY PEPPER, ERALD MOHR, FLORENCE GILL, CLARENCE ASH

dd played one of the animators we meet as Benchley kes us on a tour through the different departments of e Disney Dynasty. The live-action section was later moved when the film went into reissues and TV release, ving only the animated part of the film.

PETTICOAT POLITICS
Republic   (1941)

CREDITS

Director, Erle C. Kenton. *Producer*, Robert North. *Screenplay*, Ewart Adamson, Taylor Cavan. *Photography*, Jack Marta. *Music director*, Cy Feuer. *Running time, 67 minutes.*

CAST

ROSCOE KARNS, RUTH DONNELLY, SPENCER CHARTERS, GEORGE ERNEST, LOIS RANSON, POLLY MORAN, PAUL HURST, PIERRE WATKIN, ALAN LADD

The Higgins Family again. Here Pa has decided to retire from the candy business and, through a series of complications, is forced to run for mayor. As the son of Pa Higgins's opponent, Ladd, still playing Miss Ranson's boyfriend, puts Pa in a difficult situation. Ladd's billing was the same as in *Meet the Missus.*

Ladd, Lois Ranson, and Jeff Corey in Petticoat Politics.

41

From Paper Bullets, *which was later released as* Gangs, Inc.

PAPER BULLETS
(LATER RELEASED AS GANGS, INC.
KB Productions/PRC   (1941)

CREDITS

Director, Phil Rosen. *Producers*, Maurice Kozinsky, Fran
Kozinsky (aka King Brothers). *Story and screenplay*, Mar
tin Mooney. *Photography*, Arthur Martinelli. *Assistan
director*, Arthur Gardner. *Songs*, Vic Knight, Johnr
Lange, Lew Porter, Maurice Kozinsky. *Running time, 7*
minutes.

CAST

JOAN WOODBURY, JACK LaRUE, LINDA WARE
JOHN ARCHER, VINCE BARNETT, ALLAN (ALAN
LADD, GAVIN GORDON, PHILLIP TRENT, WII
LIAM HALLIGAN

A thriller about a girl who seeks revenge, this unpre
tentious B movie had Ladd playing an undercover re
porter, a double for a notorious gangster whose news
paper picture is posed by Ladd. He was billed as Allar
The original title, *Paper Bullets*, which referred to th
political graft portrayed, was not felt to have enoug
punch, so after release the film was renamed *Gangs, In*
"starring Alan Ladd."

THE BLACK CAT
Universal   (1941)

CREDITS

Director, Albert S. Rogell. *Producer*, Burt Kelly. *Screen*
play, Robert Lees, Fred Rinaldo, Eric Taylor, Rober
Neville. *Photography*, Stanley Cortez. *Music director*, Han
J. Salter. *Special effects*, John P. Fulton. *Suggested by*
story by Edgar Allan Poe. *Running time, 70 minutes.*

CAST

BASIL RATHBONE, HUGH HERBERT, BRODER
ICK CRAWFORD, BELA LUGOSI, GALE SONDER
GAARD, ANNE GWYNNE, CLAIRE DODD, ALAN
LADD, JOHN ELDREDGE, CECILIA LOFTUS
GLADYS COOPER

Although credit was given to the Poe story, little of it remains in this version, which is quite different from the earlier film of the same title, which starred Boris Karloff. This was another of the "old dark house" or "murder in the mansion" films, with everyone trying to discover who was doing what to whom. Hugh Herbert and Broderick Crawford play it mostly for laughs, with Hugh doing his absentminded dithering bit and Crawford being both clumsy and clever and solving the whole thing almost by accident. There was some good creepy camera work by Cortez, but it was really just an adequate movie.

The plot concerns a group of greedy heirs who gather to wait for the demise of Miss Henrietta Winslow. Ladd played Basil Rathbone's son, Gladys Cooper's stepson. Murder, yowling cats, hidden family secrets, hidden passages—things keep moving.

Lugosi played a suspicious-looking butler, with Sondergaard as a sinister housekeeper. After much confusion—screams in the night, claps of thunder, and wild gunshots—all is finally sorted out, and the heirs depart while Crawford and Gwynne plan their wedding.

Ladd's part was at least central to the plot, and he was in more than a few scenes, though he didn't have many lines. He also toted a gun around, which makes stills from this film look more natural than stills from his other bit roles.

Broderick Crawford, Ladd, Basil Rathbone, and Gladys Cooper in The Black Cat. *Ladd was billed thirteenth.*

JOAN OF PARIS
RKO Radio   (1942)

CREDITS

Director, Robert Stevenson. *Producer,* David Hempstead. *Screenplay,* Charles Bennett, Ellis St. Joseph. *Original story by* Jacques Thiery, George Kissel. *Photography,* Russell Metty. *Music director,* Roy Webb. *Running time, 91 minutes.*

CAST

MICHELE MORGAN, PAUL HENREID, THOMAS MITCHELL, LAIRD CREGAR, MAY ROBSON, ALEXANDER GRANACH, ALAN LADD, JACK BRIGGS, JAMES MONKS, RICHARD FRASER

This picture, made in 1941 and released in 1942, was part of America's preoccupation with what was going on in Europe. The Nazis were triumphant in Paris, and the English were just hanging on. It was a time of great tension in the world, and though not yet committed to war when this was filmed, America was making movies as if we were.

Ladd got lucky with this picture—there were four young flyers in Paul Henreid's squadron, and Ladd's role was the one on which plot manipulations hung and on whom audience sympathy is focused. His blond good looks stood out, and he made an impact.

The story concerns an RAF black-and-white squadron downed over occupied France. The flyers, with their leader, Henreid, make their way to Paris, though Baby (Ladd), the youngest of the group, is wounded. It is imperative that they find somewhere to hide Baby and care for his wounds. The Gestapo leader, Cregar, has already issued an order for their arrest.

Mitchell, a sympathetic, courageous priest, hides Baby in the crypts below his church, and Henreid sets out to contact British Intelligence. Instead he runs into a lissome French girl, Morgan, and decides to use her as his go-between, for he realizes he is being followed by Gestapo agents. She is able to make contact with Resistance fighters and get word out. Meanwhile, she and Henreid discover they are in love.

The shadow of the Gestapo prevents Henreid from meeting his comrades in the church crypt, and Morgan goes in his place to explain the escape plan. However, it is too late for Baby. He dies in his buddies' arms. The other three must get away fast.

Morgan is arrested by Cregar and fools him into thinking she is leading him to the flyers. Instead, she stalls long enough for Henreid and the others to escape. In the final scene Morgan is in prison, awaiting death and praying to Saint Joan, her patron.

Viewed today, this film seems loaded with the most unabashed sentimental patriotism, in both speech and action. Ladd's death scene is played for maximum pathos, with the priest murmuring and Morgan sobbing over him. This was Ladd's finest moment to date, and he gave it his all, his eyes expressive, first with pain, then widening in shock as death comes.

Joan of Paris has atmosphere and suspense and, if you can forgive some incongruities, several interesting performances. Both Ladd and the elegantly villainous Cregar were ready for better things.

Although RKO offered a contract at five-hundred dollars a week for Ladd on the strength of this film, they lost him because Paramount had a definite script to offer and Sue had read that script. She saw Ladd's future in every line of it.

Other films sometimes listed in Ladd's credits are:
NO MAN OF HER OWN   Paramount 1932. A drama with Carole Lombard and Clark Gable.

BORN TO THE WEST   Republic 1937. A western with John Wayne and Johnny Mack Brown. Reissued as *Helltown.*

RUSTLER'S VALLEY   Paramount 1937. A western with William "Hopalong Cassidy" Boyd.

Paul Henreid and Ladd in Joan of Paris

THE SUPERSTAR YEARS
1942-53

In the late summer of 1941, Bill Meikeljohn, who was then head of the talent department at Paramount, called Sue Carol to tell her an old friend, director Frank Tuttle, was looking for an unknown actor to play an important role in a new thriller. The movie in question was a film version of Graham Greene's *A Gun for Sale*, which the studio was retitling, *This Gun for Hire*. Meikeljohn was well aware of how hard Sue had been pushing her client Alan Ladd, and he thought this might be just the opportunity she was looking for.

As it turned out, the studio wasn't convinced the book would make a profitable film. The setting was pre-war England and the principal character in the plot was a psycho named Raven, a small, mean hired killer with an ugly harelip. Since this character was central to the picture, the studio heads were skeptical that an appealing film could be made around him.

Tuttle believed in the project and was determined to make the picture. He had done some rewriting and hoped to convince the studio by putting together a test that would more or less show the story's possibilities. To do this he needed the right actor, and he couldn't think of anyone already on the Paramount payroll who could fill the bill. Veronica Lake was penciled in if the picture went through, simply because she was a hot property at that moment and Paramount needed to put her in another picture as soon as possible.

Sue called Tuttle and set up the interview. Most casting directors, talent scouts, directors, and producers knew about Ladd because Sue had been trying so hard to sell him, but few believed he had star potential. However, Tuttle told her he would see Ladd.

When Sue brought Alan in for the appointment, Tuttle wasn't impressed. "He looks too much like a kid who would say, 'Tennis anyone?' He's just not right for the part." Small, blond, and boyish, Alan had always looked younger than his age, especially when he smiled. He looked *nice*.

Sue quickly opened her portfolio and selected some shots of Alan smoking a cigarette, squinting through the smoke—portraits of Alan looking aloof, even sinister. The camera did things to the boyish face. The gray-green eyes looked old somehow, older than the clean-cut college type Alan projected in person. Tuttle studied the portraits and made the decision to test Ladd.

As Teet Carle, press agent on the picture, recalls, the test was an elaborate one with three scenes. The first was a scene not in the final film, of Ladd being hired for the killing he was to do. The second showed Ladd carrying out the ruthless, emotionless slaying. The third and last was a long scene, taking place in the abandoned boxcar in the railroad yards, in which Ladd breaks down and tells the girl he has taken hostage about the ghastly childhood and desperate life that led him to become a twisted, homicidal misfit. (A misshapen wrist was substituted for the harelip.)

Ladd rehearsed and prepared for five days before the test. Robert Preston, who was being considered for a part in the picture, helped by reading cues with him. The test was sensational. The studio gave Tuttle the go-ahead on the picture, and he hired Ladd, telling Sue that the part would make Alan a star.

Raves over the test were unanimous. On screen the pleasantly handsome Ladd had become an unblinking neurotic. He was chilling, oddly sympathetic. And there was something else—an electricity, an energy, a sexual element that no one had expected. Paramount offered a contract at three-hundred dollars a week. Sue considered bargaining the five-hundred-dollar-a-week offer from RKO against it, but in the end she took the Paramount deal, afraid to dicker over something so crucial to Alan's future.

During the filming of *This Gun for Hire*, Alan caught a cold that grew worse as they shot night scenes in the chilled, damp air. He was running a high fever but wouldn't relent, grateful for his big chance and determined not to hold up production. He finally collapsed with pneumonia and had to stay in bed. The company shot around him. There was no talk of replacing him—the studio brass had seen the rushes coming off the set.

Alan and Sue were now open about their romance, and when the front office heard that the pair was planning to marry, they sent word to Sue that such a move would be disastrous to Ladd's new career. They must give up the idea. Alan had already told Teet Carle he was willing to do almost anything the studio ordered—as long as they didn't separate him from Sue. "We're a team," he told Teet, and insisted that Sue be present at all interviews. Actually, Sue's presence was practically a necessity. Alan would be so nervous that he could barely answer, and Sue would have to fill in the details. She became very adept at doing Ladd's interviews for him.

Ladd got fourth billing on *This Gun for Hire* and a special "Introducing . . ." credit, but his was the showcase role, and he was in ninety-five percent of the scenes. From beginning to end, he was nothing less than brilliant.

Even before *Gun* was released, Paramount cast Ladd in a remake of an old George Raft thriller, Dashiell Hammett's *The Glass Key*. His co-star was to be Patricia Morison, but after a few days' shooting, it was decided she was too tall to be playing opposite Ladd and she lost her big chance. Petite and seductive Veronica Lake was brought in to replace Pat. This seems to be the beginning of the great height coverup. No one had troubled much about it during the filming of *Gun* because Raven was supposed to be a small man.

Though they made only four co-starring films, the names Ladd and Lake will always be associated in fans' minds. It was unfortunate that Veronica Lake had a strong self-destructive streak and was so difficult and perverse that in the end Paramount decided she wasn't

One of the moody portraits Sue Carol showed Frank Tuttle in an effort to persuade him that Alan should play Raven in This Gun for Hire.

worth the trouble she gave. Ladd, who was seldom heard to utter an unflattering remark about anyone, admitted in the 1950s that he hadn't enjoyed working with her. Other of her co-stars were apt to put it a good deal stronger than that.

Sue set up residency in Nevada for six weeks and obtained a divorce from Wilson, leaving her free to be married to Alan in Mexico. Two months later, when his divorce from Midge became final, Ladd and Sue were married again in California to ensure legality. Sue and Alan were so close at this time that they seemed to be alter-egos—two parts of the same whole. They could exchange a look across a set and make a decision on something without a word spoken. Those who witnessed this communication were awed by it.

The studio had finally accepted Sue, if reluctantly. Obviously she was necessary to keep Ladd functioning like a star. The studio mailroom had become buried in fan response to his electrifying debut, and his success seemed assured. It would not, however, please his fans to learn their handsome new heartthrob had left his young, pretty wife for an older, experienced, much-married woman, so it was left to the publicity department to make the marriage respectable, even romantic. By skimming years off Sue's age and being vague about past marriages, the impression was given that both parties had been free when they met and had fallen in love at first sight.

The reality was perhaps more hardheaded than that, but there were elements of truth in the publicity releases. Sue was exactly what he needed at that point. Shrewd and ambitious, she exuded the confidence he lacked. She was his buffer, his helpmate and partner in all things. His was a fragile ego; he was sensitive and could become depressed when he felt he was not receiving approval.

With the success of *The Glass Key*, Paramount knew it was time to let Ladd carry a picture. Brian Donlevy had been top billed in *Key*, but Ladd had been allowed to dominate the picture. The next question was: Could the Ladd name alone bring customers into the theaters? There was another reason for rushing Ladd into a starring vehicle. He was of draft age, and World War Two had begun while he was climbing to the top of the popularity polls.

Several possible films were announced for Ladd— among them a Dashiell Hammett story called *Red Harvest*, a musical, *Incendiary Blonde*, with Betty Hutton, and *Tahiti*, with Dorothy Lamour. None of these were made with Ladd, and in fact, only *Incendiary Blonde* was made at all.

Instead, Paramount chose a Runyonesque comedy-drama called *Lucky Jordan*. It is one of Ladd's most entertaining films, and he parodied his tough-guy image well.

Lucky Jordan was a smash hit, rating high on the year's list of top grossers, and Ladd's fan mail reached a high of nearly twenty-thousand letters a week. His was the

Sexual antagonism was the most potent ingredient in the Ladd-Lake screen relationship, as seen here in Saigon.

A frequent Ladd co-star was William Bendix, who was either beating Ladd to a pulp or chumming around with him.

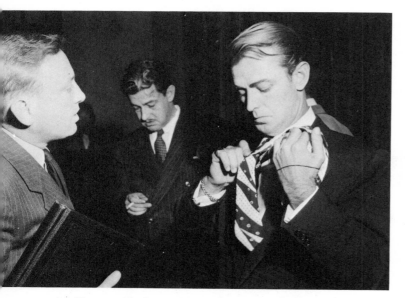

Making a quick change. Preston Sturges is in background.

sole name above the title, and he quickly proved he was the 1940s' top find.

With the draft board closing in, Paramount hurried Ladd into an action-adventure flick called *China*. His sidekick was his close friend William Bendix, and his co-star was Loretta Young. Loretta was a long-time star and her contract called for top billing, but it was obvious from the ads whom Paramount expected to sell the most tickets. Once more Ladd had a huge hit, though the critics, led by Bosley Crowther, were beginning to make some snide remarks about Ladd's typecasting as a tough guy.

During this time Ladd had a very painful ulcer; nevertheless, he was drafted. His stint in the army air force was brief. He was inducted in January 1943 and released in November the same year, medically discharged for that ulcer and a double hernia. While in the service, he filmed some government shorts used to boost morale, among them *A Letter from a Friend* and *Skirmish on the Homefront*. The fans were given no chance to forget him, with *China* playing in theaters around the country and coverage by the fan magazines, led by *Modern Screen*, which provided endless, breathless accounts of his every move.

A mild indication of how much use was made of Ladd's military service was the contest run by Paramount and *Modern Screen*. In the June 1943 issue, *Modern Screen* offered two-thousand dollars in war bonds, supplied by the studio, for writing a winning ten-word make-believe telegram to Private Ladd. Mrs. Ladd was to act as contest judge.

For Ladd's return, Paramount had ready a woman's story taken from a novel by Rachel Field. In *And Now Tomorrow*, Ladd was cast as a doctor in love with his patient—a lovely, pampered, deaf girl, played by Loretta Young. Though he carried a syringe instead of a gun, Ladd was as cool and caustic as ever. The critics were skeptical, but the public loved him.

There were plenty of new expenses at the Ladd household. Sue had given birth to a daughter, Alana, while Alan was in the service, and Carol Lee, Sue's daughter by Nick Stuart, also lived with them. Responding to the monthly fan mail cost a small fortune, requiring full-time secretarial help and postage. There was also a newly acquired ranch, Alsulana, in Hidden Valley, with its stables and upkeep. Paramount's paternalism was farily pronounced, and there was no rush to raise Ladd's salary according to his degree of importance. Paramount was keeping Ladd on a straight player's contract while they cleaned up at the box office.

After a series of action-adventure successes, the best of which was *The Blue Dahlia*, Ladd was assigned a lackluster western titled *California*. It was time to rebel. He nixed *California* and went on suspension, holding out for better scripts and more money. Sue had given up being his agent and had sold off half his contract—"I couldn't bear to part with all of it for sentiment's sake"—but she came to the set every day, knew everything that went on, and advised Alan on all career matters. The paltry

Sunning at the beach at Malibu while home on leave in 1943.

salary she had won for him as a new contractee was hardly in keeping with his superstar status and, she felt, was humiliating to someone in his position. Money was only part of the problem; his cookie-cutter roles were beginning to pall as well.

A new contract, guaranteeing him seventy-five-thousand dollars per film, was drawn up and from that point on, as Sue recalls, the studio brass stopped thinking of Alan as a nice, dumb kid and began to treat him with the respect their top money-making male star deserved.

Money represented security to Alan. He had had so little of it most of his life and he lived high for a time when the big money rolled in, buying Cadillacs and dozens of fancy ties. This first flush of successitis passed quickly, however, and he began to look for better investments. He and Sue and their daughters were still living in the house on Cromwell Avenue, which Sue had kept as part of her divorce settlement from Wilson. Alan hired an architect and plans were begun on a big new house in Holmby Hills.

Better scripts, though, were harder to secure than the material possessions. Actually, he had little belief in himself as an actor, and his only acting formula was, "You've got to think it and believe it—then it comes through." That isn't a bad formula at all, but it does presume the actor will be given something to think *about*, and Ladd's scripts generally didn't have that advantage built into them. Everything being done for him around the studio only indicated further to Ladd that he was a studio-created product, a manufactured personality made up by the publicity department and the still camera. He longed for serious recognition and at the same time feared being challenged beyond his capabilities. The more hackneyed the scripts became, the more doubt they created. Could he do anything better? Sue usually kept the more disparaging columnists' remarks out of sight because they could so easily depress him.

Sue continued to visit the set each day and to check over every detail where he was concerned. She made sure his lighting was right and his makeup suitable. When Alan finished a scene, he would usually look first at Sue for confirmation, than at the director. Her consuming interest in life was Alan Ladd, and for him she would suffer anything. Through their years together she played all the roles with him: lover, wife, friend, manager, mother. She provided the anchor, the stability he had once lacked. If later he came to lean on her too much, so that he lost his own personality, that is the danger that all too often overtakes such close, off-balance relationships.

The tough-guy roles continued. From time to time Paramount would announce that Ladd would do a musical—he had sung "My Ideal" on a 1945 bond tour and a duet with Dorothy Lamour in the all-star film *Variety Girl*, and he had a fairly good singing voice—but the musical projects did not materialize.

When he was told he would be co-starring with Lake in another actioner, *Saigon*, Alan began to wonder if he would ever get to do a worthwhile part in a worthwhile

Alan and daughter Alana.

Corporal Ladd of the Army Air Force.

53

Alan Ladd was one of the very few male actors who could be counted on to sell magazines by appearing on the cover . . . it was generally believed by publishers that only female stars made good cover material. Though other actors were used for covers now and then, Ladd was the only actor used consistently—because he was good business.

film. The stuiod brass promised him the star role in F
Scott Fitzgerald's *The Great Gatsby* if he made *Saigon*
The idea of doing Gatsby was both frightening and ex
hilarating. All he needed was a great role and a skilled
understanding director.

Saigon was cheaply done and so reminiscent of a dozer
other adventure films that it was almost embarrassing
but it did make money. However, there was some in
dication that fans were starting to take Ladd for grantec
in such mediocre stuff and were going to his films ou
of habit, expecting little more than a chance to see thei
idol.

The same year he made *Saigon*, Ladd also made *Wila
Harvest* and a Technicolor western, *Whispering Smith*.
During the filming of *Wild Harvest*, Sue was having a
difficult pregnancy with their son David. She was far
past the ideal child-bearing age, and barely survived,
but David Alan was born on February 4, 1947. Alan was
very proud of his new son, and he and Sue were as close
as ever. Alan, Jr., was a frequent visitor at the Ladds',
and Alan hoped the boy would live with them, but Alan,
Jr.'s, mother, Midge, had remarried and wasn't eager
to lose the boy. Though the two Ladd-Carol children,
David and Alana, were photographed constantly, the
other children, Carol Lee and Alan, Jr., were from marriages never mentioned to the press and therefore were
seldom seen in photos and were kept more or less out
of sight when reporters were around.

In September 1947, Alan started another potboiler,
Beyond Glory (working title: *The Long Grey Line*), and he
and Sue went off to West Point for preproduction shots.
Alan definitely did not like to travel. He had seldom
been out of California since his boyhood, making his first

*Dancing with Sue while on leave. Pat and Charles Boyer are in
background.*

trip to Chicago when he was still a hungry bit player and had a job filming a meat-packing commercial film. His second trip had been to New York for the premiere release of *This Gun for Hire*. Locations could shake him loose from his home, but even on vacations he was often no farther from Hollywood than Palm Springs. He would not fly and always went by train or, when necessary, by boat.

Beyond Glory was released in February 1948, to lukewarm reviews, and in March production was begun on *The Great Gatsby*.

For once, Alan was hopeful. Here was a strong story by a famed writer, and it was likely that Paramount would go the whole way, giving it the kind of production values too often overlooked on routine Ladd flicks. A good friend, Richard Maibaum, was producing the film, and Maibaum wanted Betty Field to play Daisy. Field had a strong reputation as an actress, stage trained and very capable, but she did not have much box-office pull.

Barry Sullivan, Macdonald Carey, Howard da Silva, Shelley Winters, Henry Hull, Elisha Cook, Jr., and Ruth Hussey made up the rest of the excellent cast. Whatever flaws the film may have had, it remains Alan Ladd's most underrated and neglected performance. Of course, few people have seen it in years because Paramount withdrew it from circulation when they made the 1974 version. The 1949 production is superior in every way and could only make the later flop look worse.

Though *The Great Gatsby* made a respectable profit, it was not considered one of Ladd's better box-office successes. Paramount returned to casting him in stereotyped tough-guy roles. He finished out the 1940s with *Chicago Deadline*, a routine adaptation of a hard-nosed Tiffany Thayer novel.

Ladd had long wanted to do a radio show of his own, but Paramount did not want him competing with himself in that way, so not until late in 1948 was he able to put together a syndicated weekly show called *Box 13*. In it he played Dan Halliday, a writer who advertised for adventure. The syndication method was ideal for a busy star; he could do the shows whenever it was convenient and not be tied to a weekly schedule. *Box 13* ran for a couple of years.

In 1951 Paramount made what for them was an unusual move: They starred Ladd with two other stellar box-office draws, Charles Boyer and Deborah Kerr, in a topical drama called *Thunder in the East* (not to be confused with an early-1930s Boyer film of the same name). *Thunder in the East* concerned India's first years of struggle with independence. Ladd's name was still above the title, but the presence of Kerr and Boyer would seem to indicate the film was more than just Ladd's usual exotic actioner. Unfortunately, whatever impact it might have had was defused because the State Department grew fearful that the subject matter might inflame a delicate political climate, and Paramount shelved *Thunder in the East*, not releasing it until 1953. It turned out to be a

Ladd looks over his pastures on his ranch, Alsulana.

(Left) The Cast of The Great Gatsby: *Barry Sullivan, Betty Field, Ladd, Ruth Hussey, MacDonald Carey, Howard da Silva.*

decided letdown.

Meantime, Alan and Sue were trying to renegotiat[e] his contract, which was coming up for renewal. Befor[e] he sighed a new contract, he wanted some changes made[.] He had too often been passed up for some part he longe[d] to play—he had been desolate when Kirk Douglas g[ot] the lead in the prestigious *Detective Story*, and he ha[d] more than once hinted that he would be the ideal *Lawren[ce] of Arabia.* Ladd felt it was time he was given some [of] the plums. As Paramount's most popular star, he cer[-] tainly deserved some consideration. The studio did agre[e] to a healthy salary hike, but they were not eager to ad[d] cast and script approval.

Alan's agent at MCA let it be known that Alan woul[d] be considering offers—and the bidding was on. At th[at] time Ladd was the world's most popular star, if one ca[n] believe all the various newspaper and magazine polls. H[e] and Esther Williams received gold Henrietta statuett[es] from the Foreign Press Association for being World Fil[m] Favorites in a poll taken of fifty foreign nations. How[-] ever, winning polls was nothing new to Alan. What [he] really wanted was to win some critical approval, and [he] was convinced that Paramount was not going to provid[e] the sort of vehicle which would make that possible.

Meanwhile, Paramount's executives were in shock ov[er] Ladd's interest in other offers. Darryl Zanuck state[d,] "There aren't any box-office stars any more except Jo[hn] Wayne and Alan Ladd," and openly hoped to sign hi[m.] But Zanuck could not beat Warner Bros.' offer: a on[e-] hundred-fifty-thousand-dollar guarantee per picture a[nd] ten percent of the gross for one picture a year for t[en] years. The deal set a precedent that later led to sta[rs] making ridiculous demands of studios already panick[ed] by the emergence of television. The fringe benefits we[re] what interested Alan most, however. He now had sto[ry] approval (and he would prove as faulty in his judgme[nt] of what was right for him as most stars do when giv[en] the chance to choose) plus residual rights and the freedo[m] to do outside pictures. There was even talk of his bei[ng] able to form his own production company.

It was a fabulous deal, but instead of giving Al[an] renewed confidence, it cut the ground from under hi[m.] His friends, the people he considered as family, were [to] be left behind. A simple, quiet man with an inexplicab[le] inferiority complex, Ladd had always been uncomfortab[le] with strangers and preferred to have the same people [on] picture crews whenever possible. The directors w[ho] worked with him knew how important familiar fac[es] were to him; he was always a bundle of doubts and fe[ars] at the start of each new picture. It took understandi[ng] and tact to make him calm and confident. Sue's pl[ace] at Paramount had long ago been established; that, to[o,] was important. But all the people at Warner Bros. kn[ew] was that Ladd was a superstar, and a high-priced one [at] that.

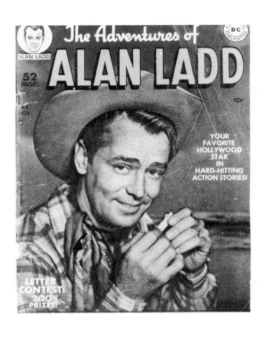

"The Adventures of Alan Ladd," a series of comic books put ou[t in] 1949 by DC publications, ran for nine issues. This is issue num[ber] one.

61

Raven checks his gun, the tool of his trade.

This Gun for Hire

Paramount   (1942)

CREDITS

Director, Frank Tuttle. *Producer*, Richard M. Blumenthal. *Screenplay*, Albert Maltz, W. R. Burnett. *Based on the novel by* Graham Greene. *Photographer*, John Seitz. *Music*, David Buttolph. *Songs*, "I've Got You," "Now You See It," Frank Loesser, Jacques Press. *Editor*, Archie Marshek. *Running time, 81 minutes.*

CAST

Ellen Graham, VERONICA LAKE; *Michael Crane*, ROBERT PRESTON; *Willard Gates*, LAIRD CREGAR; *Raven*, ALAN LADD; *Alvin Brewster*, TULLY MARSHALL; *Sluky*, MIKHAIL RASUMNY; *Tommy*, MARC LAWRENCE; *Annie*, PAMELA BLAKE; *Albert Baker*, FRANK FERGUSON; *Senator Burnett*, ROGER IMHOF; *Baker's Secretary*, BERNADENE HAYES; *Blair Fletcher*, OLIN HOWLAND; *Crippled Girl*, VIRITA CAMPBELL; *Steve Finnerty*, HARRY SHANNON: *Ruby*, PATRICIA FARR; *Rooming-house Manager*, CHESTER

A cat softens Raven as he and Ellen hide out.

CLUTE; *Salesgirl*, MARY DAVENPORT; *Night Watchman*, JAMES FARLEY; *Police Captain*, CHARLES C. WILSON; *Mr. Collins*, EARLE DEWEY; *Gates's Secretary*, LYNDA GREY; *Charlie*, EMMETT VOGAN; *Lt. Clark*, DICK RUSH

If Paramount had decided to film Graham Greene's novel as it was written, possibly the whole Ladd phenomenon would not have happened. Raven, as Greene wrote him, was a repulsive harelipped creature, deformed in feature as he was in character. Had the makeup department duplicated that description, history might have been written another way; Ladd might have been nominated for a Best Supporting Actor award. What got in the way of this being strictly a remarkable acting job was that most curious of accidents: screen chemistry.

From the moment Ladd first sits up in that sleazy bed in the rooming house, until that final closeup when his eyes roll back lifeless, the viewer is completely absorbed with him. He is surly, hostile, ruthless, and we are immediately struck by an uneasy sympathy for him. He obviously believes himself to be hard, self-contained, but he hurts, he yearns for something indefinable. "You're tryin' to make me go soft," he accuses the girl. "Well, save your oil—I don't go soft for nobody." It's a lie and he knows it and the knowledge frightens him.

In the Paramount version with Ladd, the story opens with Raven keeping an appointment to gun down two people he has never seen before. He does this with dispatch and a steely smile. As he leaves the building, he passes a small crippled child sitting on the stairs. He pauses. Has she heard the shots? She drops her ball and calls for him to retrieve it for her. He turns, his odd eye giving her a blank stare, his hand going to the concealed gun—then he picks up the ball instead and hands it her. It's a moment you remember long afterward.

Raven is paid off by a peppermint-eating fat man, Gates (Laird Cregar). When the fat man asks, with shudder, how Raven feels when he kills a stranger, Raven answers with a cold, calm, "I feel fine."

The money paid to Raven is hot—he has been double-crossed. Meanwhile, a pretty blond nightclub entertainer has just been hired by the fat man to sing in his Los Angeles nightclub. We discover she has been put on the job by a Washington senator who wants to get the goods on Gates, who is suspected of fronting for a gang of spies selling poison gas to the enemy. The blond Ellen Graham (Lake), has a cop boyfriend, Michael (Preston), who is assigned to investigate the murders committed by Raven and who has a lead on Raven because of the marked payoff money.

Raven sets off for Los Angeles to find Gates and get even. Ellen is on the same train, on her way to take the new job. By coincidence they sit together and Gates spots them and assumes they know each other and are working together to frame him.

His attempt to eliminate Ellen by inviting her out to his estate and turning her over to his chauffeur-henchman, Tommy (Lawrence), is thwarted when Raven shows up. Raven kicks the chauffeur down the basement stairs and rescues the bound and gagged Ellen. For a moment while untying her, he is close to her and the effect of her clean beauty is obvious on Ladd's face: admiration, wariness, doubt.

There follows a hairbreadth chase through a dark factory and then across a railroad yard, while Michael and his cops are hot on the heels of Raven and his hostage. Raven is still hell bent on revenge; Ellen is after the same gang for the sake of the government. She doesn't fight Raven, because she hopes he will lead her to her own objective.

In a dark, cold, abandoned railroad car, surrounded by spotlights and police, Raven and his hostage settle down to await the dawn.

A cat comes in through the window. Raven picks it up, saying, "Cats bring you luck." He strokes it and calls it Tuffy. Explaining his fondness for cats, he says "They're on their own; they don't need nobody." The

With Veronica Lake.

Raven rescues Ellen in the old house.

With Laird Cregar.

suddenly voices are heard outside as two workmen pa
by. Raven must stifle the cat's meow—and he discove
a moment later that he has smothered the animal.
killed it," he mutters bleakly. "I killed my luck."

The dead cat triggers self-revelation, and he fin
himself purging himself of his weary nightmares, tellin
everything to the quiet blond girl in the hopes that "
you tell your dream, you won't have it no more." Lil
the rest of us, Ellen is sickened by tales of the beating
he took as a child and of his bloody revenge against th
aunt who mistreated him: "I picked up a knife, and
let her have it—in the throat. They put a label on m
killer, and sent me to reform school, and they beat m
there, too. . . ."

When her pity grows too strong for her to bear, sh
reaches out, and he growls, "Get away—get away fro
me!" In this one scene alone, Ladd justifies a whol
career.

As dawn comes, Lake has persuaded Raven to hel
her catch the spies—not to kill, but to get a confession
Raven is skeptical, but by now he cannot conceal h
admiration for the girl. She hasn't whimpered or los
control. He is almost driven to trust her, though he sti
finds his own dark side easier to live with than his bette
nature. He is the total cynic: Good impulses scare him

The girl dons Raven's hat and coat and will act a
decoy so he can get away to the factory. As she turns t
run into the mist, she reaches up and kisses his unshave
cheek. Raven hesitates; his fingers touch where her lip
have brushed and his cold eyes raise with wonder. The
he snaps to and leaps out the window.

Through a ruse he gains entrance to Brewster's (Mar
shall) secret office in the gas-producing company, an
he manages to extract the confession from both Brewste
and Gates before he is forced to gun them down in self
defense. Michael is trying to reach the office by a scaffol
outside the window, and Raven lifts his gun, only to se
Ellen's stricken face as she strains to hold Michael back
He hesitates, and Michael fires. As Ellen stands by cryin
silent tears, Raven expires with a smile for her on his
lips.

Ladd came down with pneumonia during the filming
and his illness may have aided his performance, giving
him that strained, hunted look. In the boxcar scene h
looks exhausted, as if all his life force had run out.

Good camera angles, the use of wet streets and dark
shadows, the sounds of low cat cries and lonely trair
whistles, gave the picture an interesting *film noir* at
mosphere. Frank Tuttle's direction was sharp, crisp, and
well paced and drew from his principals their best per
formances. Lake seemed real for once; a world-weary
smart little cookie with tolerance for the weak and tor
mented, she was both gorgeous and sympathetic.

What started out as a routine production was greeted
by serious reviews and praise for a new star. *Liberty* mag
azine gave it three stars and called Ladd "an actor to be

reckoned with." *Life* said the film rose above the run of ordinary drama because it had two requisites of a good movie: action and original characters. "Standout attraction," stated *Life*, "is twenty-eight year old Alan Ladd, who suggests by his deadpan acting the festering bitterness of a killer who hates everything."

Family Circle predicted, "After [the film's] release, audiences will have found a new screen rave. Young Mr. Ladd gives one of the finest performances as a cold blooded killer since Chester Morris's portrayal of one in *Alibi*."

From the moment *Gun* was released, Alan Ladd was a star.

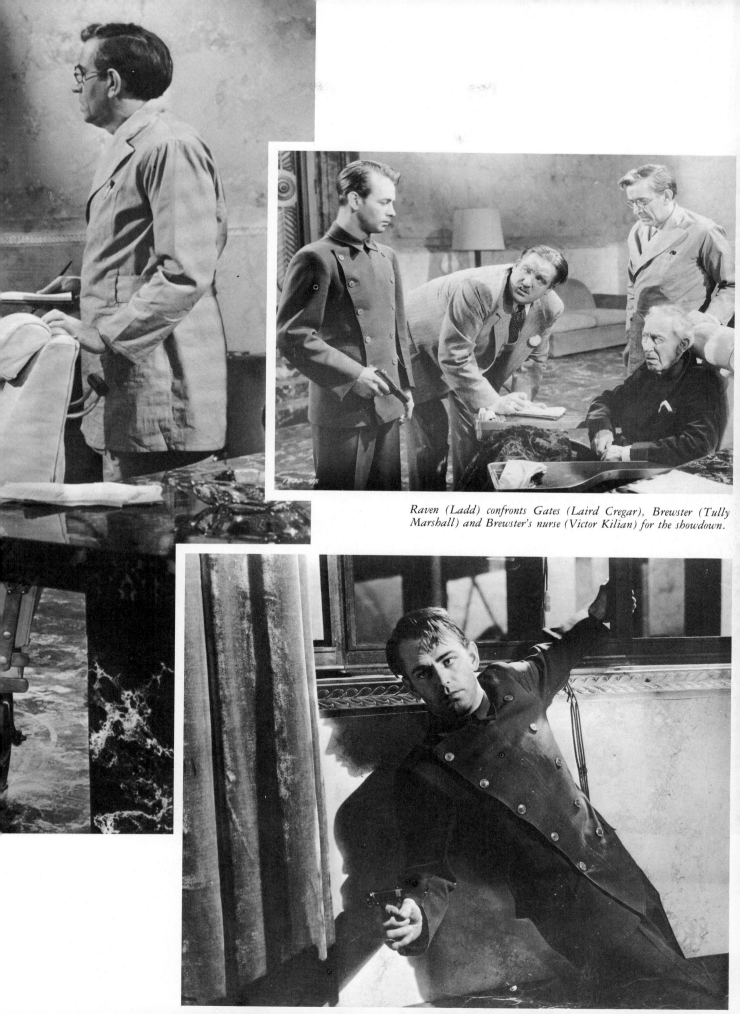

Raven (Ladd) confronts Gates (Laird Cregar), Brewster (Tully Marshall) and Brewster's nurse (Victor Kilian) for the showdown.

With Brian Donlevy.

The Glass Key
Paramount (1942)

CREDITS

Director, Stuart Heisler. *Producer*, Fred Kohlmar. *Screenplay*, Jonathan Latimer. *Adapted from a novel by* Dashiell Hammett. *Photography*, Theodor Sparkuhl. *Music*, Victor Young. *Editor*, Archie Marshek. *Running time, 85 minutes.*

CAST

Paul Madvig, BRIAN DONLEVY; *Janet Henry*, VERONICA LAKE; *Ed Beaumont*, ALAN LADD; *Opal Madvig*, BONITA GRANVILLE; *Taylor Henry*, RICHARD DENNING; *Nick Varna*, JOSEPH CALLEIA; *Jeff*, WILLIAM BENDIX; *Nurse*, FRANCES GIFFORD; *Farr*, DONALD MacBRIDE; *Eloise Matthews*, MARGARET HAYES; *Senator Ralph Henry*, MORONI OLSEN; *Rusty*, EDDIE MARR; *Clyde Matthews*, ARTHUR LOFT; *Claude Tuttle*, GEORGE MEADER; *Lynch*, JOE McGUINN; *Politician*, PAT O'MALLEY; *Gambler*, JAMES MILLICAN; *Henry Sloss*, BERNARD ZANVILLE (DANE CLARK); *Groggins*, FRANK HAGNEY

When the rushes of *This Gun for Hire* were shown, the men in the front office at Paramount wondered: Would this Ladd hit the public the way he was hitting everyone on the lot? Wouldn't it be wise to have another feature film ready for release?

The Glass Key was a property that had been kicking around for some time. George Raft had starred in a tense version of it in 1935. A Dashiell Hammett novel of the tough, sledgehammer variety, it had a dollop of romance and a barrel of action. The book's hero, Ned Beaumont (renamed Ed in the film), was a tough-talking, hardheaded type whose main virtue seemed to be loyalty. He wasn't exactly a criminal; he just wasn't fastidious about how he got things done. If it worked for Raft, it would work for Ladd.

Patricia Morison was supposed to be the leading lady in *Key*, but after a few scenes were shot, it was decided that she was too tall. Though *This Gun for Hire* had not yet been released and the public had yet to see Ladd and Lake together and the Paramount brass were not aware

(Above) Opal (Bonita Granville) and Ed Beaumont (Ladd) at Taylor's funeral. (Facing page) Ed (Ladd) confronts Madvig (Brian Donlevy), Senator Henry (Moroni Olsen) and Varna (Joseph Calleia).

of the impact the team would have, they quickly replaced Morison with Lake, simply because Lake was tiny and looked fine standing next to Ladd.

The plot of *Key* was both obvious and unfathomable, probably because of an uneven script. Donlevy plays Paul Madvig, a tough, shady political boss who has fallen for socialite Janet Henry (Lake) and has decided to back her father as the reform candidate for mayor. Janet is stringing Paul along to ensure his help for her father, but when she meets Paul's right-hand man, Ed (Ladd), she flirts behind her fiancé's back to arouse Ed's interest. He sees through her and, though he is attracted, rebuffs her.

Janet's no-good brother Taylor (Denning) has been romancing Opal (Granville), Paul's kid sister, and when Taylor is suddenly murdered, Paul is the obvious suspect because he had tried to break them up. Nick Varna (Calleia), the city's kingpin gambler, jumps at this opportunity to smear Paul and weaken his candidate.

Angered by the slander and hoping to stop it, Ed goes to Varna, pretends to have left Paul's camp, and tries to get information. It is a trap, however, and Varna turns Ed over to Jeff (Bendix), his brutish henchman, who beats him to a pulp. (This was the first of many screen beatings Ladd would endure over his years of stardom, and it remains the most thorough and the best remembered.)

(Top) A deal is discussed: Joseph Calleia, William Bendix, Brian Donlevy and Ladd.
(Bottom) Bonita Granville stares at the body of Varna's dead henchman (William Bendix)
as Callei, Eddie Marr and Ladd look on.

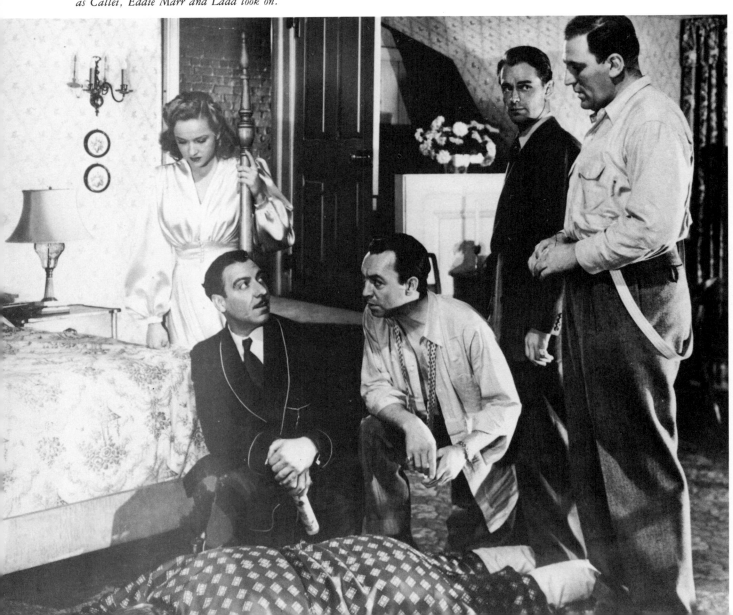

Ed escapes and manages to foul up Varna's plans to pin the murder on Paul. Yet when one of Varna's henchmen turns up dead, Paul is arrested. Ed tracks down Jeff and tricks him into bragging about the murder. Varna walks in on this confession and, in the ensuing argument, is strangled by Jeff. The police arrive and take the maddened Jeff away.

In a last-minute ruse, Ed discovers that Janet's father killed his own son in a quarrel over gambling debts. Paul, who has been protecting his fiancée's family with his silence, is freed.

Ed packs for New York, but Janet has no intention of letting him get away. Ed is still trying to resist her, when Paul intervenes and gives the pair his blessing.

The Glass Key established Ladd's drawing power and gave the fans what they wanted. An occasional critic compared it unfavorably with the 1935 version; a few liked it better. Neither opinion slowed it down at the box office.

Still, viewed today, *Key* seems a shopworn item. The dialogue is second-rate Hammett, and the key characters are unbelievable. Donlevy's political boss is so stupid, crude, and dishonest that it seems ridiculous that he could be in such a position of power. It was very likely Hammett's view of politicians, but it is a caricature, and it doesn't play.

What motivates Ladd's Beaumont is surely a mystery, for he can have little in common with the boisterous Donlevy. Throughout the film Ladd seems to change expression by affecting a strange and often inappropriate little smile. At this time Ladd was still trying to look taller—leaning back on his heels, thrusting his chin forward. Such posturing was gone by the next film. Evidently Ladd spotted what he was doing and corrected it by conscious practice.

Lake's dialogue with Ladd does not have the crackle we later came to expect of these two. She is arch and coy at the same time, and her character is as ill-defined as Ladd's. But Lake's assets were basically feline in nature and didn't rely on a polished acting technique. She could drawl a sarcasm and pout seductively, and she was nearly always interesting, even when she was mediocre.

The best performance in *Key* came from a scene stealer *par excellence*, William Bendix. His pathological bully boy is both ghastly and pitiable as he relishes such lines as "Aw, don't I get to smack Baby no more?"

Liberty magazine named Ladd Personality of the Week and stated in their review: "Fortunately Alan Ladd is an excellent actor as well as an arresting performer, compelling your attention whether he is playing a killer or, as in this film, a loyal lieutenant of a political boss. Whatever excitement *The Glass Key* can offer springs from Ladd's provocative performance."

Ed confronts Opal (Granville) about her involvement with Janet's no-good brother.

Madvig gets tough with Varna's (Calleia's) henchmen, Jeff (Bendix, on floor) and Rusty (Marr).

Lucky Jordan
Paramount   (1942)

CREDITS

Director, Frank Tuttle. *Associate producer*, Fred Kohlmar. *Screenplay*, Darrell Ware, Karl Tunberg. *Story*, Charles Leonard. *Camera*, John Seitz. *Music director*, Adolph Deutsch. *Art directors*, Hans Dreier, Ernest Fegte. *Running time, 84 minutes.*

CAST

Lucky Jordan, ALAN LADD; *Jill Evans*, HELEN WALKER; *Slip Moran*, SHELDON LEONARD; *Annie*, MABEL PAIGE; *Pearl*, MARIE McDONALD; *Ernest Higgins*, LLOYD CORRIGAN; *Angelo*, DAVE WILLOCK; *Eddie*, RUSSELL HOYT; *Herr Kesselman*, JOHN WENGRAF; *Kilpatrick*, MILES MANDER; *Gas-station Attendant*, CLEM BEVANS; *Hired Killer*, ANTHONY CARUSO; *Sergeant*, CHARLES CANE; *Little Man*, GEORGE F. MEADER; *Woman*, VIRGINIA BRISSAC; *Mrs. Maggotti*, KITTY KELLY; *Mr. Maggotti*, GEORGE HUMBERT: *Toy-shop Clerk*, GEORGIA BACKUS; *Maid at Hollyhock School*, DOROTHY DANDRIDGE; *First Killer*, AL M. HILL; *Second Killer*, FRED KOHLER, JR.; *Draft Official*, PAUL STANTON; *Commanding Officer*, WILLIAM FORREST; *Florist*, RONNIE RONDELL; *Pearl's Boyfriend*, KIRK ALYN: *Hearndon*, ARTHUR LOFT

Ladd's fan mail after the success of *This Gun for Hire* and *The Glass Key* was staggering. He could not walk down the street without being mobbed, girls screamed and swooned when he appeared at radio shows, and his face was on a dozen magazine covers.

It was time to bill him over the title and let him carry a picture himself. Strangely enough, the vehicle chosen was his only genuine comedy. Though flawed, *Lucky Jordan* is styled after Damon Runyon's work and is a very enjoyable film. Blond again after being tanned and brown haired, Ladd was at his handsome prime, and he was more animated than he was to become later after his tough-guy mold hardened around him.

Lucky (Ladd) is a gangster who "controls all the rackets in town" and who has no intention of being drafted into World War II. His mouthpiece, Higgins (Corrigan), has been trying to get him deferred, even going as far as to try to get Lucky classified 4-F by having him declared "socially undesirable." Lucky is indignant. "Whaduya

With Helen Walker.

mean, 'socially undesirable'?" he huffs, flexing his shoulders inside his zoot suit. "Dames like me!"

The solution would seem to be to hire a dependent parent, Lucky being an orphan. "There must be some old broad who won't mind callin' me Sonny for the right amount."

Mabel Paige as Annie, "the old broad," is absolutely priceless though she insists, "For that kind of dough [fifty dollars], I'd do a swan dive off the Statue of Liberty!"

The ruse fails, however, and Lucky is drafted.

At boot camp Lucky proceeds to be about the worst soldier to ever sleep in a tent. He lolls around in silk pajamas, misses roll call, and later wanders into the post canteen looking for a place to hide out for the day.

Jill (Walker) leads Lucky on, playing on his ego.

"Ma" (Paige) shares her stew with "son" Lucky.

When the canteen workers' shift changes and pretty Helen Walker comes on duty, the girl leaving indicates Lucky alone in the canteen and warns, "There's something funny about that one—he's been hanging around all day." Jill (Walker) allows as how he might be homesick. The girl shakes her head. "I don't know—something tells me he's been away from home before!"

When the MPs catch up with him, he lands in a cell but manages to escape and go AWOL. Along the way he picks up a civilian's car, that car is later hijacked by some hoodlums on the road outside camp, and Lucky winds up commandeering Jill's car when she happens along. Jill pleads with him to let her go, even threatens to throw a briefcase out of the car, but as she tosses it Lucky just grins and informs her, "It wasn't my briefcase—it belonged to the guy I swiped the car from. . . ."

Realizing his old gang had been taken over by Slip (Sheldon Leonard), a henchman never to be trusted, Lucky confronts him and learns that Slip has been selling secrets to the enemy. "I got twenty-thousand dollars for settin' fire to da *Normandy*," Slip brags.

Lucky is impressed, "You did that?"

Slip demurs, "Naw, but dey don't know I didn't!"

Lucky decides to muscle in on the take. Slip pretends to go along and tells Lucky the briefcase in the stolen car was worth plenty and it was his men who had tried to grab it. With Jill for an unwilling guide, they drive out to find it. Slip gets nasty with a gun, and Lucky kicks him unconscious.

Night comes, and when Lucky decides to park Jill in a service-station washroom so she can't escape, she manipulates the egotistical Lucky with her sex appeal, and he thinks she has fallen for him. She gets away.

Even Lucky's moll Pearl (Marie McDonald) has deserted him for Slip, so Lucky takes the briefcase and hides out at Annie's. Annie welcomes him and calls him Son, admitting that hearing herself referred to as his mother had done something to her—she has even been bragging about him to other service mothers.

Their scenes together are sheer delight. When Lucky questions her about some little luxury in her shabby flat, she says she was "just walkin' through this store and it kinda fell into my umbrella." Lucky looks down at the thin stew she has just dished up and mutters, "Too bad you and your umbrella didn't waltz past a couple of thick steaks." She immediately gives him all the meat off her own plate—and he eats it.

The last third of the picture is a disappointment. Unfortunately, the fun goes out of *Lucky Jordan* when Lucky goes after the spies. First, his motivation is a little hard to swallow—the spies beat up Annie and steal the briefcase—but in a sense, it has a certain logic. Jill has tried to appeal to his patriotism and gets a sneer for her trouble. Politics are beyond him. But violence against Ma—that he understands, and he declares he "don't want this country run by guys who beat up old ladies."

The end is satisfying. Jill helps him outsmart the spies, and as the police round them up, she turns to Lucky, eyes shining with admiration, and tells him, "Why, they'll probably give you a medal for this!" Lucky gives her a cocky grin, plainly liking the idea.

Dissolve to army camp. Lucky, dressed in fatigues with a P painted on his shirt, is reluctantly digging a ditch. "Get the lead out!" bellows the sarge. With a calm, nonchalant movement, Lucky lifts the next shovelful of dirt and neatly dumps it on the sergeant's polished boot. "Sorry," he says. "I thought it was your face." Fadeout. The end.

The reviews were mixed and seemed confused about what kind of movie it was. *Time* dismissed it with, "As sociological treatise, *Lucky Jordan* shows that U.S. gangsters are infinitely nicer than Nazis because 1) they are Americans, 2) they do not like to 'go around beating up old women.'"

Lucky in trouble. Ladd is threatened by John Wengraf as Lloyd Corrigan holds him.

Jill and Lucky hold the spies for the FBI.

Pearl (McDonald) tries to explain her defection.

Phillip Hartung in *The Commonweal* wrote, "Up to the point of Jordan's conversion, this is an unusual and interesting melodrama. Frank Tuttle directed it with a fast pace and a hard punch, and Alan Ladd plays the gangster with a relentless, self-centered toughness that carries conviction. (Ladd does these hard-boiled roles so well and so consistently that one wonders if he can do anything else, or if he's an actor at all.) Particularly interesting are [his] scenes with Annie (Mabel Paige), a Times Square panhandler whom Jordan tries to foist on his draft board as his mother. . . . However, the film's good start and exciting chase comes to naught when the script goes to pieces. Obviously it has been tampered with. . . ."

Lucky Jordan was one of the year's top grossers and a solid box-office hit, and Ladd was plainly the star of the year.

It'll Never Be Topped!

THE PARAMOUNT MUSICAL COMEDY OF THE YEAR!

'Star Spangled Rhythm'

Star Spangled Rhythm

Paramount (1942)

CREDITS

Director, George Marshall. *Associate producer*, Joseph Sistrom. *Original screenplay*, Harry Tugend. *Music*, Robert Emmett Dolan. *Camera*, Leo Tover, Theodor Sparkuhl. *Art directors*, Hans Dreier, Ernest Fegte. *Songs*, "That Old Black Magic," "Hit the Road to Dreamland," "Old Glory," "A Sweater, a Sarong, and a Peekaboo Bang," "I'm Doing It for Defense," "Sharp as a Tack," "On the Swing Shift," "He Loved me Till the All-clear Came," *by* Johnny Mercer *and* Harold Arlen. *Running time, 99 minutes.*

CAST

Pop Webster, VICTOR MOORE; *Polly Judson*, BETTY HUTTON; *Jimmy Webster*, EDDIE BRACKEN; *B. G. DeSoto*, WALTER ABEL; *Sarah*, ANNE REVERE; *Mimi*, CASS DALEY; *Hi-pockets*, GIL LAMB; *Y. Frank Freemont*, EDWARD FIELDING; *Mac*, EDGAR DEARING; *Duffy*, WILLIAM HAADE; *Sailors*, MAYNARD HOLMES, JAMES MILLICAN; *Tommy*, EDDIE JOHNSON; *Petty Officer*, ROD CAMERON; *Guest stars and novelty numbers*: BING CROSBY, BOB HOPE, FRED MacMURRAY, FRANCHOT TONE, RAY MILLAND, LYNNE OVERMAN, DOROTHY LAMOUR, PAULETTE GODDARD, VERONICA LAKE, ARTHUR TREACHER, WALTER CATLETT, STERLING HOLLOWAY, TOM DUGAN, RICHARD LOO, PAUL PORCASI, VERA ZORINA, JOHNNIE JOHNSTON, FRANK FAYLEN, MARY MARTIN, DICK POWELL, ALAN LADD, MACDONALD CAREY, EDDIE "ROCHESTER" ANDERSON, KATHERINE DUNHAM, WOODROW "WOODY" STRODE, JERRY COLONNA, WILLIAM BENDIX, MARION MARTIN, DONA DRAKE, SUSAN HAYWARD, MARJORIE REYNOLDS, BETTY RHODES, DON CASTLE, GARY CROSBY, C. B. DeMILLE, PRESTON STURGES, ALBERT DEKKER, CECIL KELLAWAY, ELLEN DREW, JIMMY LYDON, FRANCES GIFFORD, SUSANNA FOSTER, ROBERT PRESTON, GOLDEN GATE QUARTETTE

Really just an excuse to run all the stars on the lot through a series of skits and song numbers, *Star Spangled Rhythm* had a slight plot concerning a crazy blond Paramount secretary (Hutton) and the need to keep her sailor boyfriend (Bracken) from discovering that his dear, bumbling old father (Moore), who is in reality the studio

With Macdonald Carey in a skit.

gatekeeper, is not the head of the studio as "Pop" has been bragging to the boy. This involves subterfuges of the most absurd kind, from taking over the absent studio boss's office, to making false calls to directors such as De Mille and Sturges. It is all wild and hectic and entirely improbable, even to the slight veiling of Buddy De Sylva's name by calling the studio boss B. G. DeSoto.

The film's finale is provided by a big show Betty and Pop organize to entertain Bracken's shipmates. The show includes just about every Paramount star working on the lot at that time, some doing production numbers, such as Crosby's rendering of "Old Glory," others involved in comedy sketches.

Ladd's main bit was a skit: the curtain opens on a poolhall, Macdonald Carey is cowering beside a pool table saying something like, "No, no Scarface—I didn't mean to—!" and Ladd in trenchcoat and hat is bearing down on him, muttering, "You dirty double-crossin' squealer . . ." Ladd then reaches slowly into his coat and pulls out . . . a bow and arrow, with which he shoots the trembling Carey.

An ad for China.

China

Paramount   (1943)

CREDITS

Director, John Farrow. *Producer*, Richard Blumenthal. *Screenplay*, Frank Butler. *Based on the unproduced play Fourth Brother by Archibald Forbes. Photography*, Leo Tover. *Editor*, Eda Warren. *Special photographic effects*, Gordon Jennings. *Running time, 78 minutes.*

CAST

Carolyn Grant, LORETTA YOUNG; *Mr. Jones*, ALAN LADD; *Johnny Sparrow*, WILLIAM BENDIX; *Lin Cho*, PHILLIP AHN; *Kwan Su*, IRIS WONG; *Lin Wei*, (VICTOR) SEN YUNG; *Tan Ying*, MARIANNE QUON; *Student*, JESSIE TAI SING; *Lin Yun*, RICHARD LOO; *"Donald Duck,"*, IRENE TSO; *Chang Teh*, CHINGWHA LEE; *Tai Shen*, SOO YONG; *Captain Tao-Yuan-Kai*, BEAL WONG; *Aide to Captain*, BRUCE WONG; *Woman*, TALA BIRELL; *Nan Ti*, BARBARA JEAN WONG; *Japanese General*, CHESTER GAN

With a good director and plenty of action, *China* comes off better than it should. Though the script bogs down periodically with the most blatant sort of propagandizing, it isn't very different from dozens of other wartime films that waved the flag and unashamedly lectured on freedom and decency while blasting the hell out of the enemy. At the time—1943—we expected films to sound like that, and no one quibbled much about getting a good dose of patriotism with their entertainment.

Regardless of its noble noises, *China* was not a serious attempt to explore the Chinese problem or to examine what led us to the calamity of Pearl Harbor. Nor are the characters very believable. By mouthing all the righteous and high-minded platitudes, they manage to make a mockery of everyone concerned: the Chinese, whose situation in the face of Japanese terrorism was very grim indeed; the Americans, personified by Alan Ladd as surly, conniving, self-serving, and greedy; and Lady Bountifuls, portrayed with stern but sugary do-gooder zest by Loretta Young. The only character with no ax to grind, and therefore the one with the most credibility, is lovable William Bendix, though it is a puzzle how he came to be in China and why he hangs around the generally antisocial Mr. Jones (Ladd).

China was something of a rush job—Paramount had no intention of letting their hottest new star cool off for the duration and wanted something to tide the fans over while Ladd was away in the service. What was needed

Plotting a raid with Lin Wei (Yung) and Lin Cho (Phillip Ahn).

Ready to blast, Johnny and Mr. Jones wait for the Japanese convoy.

Mr. Jones (Ladd) discovers that his truck is full of schoolgirls.

was a timely adventure story with plenty of action and a chance for Ladd to act hard-boiled and virile, the way the fans liked him. According to those requirements, *China* was a smash success.

The movie begins with bombs being dropped on a Chinese village and Bendix picking up a crying baby

from the rubble as he goes in search of his pal Jones Jones is with a blonde B-girl, but when he hears of th bombing, he grumbles to Bendix to dump the baby ar goes off to pick up his truck so they can drive to Shangh to sell a load of oil to the Japanese. He makes it cle he doesn't much care that it is the Japanese who a dropping the bombs. It isn't his war, and anyway, "Th Japs are good business."

Rain is falling, and the roads are clogged with refu gees. In the dark the truck is stopped and commandeer by a beautiful American girl, Carolyn Grant (Young who, with the aid of a young Chinese guerrilla, forc Jones to take a load of female Chinese students into t back of the truck. Jones discovers that Johnny (Bendi has brought the baby along after all and that they ne milk for it.

One of the girl's parents has a farm nearby, and the "Donald Duck," as Johnny has dubbed the baby, ge food and a bath. The group decides to leave the bal at the farm, and Jones has agreed to take the girls as f as a temple up the road, where he can then turn off f Shanghai. No amount of persuasion will convince hi to take them farther. Guerrilla fighting in the hills brin the war close to the truck—then it is discovered one the girls is missing—young Tan Ying has returned the farm to be with her parents. Over Jones's protest Carolyn insists on going back for her, intimating wh the Japanese soldiers would do to a young girl the found.

At the farm, Carolyn and Jones discover devastation— which breaks down Jones's last resistance to involvemen Tan Ying's parents and the baby are all dead, and Ta Ying has been raped and beaten. Jones takes up a machin gun and shoots the three soldiers they find in the hous confessing later to Carolyn that he enjoyed it—"I've g no more feelings about it than if they had been thre flies on a pile of manure." (It was exactly this sort casual violence that made critics so nervous about Ladd popularity with young people.)

The injured girl dies, and this hardens Jones's resolv to get back at the Japanese. He and the guerrilla ban headed by First Brother, set out to steal dynamite fron a Japanese bridge-building crew, with the idea of blow ing up a mountain pass the Japanese are using. The raid carried out in stealth at night, is successful though costly taking too many lives, including young Lin Wei (Se Yung), Third Brother, whom Jones has come to admir for his sass and his courage.

Back at the temple, Jones confesses to Carolyn tha he loves her, unaware that Johnny has made his ow shy, stumbling proposal to her and has been turne down. Carolyn does not reject Jones, however, and i the back of the truck they spend the night talking an making love, knowing that time is running out.

At dawn Jones and what is left of the guerrilla ban go off to set the charges in the side of the mountain but before he can get the dynamite rigged, the Japanes vehicles are spotted. He instructs the others when to se off the charges and then strides down the mountain t

...) and Carolyn (Young) comfort Tan Ying (Marianne Quon) after she's been attacked.

stall the lead jeep.

Jones stops the motorcade, and in the ensuing confrontation with the jeep's passenger, a general (Gan), he defiantly flips a cigarette in the general's face. A shot rings out and Jones is killed, but at the same moment the whole mountain explodes and buries the convoy. Johnny and Carolyn are left to carry on the work for a free China and to remember Mr. Jones as "a great guy."

At the time *China* was filmed, Loretta Young's contract gave her top billing. The ads, however, made no pretense as to whom the fans would come to see. Studio artists air-brushed an absurd set of muscles on a tough-looking, bare-chested Ladd and he was featured as out to get "the rapacious Japs!"

Time's review stated, "[*China*] stars recently drafted Alan Ladd and gazelle-eyed Loretta Young in as thick a glossary of clichés as may be collected currently from any U.S. screen."

The Commonweal said, "Alan Ladd plays this role with a lack of conviction, not so much through his fault as through a badly written characterization," and added, "We praise [*China*'s] honest intention, regret its ten-twenty-thirty execution."

It was in a review of *China* that *Newsweek* referred to Ladd as "that boyish specialist in mildly abnormal behavior"—a description that was to haunt him during the rest of the 1940s.

And Now Tomorrow

Paramount (1944)

CREDITS

Director, Irving Pichel. *Producer*, Fred Kohlmar. *Screenplay*, Frank Parton, Raymond Chandler. *From the novel by* Rachel Field. *Photography*, Daniel Fapp, Farciot Edouart. *Music*, Victor Young. *Running time, 86 minutes.*

CAST

Doctor Merek Vance, ALAN LADD; *Emily Blair*, LORETTA YOUNG; *Janice Blair*, SUSAN HAYWARD; *Jeff Stoddard*, BARRY SULLIVAN; *Doctor Weeks*, CECIL KELLAWAY; *Aunt Em*, BEULAH BONDI; *Uncle Wallace*, GRANT MITCHELL; *Peter Gallo*, ANTHONY CARUSO; *Angeletta Gallo*, HELEN MACK; *Joe*, DARRYL HICKMAN; *Doctor Sloane*, JONATHAN HALE: *Meeker*, GEORGE CARLETON; *Hester*, CONNIE LEON; *Jan Vankovitch*, LEO BULGAKOV

Vance and Janice (Hayward) watch deaf Emily try to dance with her fiancé, Jeff (Sullivan).

Vance administers one of many injections to Emily.

After approximately eleven months in the army air corps, Alan Ladd was medically discharged and returned to to at Paramount. The studio had a drama of a different type for him—a romantic "woman's picture." Based on a popular novel by Rachel Field, the film was a series emotional clichés that were nevertheless welcomed by the hordes of eager Ladd fans—and this time he received top billing over Young. The film was among the top ten grossers of the year.

The story concerned a rich, snobbish deaf girl and surly, handsome, born-on-the-wrong-side-of-town doctor. Emily Blair (Young), whose family owns the Blairstown Mill and practically everything else in Blairstown, Massachusetts, has been deaf since she contracted meningitis, and she has made the rounds of the best known doctors, all to no avail. Discouraged, she has come home to resume her life in the family home at the top of the hill.

Emily reads lips, but she is not prepared for what she reads on the lips of a rude young man she jostles in the railroad station. He introduces himself as Dr. Mere Vance (Ladd).

Doctor Vance turns out to be the protegé of Doctor Weeks (Kellaway), the Blairs' family doctor, and he brings young Vance along when he comes to dinner at the Blair mansion. Vance meets Janice (Hayward), Emily's sister, and Jeff (Sullivan), Emily's fiancé. Vance misses very little, including the undertones passing between sister and fiancé. Later he tells Emily of first seeing her as a rich child passing out gifts at the company Christmas party, patronizing the Mill's poor children. He had been named Vankovitch then—and he had hated her for being a spoiled member of the rich Blair family.

Vance has been working on a new serum to treat deafness, and Doctor Weeks persuades Emily to take injections secretly. She has put off marrying Jeff on the theory that it would be unfair to go to him handicapped. She and Vance do not get on well, but his serum has given her renewed hope, and she continues to visit him despite their antagonism.

One night she accompanies Vance on a call to Shantytown where he must perform an emergency operation on a little boy with a mastoid infection. She helps, gaining Vance's respect.

Vance must finally tell Emily that his treatments are not working. Aware of the affair between her sister and her fiancé, Vance makes a pitch of his own, but Emily rejects his overtures, accusing him of making love to her as compensation for his failure to cure her. "Who are you a man can't make love to you?" he sneers, "Some princess in an ivory tower?" Piqued, Emily immediately announces that she and Jeff will set a date, since there seems to be no more reason to hope for miracle cures.

Emily then discovers that Vance is working on yet a new serum, still in the experimental stages, and she persuades him to use it on her. "Emily Blair—no better than a charity patient?" he muses, but he gives in to her appeals—only to have her faint in an unexpected reaction to the injection.

Dr. Weeks discovers that Emily has been playing guinea pig.

She wakes in her own room to the sounds of rain pelting the windowpane and a fire crackling in the hearth. She can hear! Before she can rejoice too much, she overhears a hushed conversation between Janice and Jeff and learns the truth about their affair. She is disappointed to learn that Doctor Vance has returned to his clinic in Pittsburgh. Dissolve to Pittsburgh. Emily has arrived to tell Vance her news: she can hear and she owes it all to him and she has come to work with him, to be his proof of success, to be anything he wants her to be, to . . . they go into a clinch.

Bosley Crowther, writing in the *New York Times* reported, "Ladd plays the doctor with a haughty air that must be tough on his patients—and is likely to be equally tough on yours."

Time magazine, which took potshots at Ladd at every opportunity, did not pass up *And Now Tomorrow*: "The one thing that gives this thousandth version [of the skirmishing of the sexes] any novelty is Alan Ladd's triple-chilled proficiency at handling all the tricks of making love in reverse gear. This is as interesting to look at, in a simpleminded way, as someone drinking a glass of beer standing on his head. But it probably takes a great deal more talent."

Philip Hartung in *The Commonweal* said, "In portraying this doctor, Ladd contributes little more to the story's visualization than his own personal magnetism."

Well, Ladd had plenty of that.

Salty O'Rourke

Paramount   (1945)

*The loveliest of Ladd's leading ladies was fragile Gail Russell,
the perfect foil to Ladd's hard-edged toughness.*

CREDITS

Director, Raoul Walsh. *Producer*, E. D. Leshin. *Story and screenplay*, Milton Holmes. *Photography*, Theodor Sparkuhl. *Editor*, William Shea. *Music*, Robert Emmett Dolan. *Running time, 100 minutes.*

CAST

Salty O'Rourke, ALAN LADD; *Barbara Brooks*, GAIL RUSSELL; *Smitty*, WILLIAM DEMAREST; *Johnny Cates*, STANLEY CLEMENTS; *Doc Baxter*, BRUCE CABOT; *Mrs. Brooks*, SPRING BYINGTON; *Babe*, REX WILLIAMS; *Sneezer*, DARRYL HICKMAN; *Lola*, MARJORIE WOODWORTH; *Hotel Proprietor*, DON ZELAYA; *Dignified Salesman*, LESTER MATTHEWS; *Racing Secretary*, WILLIAM FORREST; *Bennie*, WILLIAM MURPHY; *Murdock*, DENIS BROWN

Babe (Williams) and Doc (Cabot) threaten Salty (Ladd) and his pal Smitty (Demarest).

Perhaps the great puzzle about Ladd vehicles such as *Salty O'Rourke* was how Alan Ladd managed to play despicable, dishonorable characters and always make them sympathetic, even devastatingly attractive. It's quite a trick. As *The Commonweal* put it, "You have to keep in mind of course that Alan Ladd is never allowed to be as thoroughly bad as the script makes him out to be." *Salty O'Rourke* was another of the studio's efforts to give the fans the Ladd they wanted to see.

Once more Ladd is tough as nails, devious, and cunning, if not downright crooked. He and his pal Smitty (Demarest) are being threatened by Doc Baxter (Cabot), a hood who wants a sum of money Salty owes. They have one month.

Salty knows there is a fast horse for sale that no jockey can ride—except for one. Salty and Smitty track down Johnny Cates (Clements), an unscrupulous if talented rider who has been barred from American tracks, and by using Johnny's younger brother's birth certificate, they are able to register Cates for the big race, the Denington Handicap.

Johnny is twenty-two, but the brother he is pretending to be is only seventeen, which means Johnny must attend the track's school. Cates is aghast at the idea. "Listen," he tells Salty, "I got all the education I need, and I ain't gonna overdo it." The big purse is persuasive, however, and Johnny goes to school, where he encounters lovely, naïve Barbara Brooks (Russell), whom he im-

mediately offends. He is so patently obnoxious that she suspends him the first day.

Salty must get him reinstated, and oozing charm the way a sandwich oozes jam, Salty goes to work on Barbara Brooks and her fluttery mother (Byington). The more Johnny gets his foot caught in his mouth, the more Salty must see of Barbara, causing Johnny to become unhappy and jealous, break training, and act like the cheap little weasel he is. So Salty persuades Barbara to be Johnny's date at the Jockeys' Ball. Johnny takes the opportunity to propose. Dismayed, Barbara reveals it is Salty she loves, which sends Johnny off on a bender with his floozy (Woodworth).

Now it is Salty who discovers he is in love—for Barbara has let him know just what she thinks of a man who would use a friend in such a ruthless way—and Johnny is no more sensitive to Salty's newfound emotions than Salty was to his. Johnny arranges a neat double cross with Baxter. He will lose the race for Salty, and Baxter will close in for the kill.

When Barbara gets wind of what is happening, she pleads with Johnny to do the decent thing. Touched by her tears, Johnny relents at the last moment and handily wins the race, thus double crossing Baxter. Baxter's henchman guns Johnny down before he can leave the track. Johnny dies in Salty's arms.

Salty then goes after Doc and, in a fast shoot-out, gets both Doc and his henchman, just as the police arrive. Barbara, terrified at losing Salty, who has confessed that he loves her, has called the cops. With Smitty driving, she and Salty take off in his little roadster. Salty tosses

his gun away as they cross the first bridge to the fu...

Salty O'Rourke had a breezy sort of charm, even tho... it dealt with race-track low-life. Ladd was very goo... Salty, best in his scenes with Stanley Clements, ... nearly steals those scenes, although it is hard to st... scene from Ladd. Ladd seems to do nothing to cal... tention to himself—no mugging or obvious mar... isms—yet he has so much screen presence that our ... just naturally follow him.

Phillip Hartung in *The Commonweal* commer... "Raoul Walsh excels in directing the big scenes ar... the episodes involving Ladd, Clements and the tra... played by William Demarest, with a wonderful sen... humor. The dissolving of the plot is too cheap for se... consideration, but the characterizations will hold ... interest."

There is one interesting Ladd-like piece of dial... in *Salty O'Rourke* which seems to sum up the pu... idea of Ladd's screen persona. When Gail Russell ... the gun tucked in Ladd's belt she asks about it an... tells her: "Don't call it a gun. That's my friend, ... Roscoe. When I need him, he speaks up for me; he'... persuader. You see," he explains as pretty Gail ... puzzled, "with your friends you can sway them ... words and they listen. But with your enemies . . . ... that's where my friend John Roscoe comes in. He ... suades my enemies."

Paramount was able to build a good dozen more ... around the character that such dialogue helped ch... terize.

Smitty has had enough of Johnny's high-handedness and complains to Salty.

The Blue Dahlia

Paramount   (1946)

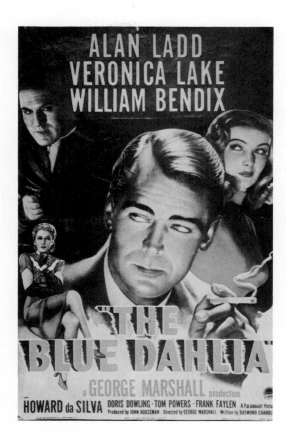

CREDITS

Director, George Marshall. *Producers*, George Marshall, John Houseman. *Screenplay*, Raymond Chandler. *Photography*, Lionel Lindon. *Music*, Victor Young. *Editor*, Arthur Schmidt. *Running time: 99 minutes.*

CAST

Johnny Morrison, ALAN LADD; *Joyce Harwood*, VERONICA LAKE; *Buzz Wanchek*, WILLIAM BENDIX; *Eddie Harwood*, HOWARD da SILVA; *Dad Newell*, WILL WRIGHT; *George Copeland*, HUGH BEAUMONT; *Helen Morrison*, DORIS DOWLING; *Captain Hendrickson*, TOM POWERS; *Corelli*, HOWARD FREEMAN; *Leo*, DON COSTELLO; *The Man*, FRANK FAYLEN; *Heath*, WALTER SANDE; *Blond*, VERA MARSHE; *Maid*, MAE BUSCH; *Marine*, ANTHONY CARUSO; *Photographers*, JAMES MILLICAN, ALBERT RUIZ; *Hotel Clerk*, PERC LAUNDERS; *Hat-check Girl*, NOEL NEILL

The Blue Dahlia is considered one of the four or five best movies Ladd made, and it has become something of a cult favorite, owing to Raymond Chandler's original screenplay. Chandler, a pulp-detective-story writer turned successful novelist, had worked on one Ladd screenplay, *And Now Tomorrow*, in 1944. He started *Dahlia* as a novel, and when it bogged down, he sold it to Paramount, unfinished, as a Ladd vehicle. For all its crisp dialogue and intriguing atmosphere, *Dahlia* is a mystery plot with many weak situations and a solution that is positively ventilated.

Johnny Morrison (Ladd) and his buddies George and Buzz (Beaumont and Bendix) have just been discharged from the navy and are back in Los Angeles. Buzz and George go off to find an apartment, and Johnny heads for a classy bungalow court and his wife.

The homecoming is a disaster. Helen (Dowling) is throwing a party, and Johnny catches her kissing her fill-in boyfriend, Eddie Harwood (da Silva), a shady character who owns the Blue Dahlia nightclub. The party breaks up when Johnny socks Eddie. Helen drinks too much, and she admits that she was driving while drunk the night their son Billy was killed. Johnny is fed up. He pulls out his service gun but tosses it aside, deciding that Helen isn't worth shooting. He exits.

Hours later a maid finds Helen's dead body and calls Dad Newell (Wright), the house dick, who notifies the police. Johnny is the number-one suspect.

Meanwhile, Johnny has been trying to thumb a ride in the rain. He is picked up by a blond who tells him she is headed for Malibu, "if that's any use to you."

Some wonderfully atmospheric shots of wet streets reflecting neon and flashing car lights, as well as the gritty reality of Los Angeles' less attractive settings—seedy hotels, stucco bungalows, tacky motels—add a good deal of flavor to the grim proceedings. The scene played out in the confines of Lake's little convertible coupe is pure Ladd-Lake chemistry, the sort of moment that explains their phenomenal popularity as a pair.

The blond (Lake) is in a teasing, ironic mood. "Why

Johnny (Ladd) confronts his no-good wife (Dowling).

Malibu?" Johnny asks, not really caring.

"I tossed a coin," she replies wryly. "Heads I go to Malibu; tails I go to Laguna."

His heavy-lidded eyes slide from the rain-streaked window to her face. "What if the coin rolls under the davenport?" he asks.

"Then I go to Long Beach," she answers.

When he points out that they have passed Malibu, she shrugs and keeps driving. They have not exchanged names, but a certain sexual interest runs under all this off-hand dialogue. Yet it is plain that each is running away from some personal problem, and the mutual attraction goes nowhere.

In the subsequent murder investigation, George an Buzz are questioned by the police, as are Eddie Harwoo and Dad Newell. Buzz is belligerent (having a shor temper because of a plate in his head, which causes muc pain), George is mum, Eddie is seemingly cooperative and Dad is shifty. But Johnny's gun is the main evidence

Dad, in fact, tries out a little blackmail on Eddie an quickly finds out, in one of the better-played scenes i the movie, that Eddie's civilized, courteous manner sug gests more menace than a small-time hustler like Da cares to handle.

Holed up in a fifth-rate hotel, Johnny discovers tha Helen had a hold on Eddie, a secret about his past tha could have meant blackmail. When he goes to Eddie' place hoping to learn whether Harwood killed Helen he finds that the blond who picked him up in the rai is none other than Harwood's estranged wife. Therefore she, too, could be involved.

Eddie, fearing what Johnny knows about him, ha Johnny kidnapped, but in the rough and tumble tha follows Johnny's confinement in a lonely lodge, Eddi and his partner, Leo (Costello), are killed. Johnny stil has no idea who killed Helen, but he is sure it wasn' Eddie.

The denouement takes place in the Blue Dahlia night-club, where Buzz is on the verge of a crackup and ha become the prime suspect because he cannot recall wher he was the night of the murder. Johnny arrives to tak the pressure off Buzz and is told that he is no longer suspect; Mrs. Harwood has told the police that she and Johnny were together at the time of the murder. That leaves Dad Newell, the cheap blackmailer, who turns on them all with a gun and is shot. His motive? Helen laughed at him for being a penny-ante crook, spying on bungalow tenants.

Visually, this is one of Ladd's more interesting films. It is full of the kind of background settings and atmosphere that lend a feeling of the tacky, postwar world the story occupies. The film is fast paced, and there are plenty of memorable scenes, but they cannot quite bring the picture into the category of first-rate screen fare. There are too many coincidences, too many broken threads of plot to pull together, and *The Blue Dahlia* seems both slickly sophisticated and at the same time, oddly oversimplified. There is evidence that Chandler had another ending in mind altogether and that when the Navy Department protested that they did not approve of wounded returning veterans portrayed as potential killers, Chandler dropped the Buzz character as his fall guy and had to scramble to find a new patsy. Dad Newell is not a credible substitute.

Lake's role is superfluous to the plot—she is there simply to provide the obligatory love interest for Ladd and another minor suspect for the murder. Since she is barely noticed by the Chandler script, we are at a loss

The law catches up with Johnny. (Jack Clifford and Tom Powers

Johnny joins Joyce, saying, "Every guy's seen you before, somewhere—the trick is to find you. . . ."

Johnny checks out his wife's boyfriend, Eddie (da Silva).

to know why she seems so interesting a type. Chandler thought Lake a dreadful actress and dubbed her Moronica Lake, but she certainly made more of the part of Joyce Harwood than he gave her.

Perhaps the best acting in the film rests in the skills of Howard da Silva, who admirably captured the played-out, dapper, reluctant underworld figure who knows he must lie in the bed he has made for himself. Bendix was also fine as the stammering vet with a plate in his head. Ladd's performance was solid, controlled, entirely suitable. Johnny, like so many of Chandler's best heroes, is tough, resilient, and true to his own firm code of morality, a man who will not admit to needing anyone and who gains audience sympathy by his very aloneness.

Manny Farber in *The New Republic* stated, "Chandler makes the mayhem, drinking and talking stylized and arty; never allows his gangsters to lose their suavity, presence of mind, grace, sartorial elegance, wit in any kind of catastrophe. . . . The film is well acted from top to bottom and especially in the in-between roles."

The Blue Dahlia grossed more than $2.75 million—a lot of profit in 1946.

Facing page: (top) Bendix, Anthony Caruso and Ladd. (Bottom) Ladd in for trouble with Walter Sande and Don Costello.

With Veronica Lake.

With Veronica Lake.

Duffy's Tavern
Paramount   (1945)

CREDITS

Director, Hal Walker; *Producer,* Danny Dare; *Original screenplay,* Melvin Frank, Norman Panama, *based on characters created by* Ed Gardner; *Sketches by* Frank Panama, Abram S. Burrows, Barney Dean, George White, Eddie Davis, Matt Brooks; *Music Director,* Robert Emmett Dolan; *Photography,* Lionel Lindon; *Dance Director,* Billy Daniel; *Art Directors,* Hans Dreier, William Flannery; *Songs,* "Swinging on a Star," "The Hard Way," *by* Johnny Burke, Jimmy Van Heusen, "You Can't Blame a Girl for Tryin'," *by* Ben Raleigh, Bernie Wayne. *Running time,* 98 minutes.

CAST

Himself, BING CROSBY; *Archie,* ED GARDNER; *Peggy O'Malley,* MARJORIE REYNOLDS; *Danny Murphy,* BARRY SULLIVAN; *Finnegan,* CHARLES CANTOR; *Eddie the waiter,* EDDIE GREEN; *Miss Duffy,* ANN THOMAS; *Bing's father,* BARRY FITZGERALD; *Doctor,* BILLY deWOLFE; *Director,* WALTER ABEL; *Dancer-Waiter,* JOHNNY COY; *Dancer,* MIRIAM FRANKLIN; *Ronald,* CHARLES QUIGLEY; *Gloria,* OLGA SAN JUAN; *Masseur,* ROBERT (BOBBY) WATSON; *Customer,* FRANK FAYLEN. *Guest Stars and Novelty Numbers:* BETTY HUTTON, PAULETTE GODDARD, ALAN LADD, HOWARD da SILVA, DOROTHY LA-MOUR, VERONICA LAKE, CASS DALEY, SONNY TUFTS, ARTURO de CORDOVA, DIANA LYNN, ROBERT BENCHLEY, WILLIAM DEMAREST, GARY, PHILLIP, DENNIS, and LINDSAY CROSBY, BRIAN DONLEVY, EDDIE BRACKEN, WILLIAM BENDIX, JOAN CAULFIELD, HELEN WALKER, JAMES BROWN, GAIL RUSSELL, JEAN HEATHER, MAURICE ROCCO.

Once more Paramount tossed all their stars into a variety-show concoction, this one based on a popular radio show. The plot was flimsy, built around ex-servicemen who can't get jobs until the stars stage a benefit for them.

Ladd's bit was a quick sketch where he encounters Howard da Silva giving Veronica Lake several hard slaps. Ladd is grim. He puts his hands into his trenchcoat pockets as he looks on. "I dare you to do that again," he says to da Silva in harsh tones. Da Silva proceeds to slap Veronica. Finally, just as we expect Ladd to step in and wipe up the floor with da Silva, he instead turns to Lake and says, "Lady, you better get outta here before you get your teeth kicked in!"

Pictures like this were not memorable, nor did they interest the critics much. They did make a great deal of money, however.

O.S.S.
Paramount   (1946)

With Geraldine Fitzgerald

In OSS training school with Richard Benedict, Richard Webb.

Ellen (Fitzgerald) and John (Ladd) set the charge to blow up the tunnel.

CREDITS

Director, Irving Pichel. *Producer*, Richard Maibaum. *Screenplay*, Richard Maibaum. *Photography*, Lionel Lindon. *Editor*, William Shea. *Running time, 105 minutes.*

CAST

John Martin, ALAN LADD; *Ellen Rogers*, GERALDINE FITZGERALD; *Commander Brady*, PATRIC KNOWLES; *Colonel Meister*, JOHN HOYT; *Parker*, RICHARD WEBB; *Bernay*, RICHARD BENEDICT; *Gates*, DON BEDDOE; *Amadeus Braun*, HAROLD VERMILYEA; *Colonel Crawson*, GAVIN MUIR; *Field*, ONSLOW STEVENS; *General Donovan*, JOSEPH CREHAN; *Marc Aubert*, EGON BRECHER; *WAC Operator (Sparky)*, GLORIA SAUNDERS; *Madame Prideaux*, JULIA DEAN; *Gerald*, BOBBY DRISCOLL; *Arnheim*, CRANE WHITLEY; *Lieutenant Colonel Miles*, LESLIE DENISON; *Gracie Archer*, ROBERTA JONAY; *Brady's Secretary*, JEAN RUTH; *Trainee*, PAUL LEES

More than thirty-five years ago, General William Donovan organized and commanded a finely trained army of more than two-hundred American spies, agents of the Office of Strategic Services (OSS), the predecessor of today's CIA. These agents were dropped by parachute behind enemy lines inside such Nazi-occupied countries as France, Italy, Belgium, and Norway and managed to set up a vast and efficient espionage network during the last years of World War II.

Paramount was out in front in the race to capture the OSS files on screen and got thirty actual OSS heroes to act as technical advisors on the film, lending authenticity to the production.

In the beginning of the film John Martin (Ladd) is in training as part of an OSS team called Applejack. The other members of the team are Gates (Beddoe), a former American railroad equipment salesman in France; Bernay (Benedict), a well-known hockey player; and Ellen Rogers (Fitzgerald), an attractive sculptor who had spent many years in France.

The team is dropped by parachute into occupied France. Their job is to destroy the French railway system, in particular the vital Corbett Mallon tunnel.

Though Martin has been gruffly doubtful about taking a woman on such a dangerous mission, Ellen proves valuable. She has met a German officer, Colonel Meister (Hoyt), and he is smitten. She does a clay bust of him when he professes an interest in art.

When Ellen learns that Meister will be on a train that passes through the target tunnel, she talks the colonel into taking her along. She and Martin re-create the bust in explosive clay, which they intend to detonate as soon the underground agents stall the train in the Corbett Mallon tunnel. They succeed, but only by a hairbreadth, because Martin goes into the tunnel to bring Ellen out, and she tells him, "Never come back for me again—do you understand? *Never* come back."

The tunnel is destroyed, and Martin and Ellen join the stream of refugees on the road—and are accosted by Gestapo. The leader Amadeus Braun (Vermilyea) offers to sell information to them. An elaborate relay system is set up, and the information is transmitted to England via Bernay's wireless.

Suddenly Colonel Meister shows up, minus an eye and obsessed with revenge. Bernay is killed, Braun is arrested, and Ellen and Martin escape. Commander Brady (Knowles) has asked them to stay on the job and find an agent who is stranded and who has vital information to pass along.

They take refuge in a farmhouse with an old lady and her grandson (Dean and Driscoll). By now Martin and Ellen are deeply in love but must put the mission first. When a band of drunken Nazi soldiers invade the farmhouse and knock him around, Martin recognizes Parker, a fellow agent who is posing as a German. Parker takes Ellen aside and repeats a list of facts and figures for her to memorize, information concerning the Normandy invasion.

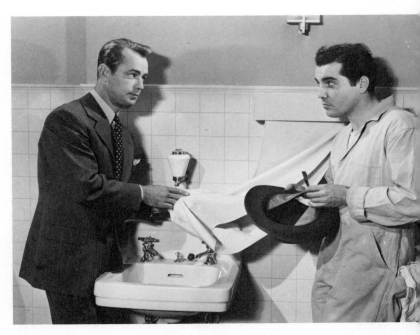
The microfilm is passed to Bernay (Benedict).

After the soldiers are gone, Ellen revives Martin and gives him the information. He transmits it to a low-circling aircraft but is interrupted by the news that the Gestapo has taken away Ellen and the old woman.

Martin continues to transmit, remembering Ellen's words, "Never come back for me!" When finished, he races back to the farmhouse and frantically searches the rooms—but it is too late. Clutching Ellen's discarded sweater, he collapses into a chair, his sobs the only sound in the empty house.

Later, he and Commander Brady watch the allied troops and tanks cross the Rhine.

The overall tone of the film is one of gray tension, heightened by some excellent black and white photography. Geraldine Fitzgerald does an admirable job, and Harold Vermilyea as the German traitor is marvelously oily, blinking his lashless, piggy eyes as he hisses his suggestions of betrayal. Ladd is also excellent, inspired, perhaps, by an understanding director and a crisp script. He had some misgivings about the scene in which he breaks down in tears over the girl, but that moment proved to be among the most touching and effective in the picture.

Phillip Hartung in *The Commonweal* stated, "*OSS* suffers by comparison with *The House on 92nd Street* because it lacks the documentary air of the film about the FBI, but it is still a good thriller in its own right."

Said A. H. Weiler in the *New York Times*, "Ladd makes a convincing, intelligent, and hard undercover agent, whose histronics are simple and acceptable."

Bron in *Variety* said, "Ladd suggests the intelligent,

Signaling the contact plane.

resourceful operative without resort to heroics, while Miss Fitzgerald is a good teammate in a quiet, intense style." And *Newsweek* praised Ladd because he "comes out of his deadpan gunman's cocoon and gives a good solid performance, punctuated by occasional flashes of emotion which are perfectly justified."

Once more a Ladd film cleaned up at the box office, and this one garnered more than a few warm reviews.

With Geraldine Fitzgerald

Being questioned by, among others, Pat McVey (center) and James Westerfield (second left).

Two Years Before the Mast

Paramount (1946)

CREDITS

Director, John Farrow. *Producer,* Seton I. Miller. *Screenplay,* Seton I. Miller, George Bruce. *From the novel by* Richard Henry Dana, Jr. *Photography*, Ernest Laszlo. *Music*, Victor Young. *Art direction*, Hans Dreier, Franz Bachelin. *Special effects*, Gordon Jennings, J. D. Jennings. *Running time, 98 minutes.*

CAST

Charles Stewart, ALAN LADD; *Richard Henry Dana*, BRIAN DONLEVY; *Amazeen*, WILLIAM BENDIX; *Dooley*, BARRY FITZGERALD; *Captain Francis Thompson*, HOWARD da SILVA; *Maria Dominguez*, ESTHER FERNANDEZ; *Brown*, ALBERT DEKKER; *Foster*, LUIS VAN ROOTEN; *Sam Hooper*, DARRYL HICKMAN; *Macklin*, ROMAN BOHNEN; *Gordon Stewart*, RAY COLLINS; *Bellamer*, TOM POWERS; *Hansen*, FRANK FAYLEN; *Hayes*, THEODORE NEWTON; *Mexican Captain*, DUNCAN RENALDO

Along with trying to keep Ladd tough and tall, Paramount was also concerned with keeping audience sympathy focused on him and they seemed to find it necessary to have him mauled, shot or beaten in picture after picture, presumably so he could triumph by wiping up the floor with every crook in sight. The formula was taken to its ultimate extreme in Paramount's filming of *Two Years Before the Mast*. The movie is a grim affair featuring floggings and other assorted tortures.

Richard Henry Dana's book was an exposé aimed at reform. It was not meant to be a swashbuckling adventure, and therefore it had no single protagonist. The book concerned all the men aboard the *Pilgrim*, and in the context of a movie there are just too many stories for us to become satisfactorily involved.

First there is the story of Charles Stewart (Ladd), the careless playboy son of the rich shipowner, Gordon Stewart (Collins), whose ship the *Pilgrim* is back in port after a record-breaking voyage.

The next story concerns Captain Thompson (da Silva) of the *Pilgrim*, a grim-faced martinet who cares only for breaking records and isn't particular how he does it. When Thompson brings a ship in from California in 130 days, it puts much money into the elder Stewart's pock-

Charles Stewart (Ladd) talks it over with Dana (Donlevy).

ets, so Stewart has little interest in questioning Thompson's methods, though men have died during the voyage.

Yet another story concerns a man who signs on the *Pilgrim* because he intends to write a book that will expose conditions in the United States maritime service. This man is Richard Henry Dana, Jr. (Donlevy), whose brother died from the rigors of sailing with Captain Thompson.

As Captain Thompson and his first mate, Mr. Amazeen (Bendix), set out to sea with still another cargo, a number of new sailors are waking in dismay at their surroundings. Among them is Charles Stewart, who, while gambling, drinking, and generally slumming along the docks, has been shanghaied with the rest. Even though he is the shipowner's son, Captain Thompson has no intention of turning around and taking him back.

Stewart is about to be flogged for stealing food.

(Top) Amazeen (Bendix) flogs Charles (Ladd) as the Captain on (Da Silva). (Bottom) Dooley and Dana (Barry Fitzgeral Brian Donlevy) tend to the victim's wounds.

They are at sea, and the captain is in full command.

Endless hours of work, wormy salt pork, and harsh living conditions make ship life a misery. "A seaman is nothing but an animal," Dana mutters, "worked to death, starved, flogged. It's come down that way from the days of galley slaves, but it's going to change some-day."

Even when he anchors near port to pick up a lady passenger, Captain Thompson refuses the men's pleas for fresh food and supplies. Scurvy breaks out, and men die. Finally Charles takes matters into his own hands, steals two guns, and takes over the ship. The mutiny attempt is foiled, however, and Charles winds up in irons.

When even Mr. Amazeen turns against his cruel captain, Thompson kills him. Incensed, the men kill Thompson and free Charles, thinking no further than escape. Now Dana and Charles must persuade the men to return the ship to Boston and face charges—because "what we did was justified." The trial causes great controversy, reaching the Senate. New laws are enacted to protect the rights of seamen, and Dana's book is published. Charles, no longer a spoiled fop, is ready to settle down with Maria (Fernandez), the ship's lovely woman passenger.

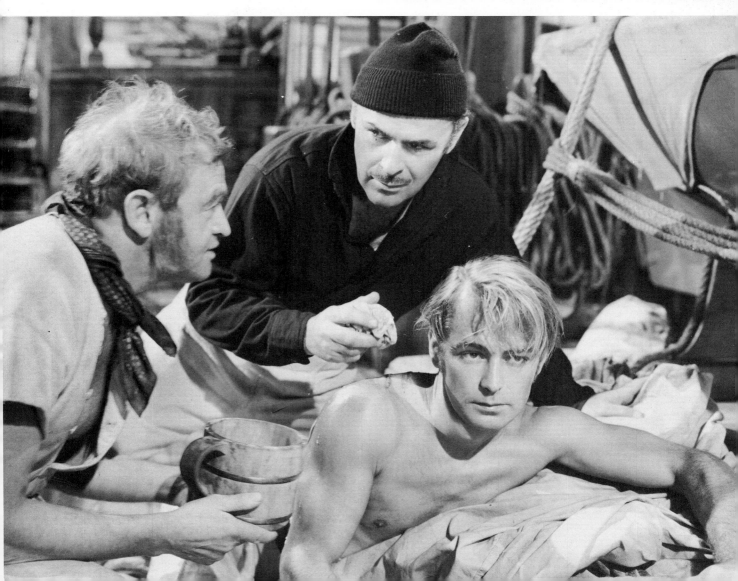

Charles fingers a newly-acquired gold coin. Looking on in awe are Daryll Hickman, Barry Fitzgerald and Esther Fernandez.

Facing page: (top) Charles and Dana are restrained from fighting. (Bottom) Charles is faced by the Captain (Da Silva) flanked by Blackie Whiteford and Bendix.

The film was unremittingly dreary, full of suffering, and the patched-in romance was conspicuously out of place. Paramount couldn't seem to decide whether this was a documentary or an entertainment, so it turned out to be neither. By exploiting the novel's physical violence and adding the extraneous romance, the film fails to drive home the point of reform Dana was trying to make. However, director John Farrow made sure the seagoing moments were genuine, and there is a kind of tough authenticity in the wild sea storms and endless days on the water.

Newsweek stated, "Da Silva is magnificent; Bendix gives an intelligent performance as his hard-boiled first mate; and Fitzgerald does his usual fine job as the ship's cook. Ladd and Donlevy are highly satisfactory."

John McCarten in the *New Yorker* said, "A fine, rousing adaptation of Richard Dana's classic. . . . Although Mr. da Silva dominates the film, the others in the cast are by no means lost. . . . William Bendix, Barry Fitzgerald, Alan Ladd and Brian Donlevy {are} excellent performers."

And Stall in *Variety* echoed that with: "[Da Silva] walks off with the blue ribbon. . . . Rest of cast, from leads to minor bits, perform excellently. Ladd does a nice job. . . ."

Calcutta
Paramount   (1947)

Neale romances Virginia (Gail Russell).

CREDITS

Director, John Farrow. *Producer,* Seton I. Miller. *Screen-play,* Seton I. Miller. *Photography,* John Seitz. *Music,* Victor Young. *Song "This Is Madness,"* Bernie Wayne, Ben Raleigh. *French lyrics,* Ted Grouya. *Theme "Madness Reprise,"* Charles W. Bradshaw. *Editor,* Archie Marshek. *Special Effects,* Gordon Jennings. *Running time, 83 minutes.*

CAST

Neale Gordon, ALAN LADD; *Virginia Moore,* GAIL RUS-SELL; *Pedro Blake,* WILLIAM BENDIX; *Marina Tanev,* JUNE DUPREZ; *Eric Lasser,* LOWELL GILMORE; *Mrs. Smith,* EDITH KING; *Mul Raj Malik,* PAUL SINGH; *Inspector Kendricks,* GAVIN MUIR; *Bill Cunningham,* JOHN WHITNEY; *Clerk,* BENSON FONG; *Jack Collins,* DON BEDDOE; *Desk clerk,* MILTON PARSONS; *Chinese radioman,* LESLIE FONG; *"Mac," mechanic,* JIMMY AUBREY; *Kim,* LEE TUNG FOO; *Lasser's bodyguard,* JOEY S. RAY

Ladd and Bendix worked so well as soldiers of fortune in *China* that Paramount decided to move the duo to India for more exotic intrigue and adventure, "Terry and the Pirates" style.

The film opens with buddies Ladd and Bendix flying cargo between Chungking and Calcutta. There is a third buddy, Bill (Whitney), who also flies and who spoils their wandering adventurers' unity by announcing to his friends Neale (Ladd) and Pedro (Bendix) that he is getting married.

Later, back in Calcutta, Pedro and Neale check in to the cargo office and learn that while they were finishing

Flashing a stolen broach, Neale questions Mrs. Smith (King).

their last run, their friend Bill was murdered—strangled and left in an alley.

Neale wants to solve the murder of his friend, and he and Pedro start their investigation at the Chalgani Club, owned by Eric Lasser (Gilmore), where Marina (Duprez), Neale's sometime girlfriend, is a singer.

Neale looks up Virginia Moore (Russell), Bill's American fiancée. He knocks on her hotel-room door, waits, then turns to go back down the stairs. A voice says, "Were you looking for me?" and he swings around to see a vision of a girl leaning on the railing, her darkne enhanced by a white dress and the white lacey arch cur ing behind her. Her beauty affects Neale; he is mor suspicious than ever. When he questions details of he story, she flares up at him.

His checking leads to Mrs. Smith (King), a fat, ciga smoking blond woman who owns a jewelry store whe Bill purchased an expensive diamond for Virginia.

The plot thickens: There is a smuggling racket i operation and the jewels have been stashed in the carg planes. Neale finds a hidden bag of valuable jewelry o one of the company planes and is nearly killed by a thug He also has a run-in with Inspector Kendricks (Muir who suspects him of the murder of a Hindu who die in the corridor outside Neale's room.

Virginia has moved to a room across town, frightene because her hotel room had been ransacked. Neale tell her of the jewels. He has fallen for her and she for him

Neale later finds that Virginia has lied to him o several counts. Though she is all softness and silky sin cerity, a couple of hard slaps from Neale get the trut from her. She and Lasser were running the smugglin game, with Virginia acting as a diversion for the flyers Bill saw too much one night, and Lasser eliminated him

Lasser walks in on the pair with a gun, gets caugh off-balance, and is killed. Neale picks up the phone t summon the inspector, while Virginia stares in disbelief

"You said you were crazy about me," she reminds him seductively.

"Not that much," Neale answers coolly.

Her last words to him? "I would have hated to hav killed you."

Shades of *The Maltese Falcon*. However, the twist a the end doesn't work because Gail Russell was far too nice. Being a seductress was difficult enough for her being a villainess was nigh impossible. Still, as a Lad co-star, Gail Russell was ideal. Her fragile, dusky beauty made her the perfect foil for his sleek, blond good looks and the contrast between their personalities added pi quancy to their romantic encounters.

Ladd's romantic habit of removing the cigarettes from his ladies' fingers before reaching for a kiss was an in teresting sexy touch, à la *Now Voyager*. Ladd's persona magnetism was strong enough to carry him through the more artificial aspects of strong-jawed hero and there are some fascinating supporting performances, primarily from Bendix and from Broadway actress Edith King as the hard-boiled mama.

Time magazine summed it up as: "A conventional, well-made melodrama. . . . "Alan Ladd handles both girls and perils with his customary cold, efficient grace."

Calcutta was scarcely art, but it did good, brisk busi ness at the box office and if one were to choose one film as the most typical of the Ladd vehicles of this period, the choice would likely be *Calcutta*.

ALAN LADD
GAIL RUSSELL
WILLIAM BENDIX
in

"CALCUTTA"

with JUNE DUPREZ · LOWELL GILMORE
EDITH KING

Produced and Written for the Screen by SETON I. MILLER · Directed by JOHN FARROW

A PARAMOUNT PICTURE

Neale finally comes to trust Virginia—to his regret.

Joe meets Fay (Lamour), the local farmer's niece.

Wild Harvest
Paramount   (1947)

CREDITS

Director, Tay Garnett. *Producer,* Robert Fellows. *Screenplay,* John Monks, Jr. *From an unpublished story by* Houston Branch. *Photography,* John Seitz. *Process Photography,* Farciot Edouart. *Music,* Hugo Friedhofer. *Editor,* Billy Shea. *Running time, 92 minutes.*

CAST

Joe Madigan, ALAN LADD; *Fay Rankin,* DOROTHY LAMOUR; *Jim Davis,* ROBERT PRESTON; *Kink,* LLOYD NOLAN; *Mark Lewis,* DICK ERDMAN; *Higgins,* ALLEN JENKINS; *Mike Alperson,* WILL WRIGHT; *Rankin,* GRIFF BARNETT; *Pete,* ANTHONY CARUSO; *Long,* WALTER SANDE; *Nick,* FRANK SULLY

Wild Harvest was another two-fisted Ladd adventure—this time concerning the itinerant combine crews who followed the golden wheat harvest from Texas to Canada each July.

During the filming of *Wild Harvest,* in December 1946, a strike staged by the Conference of Studio Painters and Carpenters Unions kept things tense around the studio. Actors working on scheduled pictures stayed on the lot and slept in their dressing rooms to avoid having to cross picket lines.

However grim the reasons for their confinement, the cast and crew of *Wild Harvest* thoroughly enjoyed the jovial camaraderie of being studio bound. Director Tay Garnett, who liked a good time, made the work fun, and there was plenty of partying each evening after the shooting stopped.

The story begins with Joe (Ladd) organizing a combine crew, having already laid out down payments on the necessary machines. He is short of cash to pay the freight, however, and rival crew boss Alperson (Will Wright) is ready to buy him out. Here enters boisterous, pleasure-loving Jim (Preston), a good buddy who is always ready for action. Jim supplies the money to get the crew moving, and they begin cutting through Texas. Joe's right-hand man is Kink, played by Lloyd Nolan with his usual competence, and the advance man is Dick Erdman.

The crew is doing fine until they have some machine breakdowns, and Jim, the man who knows engines, is too often in town having fun with "booze and broads" to ensure efficiency. Joe and Jim have words over Jim's lack of responsibility, but they soon make it up. The pressure of Alperson's cutthroat competition keeps them on their toes, and a raging wheat fire slows them down only briefly.

In Kansas Joe meets the proverbial farmer's daughter—in this case, the farmer's niece—in the person of Fay (Dorothy Lamour), and real trouble starts when she decides to make a play for him. His rebuffs only seem to intrigue her more, and she turns up everywhere, getting in his way. He gives her a momentary bit of attention, but he knows she is trouble. She turns to Jim in order to hassle Joe, and he allows her to talk him into marriage. It is the one way she can be sure of going

Joe (Ladd) talks over the route with Kink (Nolan), Jim (Preston), and Mark (Erdman).

In acting there are several things that count. Appearance is quite important, and Alan certainly had that. He had grace, a good walk; he looked well in his clothes. All these things count. He knew his lines, and he read them well. But I couldn't say he was a great actor. The sum total, however, was very effective.

LLOYD NOLAN

Jim, Joe, Kink and Fay have a confrontation during a friendly game of poker (Robert Preston, Ladd, Lloyd Nolan and Dorothy Lamour).

along when the crew moves on.

Meanwhile, the rivalry between Alperson and Joe gets out of hand when a wild free-for-all breaks out at a small-town dance. Fay eggs Jim into spending more and more money on her, and he begins high-grading the wheat—skimming bushels off the top of each load and selling it. Joe confronts Jim and learns the truth. He must either turn his friend in or cover up and run. He chooses to run, while a horde of angry farmers give chase.

When Joe catches up with Jim and Fay, he takes Jim's high-grading money and tells Kink to return it to the farmers. The last payment on the combines is due, and the company is ready to reclaim the machines. Jim sells Fay's car. When she baits him, taunting him about Joe, he and Joe fight, clearing the air and wiping out Fay as a point of contention between them. The two buddies exit the saloon together, ready to get the combines rolling again.

Ladd played his usual tight-lipped, authoritative hero, quick to protect a buddy and even quicker to cold-shoulder a pretty girl. It almost seemed with this picture as if the tough-guy mold had hardened into cement.

A little dalliance with Fay doesn't distract Joe for long.

1. WILLIAM BENDIX 9. GEORGE REEVES 17. DOROTHY BARRETT 25. VIRGINIA FIELD 33. GARY COOPER 41. LUCILLE BA
2. HOWARD DA SILVA 10. WILLIAM DEMAREST 18. JUNE HARRIS 26. BURT LANCASTER 34. DOROTHY LAMOUR 42. NANETTE P
3. MACDONALD CAREY 11. RICHARD WEBB 19. PATRIC KNOWLES 27. LIZABETH SCOTT 35. JOAN CAULFIELD 43. WANDA HEN
4. BARRY FITZGERALD 12. JOHNNY COY 20. MAVIS MURRAY 28. BOB HOPE 36. WILLIAM HOLDEN 44. MONA FREE
5. CECIL KELLAWAY 13. RAE PATTERSON 21. JOHN LUND 29. OLGA SAN JUAN 37. SONNY TUFTS 45. STANLEY C
6. MARILYN GRAY 14. ROGER DANN 22. MIKHAIL RASUMNY 30. MARY HATCHER 38. SALLY RAWLINSON 46. ANDRA VER
7. STERLING HAYDEN 15. BILLY DeWOLFE 23. FRANK FAYLEN 31. BING CROSBY 39. ALAN LADD 47. GAIL RUSS
8. CATHERINE CRAIG 16. RENEE RANDALL 24. ARLEEN WHELAN 32. JANET THOMAS 40. VERONICA LAKE 48. PAT WHITE

The stars of Variety Girl.

Variety Girl

Paramount   (1947)

Ladd and Dorothy Lamour team up on a "Tallahassee" duet.

CREDITS

Director, George Marshall. *Producer,* Daniel Dare. *Original screenplay,* Edmund Hartmann, Frank Tashlin, Robert Welch, Monte Brice. *Special Puppetoon sequence, in Technicolor,* Thorton Hee, William Cottrell. *Music,* Joseph J. Lilley, *assisted by* Troy Sanders. *Photograph,* Lionel Lindon, Stuart Thompson. *Art directors,* Hans Dreier, Robert Clatworthy. *Choreography,* Billy Daniel, Bernard Pearce. *Assistant director,* George Templeton. *Editor,* LeRoy Stone. *Songs,* "Tallahassee," "He Can Waltz," "Your Heart Calling Mine," "I Must Have Been Madly In Love," "I Want My Money Back," "Impossible Things," "The French," Frank Loesser, "Harmony," Johnny Burke, Jimmy Van Heusen, "Tired," Allan Roberts, Doris Fisher, "Romeow and Julicat," Edward Plumb, "Mildred's Boogie," Mildred *and* Jim Mulcay, "Tiger Rag," The Original Dixieland Jazz Band. *Running time, 83 minutes.*

CAST

Catherine Brown, MARY HATCHER; *Amber LaVonne,* OLGA SAN JUAN; *Bob Kirby,* DeFOREST KELLEY; *Barker,* WILLIAM DEMAREST; *Stage manager,* FRANK FAYLEN; *J. R. O'Connell,* FRANK FERGUSON; *Bill Farris,* GLENN TRYON; *Mrs. Webster,* NELLA WALKER; *Headwaiter,* TORBEN MEYER; *Guest Stars and Novelty Numbers:* BING CROSBY, BOB HOPE, RAY MILLAND, ALAN LADD, DOROTHY LAMOUR, BARBARA STANWYCK, PAULETTE GODDARD, SONNY TUFTS, JOAN CAULFIELD, WILLIAM HOLDEN, LIZABETH SCOTT, BURT LANCASTER, GAIL RUSSELL, DIANA LYNN, STERLING HAYDEN, ROBERT PRESTON, VERONICA LAKE, JOHN LUND, WILLIAM BENDIX, BARRY FITZGERALD, CASS DALEY, HOWARD DA SILVA, MACDONALD CAREY, BILLY DE WOLFE, PATRIC KNOWLES, MONA FREEMAN, CECIL KELLAWAY, ARLEEN WHELAN, VIRGINIA FIELD, RICHARD WEBB, JOHNNY COY, STANLEY CLEMENTS, CECIL B. DE MILLE, MITCHELL LEISEN, FRANK BUTLER, GEORGE MARSHALL, PEARL BAILEY, SPIKE JONES AND HIS CITY SLICKERS, JIM AND MILDRED MULCAY, WANDA HENDRIX, MIKHAIL RASUMNY, GEORGE REEVES, SALLY RAWLINSON, MARY EDWARDS, VIRGINIA WELLES, PATRICIA WHITE (BARRY), NANETTE PARKS, JACK NORTON, BARNEY DEAN

Like *Star Spangled Rhythm,* this is another studio variety show with the various stars of Paramount going through their paces as singers, dancers, and comedians—whether those roles were comfortable for them or not. The thin plot line concerns the history of the variety clubs, and the climax is an all-star charity show for these clubs. Woven through this is the old story of a young hopeful in Hollywood, Mary Hatcher, who tries to break into pictures by dubbing the voice for a big star who can't sing. Olga San Juan is her crazy starlet pal.

Alan Ladd is one of many top stars who appears briefly. Paramount was aware that he had done some singing in high school and that he had a good, mellow, if untrained voice. He was teamed with Dorothy Lamour in a quick-twist sketch. Dorothy is a stewardess on an airliner, and Ladd is the pilot. The plane seems to be in trouble, and Ladd comes on looking grim and menacing. He and Dorothy suddenly burst into a duet rendition of the song "Tallahassee."

Pete and Susan are passengers (Wally Cassell and Veronica Lake),
Douglas Dick is the co-pilot and Ladd is the pilot.

Saigon
Paramount   (1948)

CREDITS

Director, Leslie Fenton. *Producer,* P. J. Wolfson. *Screen-play,* P. J. Wolfson, Arthur Sheekman, *Based on a story by* Julian Zimet. *Photography,* John F. Seitz. *Costumes,* Edith Head. *Music,* Robert Emmett Dolan. *Editor,* William Shea. *Running time, 93 minutes.*

CAST

Major Larry Briggs, ALAN LADD; *Susan Cleaver,* VE-RONICA LAKE; *Captain Mike Perry,* DOUGLAS DICK; *Sergeant Pete Rocco,* WALLY CASSELL; *Lieutenant Keon,* LUTHER ADLER; *Alex Maris,* MORRIS CARNOV-SKY; *Hotel clerk,* MIKHAIL RASUMNY; *Simon,* LUIS VAN ROOTEN; *Boat Captain,* EUGENE BORDEN; *Surgeon,* GRIFF BARNETT; *Café Singer,* BETTY BRYANT

With Veronica Lake.

Completed in January 1947, *Saigon* was not released until March 1948. It is easy to confuse *Saigon* with *Calcutta* simply because they are cut from the same formula, though *Calcutta* is the far better picture. The cheap sort of carelessness that went into the making of *Saigon* was apparent even to the casual Ladd fan.

The picture begins in the rain in postwar Shanghai. Recently discharged from the air corps, Major Larry Briggs (Ladd) has just learned his young, cleancut flying buddy, Mike (Dick), has only a short time to live, despite several operations and a doctor's attempt to save him by implanting a plate in his skull. In a waterfront café, Larry and a third buddy, Pete (Cassell), decide not to tell Mike the truth about his condition. Instead, they plan to make his last days one big joy ride. First, though, they must finance the ride—which entails accepting a risky but highly profitable flying job offered by Alex

Maris (Carnovsky), a suavely evil type.

The job is a no-questions-asked deal, and when police interfere at takeoff time, Larry hustles Maris's blond secretary, Susan Cleaver (Lake), into the ancient DC-3 and leaves without Maris. Mike is immediately smitten with the bad-tempered Susan. When the plane must be ditched, Larry lands it in a rice paddy, and the party proceeds by oxcart and boat to Saigon.

Larry breaks open the suitcase Susan has been carrying and discovers stacks of money. Larry sees Susan as pure trouble and orders her to take the next ferry to Saigon. Mike's heartbroken reaction to Susan's disappearance causes the men to take the ferry also. Larry blackmails Susan into being nice to Mike and mails the money to himself at Saigon General Delivery.

While keeping Mike aglow with her romantic attentions, Susan discovers signs of jealousy in Larry. "I'm

125

The clerk (Rasumny) shows Susan, Mike, Larry, and Pete to their rooms.

"I'm not like Mike—I'm like you," Susan whispers.

like *you*," she whispers to Larry on the terrace of the Saigon hotel, "not like Mike...." And he knows she is right.

In the final scenes, Maris shows up to demand his money (he is a nasty war profiteer), and Pete is killed; then Mike is caught in the crossfire when Maris goes after Susan for double-crossing him. The last scene is at the cemetery, with the implication that Susan and Larry are now free to find a future together.

The sets in *Saigon* are patently phony, sound-stage arrangements, the direction is sluggish, and the screenplay is full of stereotypes. Ladd's good-bad guy has our sympathy because his intentions are noble, even if his methods are not, but Lake couldn't find the right tone, and her Susan is an empty, unlikable doll. Luther Adler, however, makes his Lieutenant Keon both enigmatic and fascinating.

Newsweek defined *Saigon* as "the kind of loud but tuneless music Ladd and Lake seemed inclined to make together," and Bosley Crowther of the *New York Times* said, "[Ladd] does little more than act superior and soothe his disdain with cigarettes."

Saigon was ordinary, and though it made money, it marked the end of the Ladd-Lake teaming.

At the cemetery Larry, Susan, and Lieutenant Keon say their farewells to Pete and Mike.

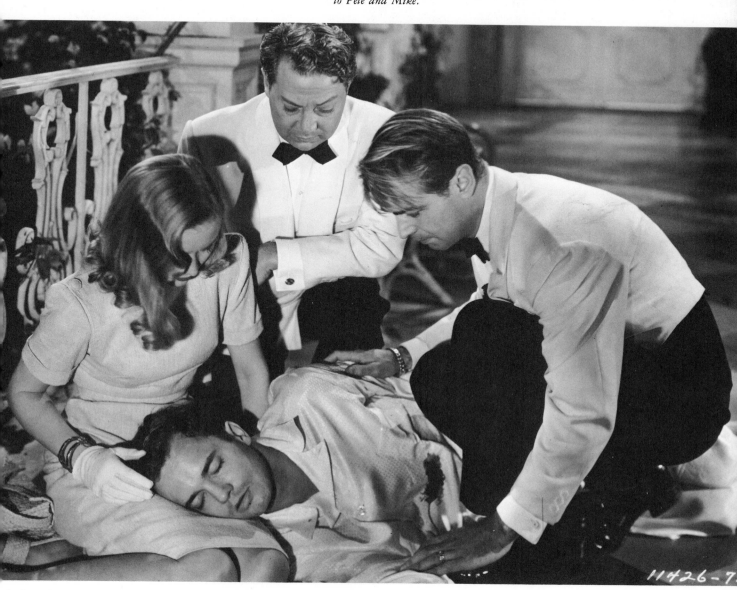

in Susan's arms as Lieutenant Keon (Luther Adler) and

Disciplining young cadet Denmore (Conrad Janis).

Beyond Glory

Paramount   (1948)

CREDITS

Director, John Farrow. *Producer*, Robert Fellows. *Screenplay*, Jonathan Latimer, Charles Marquis Warren, William Wister Haines. *Photography*, John Seitz. *Music*, Victor Young. *Editor*, Eda Warren. *Running time, 82 minutes.*

CAST

Rockwell (Rocky) Gilman, ALAN LADD; *Ann Dan...* DONNA REED; *Major General Bond*, GEOR... MACREADY; *Lew Proctor*, GEORGE COULOU... *Raymond Denmore, Sr.*, HAROLD VERMILYEA; *Dewing*, HENRY TRAVERS; *Dr. White*, LUIS V... ROOTEN; *Henry Daniels*, TOM NEAL; *Raymond ... more, Jr.*, CONRAD JANIS; *Cora*, MARGARET FI... (MAGGIE MAHONEY); *Miller*, PAUL LEES; *C... Sergeant Eddie Loughlin*, DICK HOGAN; *Thomas, ... DIE MURPHY; *Mrs. Daniels*, GERALDINE W... *Mr. Julian*, CHARLES EVANS; *Cadet*, RUSSELL WA... *John Craig*, VINCENT DONAHUE; *General Pres... STEVE PENDLETON; *Colonel Stoddard*, HARLA... TUCKER; *Cadet*, EDWARD RYAN

Rocky cuts in on Cadet Thomas's (Murphy's) dance with Ann (Reed).

riginally titled *The Long Grey Line*, this picture about West Point and one cadet in trouble was intended as a ramatic breakthrough for Ladd. The role was quite different from his usual trenchcoated tough guy, but in the nal analysis it proved less than an improvement.

In making the film, the cast and crew spent two weeks West Point filming extensive background, exterior, d "key" scenes, as well as parades, cadet formations, d classes.

Rocky Gilmore (Ladd) has had a shaky return to the vilian world after a life-and-death battle in Tunisia in hich his commanding officer, Captain Daniels (Neal), as killed. The death haunts Rocky, because there were ree minutes in that battle he cannot account for. He convinced he cowered in fear and failed to give the der that might have saved the officer's life. Discharged, ocky has wandered from job to job, unable to readjust d becoming increasingly depressed.

Finally he goes to the officer's widow (Reed), in the ope of purging himself by helping her. He falls in love ith her and she with him, and she encourages him to ter West Point. Rocky feels that he can vindicate imself by making good at the academy.

He is doing brilliantly in his studies and hoping to arry the lovely widow, when he is suddenly hauled efore a congressional board of investigation on charges having forced a certain young plebe, spoiled Raymond enmore (Janis), to resign from the Point. Denmore's wyer (Coulouris) accuses Rocky of being "untruthful, erhaps even criminal, and certainly immoral." He sets t to prove it with the help of an army psychiatrist who aims he heard Rocky admit to causing Captain Daniels's eath.

The trial is nearly Rocky's undoing; he is close to a ervous breakdown, though Ann and kind-but-tough old op Dewling (Travers), the man who looked after him hen he was a boy, encourage and support him. Rocky

Accused by lawyer Proctor (George Coulouris).

Rocky returns to New York to talk it over with Ann and Pop (Travers).

Older than the other cadets, Rocky (Ladd) learns to take the hazing from upper classmen (Dick Hogan and Edward Ryan).

does nothing to defend himself. Finally, under stres Rocky leaves the academy, though he has been confine to quarters, and goes to New York to tell Ann he leaving the Point. She and Pop persuade him to retur

His absence has given the prosecution powerful an munition, and they insist he be court-martialed. Po steps in at this stage with a new witness, Cadet Loughl (Hogan), who served with Rocky at Tunisia. Loughl tells how German tank fire kept them pinned down an how Rocky passed out for about three minutes after bein wounded. When Rocky came to and gave the order th wiped out the tank, Captain Daniels was already dead

Rocky turns to Loughlin and asks, "Why didn't y tell me this before?"—which must have provoked qui a number of people in the audience into answering f Loughlin, "You never *asked* me!"

If the involved flashbacks haven't worn you out, th final denouement will make you laugh. It's a sham because the picture is well acted all the way and has t added interest of starring young Audie Murphy, Ame ica's most decorated World War II soldier, in a sma role.

Whispering Smith

Paramount   (1948)
Technicolor

CREDITS

Director, Leslie Fenton. *Producer*, Mel Epstein. *Screenplay*, ...ank Butler, Karl Kamb. *From a novel by* Frank H. ...earman. *Photography*, Ray Rennahan. *Music*, Adolph ...eutsch. *Song "Laramie,"* Jay Livingston, Ray Evans. *Art ...rection*, Hans Dreier, Walter Tyler. *Special effects*, Gor-...n Jennings, Farciot Edouart. *Running time, 88 minutes.*

CAST

...ke "Whispering" Smith, ALAN LADD; *Murray Sinclaire,* ...OBERT PRESTON; *Marian Sinclaire,* BRENDA ...ARSHALL; *Barney Rebstock,* DONALD CRISP; *Bill ...ansing,* WILLIAM DEMAREST; *Emmy Dansing,* FAY ...OLDEN; *Blake Barton,* MURVYN VYE; *Whitey ...uSang,* FRANK FAYLEN; *George McCloud,* JOHN ...LDREDGE; *Leroy Barton,* ROBERT WOOD; *Bill ...ggs,* J. FARRELL MacDONALD; *Doctor Sawbucks,* ...ON BARCLAY; *Sheriff McSwiggens,* WILL WRIGHT; ...y, GARY GRAY

...dd's first color film and his first starring western came ...gether in the 1948 release *Whispering Smith*. Ladd had ...stable of horses on his ranch, Alsulana, had become ...mething of a horseman, and he was eager to freshen ...s image by moving it west.

...Taken from a novel by Frank Spearman, *Whispering ...ith* concerned a real-life figure of legend, a railroad ...tective who earned the nickname of "Whispering" ...ith because he was fast on the draw and spoke in a ...w, hard voice. The real Smith was neither hero nor

With Brenda Marshall

With William Demarest and Brenda Marshall.

Smith confronts Murray (Preston) in front of McCloud (Eldredge) and his worker (Ethan Laidlaw).

heel, though some historians felt he was perhaps more the latter than the legend allows.

Smith was, in fact, exactly the sort of ambiguous character Ladd played so well, but this time the scriptwriters decided to purify him, and *Whispering Smith* marks the beginning of Ladd's decent, stalwart roles—though it would be a while before he settled into a good-guy groove.

The Screen Writers Guild nominated *Whispering Smith* for their award as Best Written America Western of the year.

(There had also been a silent version of *Whispering Smith,* produced by Signal Films and starring J. P. McGowan as Smith, with Helen Holmes as Marion Sinclair. In 1936 George O'Brien did a film called *Whispering Smith Speaks,* but it had little to do with the original character.)

Though the picture is a perfectly enjoyable, colorful western, one must suspect that it was intended to be much more. There is something downright uncanny in the way *Smith* presaged the production of *Shane,* which

would follow nearly five years later. Certainly the Shane qualities are more than suggested in the Smith character.

The film presages *Shane* visually as well. First there is the opening shot: The titles roll over a panorama of majestic hills rimmed by snow-covered mountains. Far to the top right of the screen is a tiny figure on a horse, riding toward us. The music swells, and the figure is closer, out of the snow now and into the green valley, then crossing a spring meadow. The scenery is breathtaking. As the music fades with the last credit, we see a gun drawing a bead on the lone rider, who is still some distance away.

There are other similarities. The unavailable women in both *Smith* and *Shane* have the same name: Marian. And Smith's gentle way with children, his loyalty to a friend, his need to hide his emotions and do what must be done—all beg to be compared to *Shane.*

Murray (Preston) explains the character of Smith at the outset. A train is rumbling through the rain-swept night, and some railroad men gathered in a boxcar are discussing a series of recent train robberies. A telegram has come telling the men to expect Whispering Smith, a railroad detective who has been assigned to the case.

"Good ole Smitty!" Murray exclaims as he folds the telegram. One of the younger men asks about the detective's odd name. Murray laughs. "Sonny," he tells the man, "if you ever run off with the company payroll and you hear someone behind you one night talkin' low and quiet, that's Whispering Smith, and you're in trouble!"

As it turns out, Smith, whose horse was shot out from under him, flags down the train and boards, coming up behind the men in the boxcar. A short time later the train is held up, and there follows a rousing gunfight in the rain, played in and out of the cars and ending when the last bandit rides off and Smith falls unconscious from his wounds.

He wakes up in Murray's house, tended to by Murray's lovely wife, Marian (Marshall), and the look in his eyes tells you the girl is more to him than the old friend they both pretend. It develops that Murray is in trouble, running around with the Rebstock gang, led by Barney Rebstock (Crisp), a neighbor. The Rebstocks are suspected of being tied in with the Bartons, evil brothers who are notorious robbers and murderers.

Everyone appears to find Murray lovable and boyish, if a bit boisterous. What we see is a crude, boorish type who is insensitive to his wife, high-handed with his friends, cavalier to his boss, and downright dishonest with the railroad where he is employed, and it is difficult to understand why Smith works so hard to save Smith from himself.

After Murray is fired from the railroad for looting a wrecked train, he joins Rebstock in wrecking trains. Naturally, Smith must go after him and the gang and reassures Marian before going.

In the final scene Smith and Murray face each other at Murray's ranch. When Smith shows concern for Murray's wound, Murray pulls a gun. However, Murray's wound gets the best of him, and he drops.

Smith mutters things like, "If there had been any other way, Murray . . . The only cards I had to play were the ones you dealt me. . . ." Given the Murray character, this seems very forced and unduly sentimental, weakening the film's ending.

Ladd looks marvelous in color. He manages to be strong, noble, warm, wistful, steady, self-sufficient, and tender, while remaining a man alone and apart.

Newsweek stated that the film was "a deserving if desperately orthodox Western. . . . Facially and vocally, the new role fits Ladd to perfection and, for all his deceptive dead pan and almost fastidious gunplay, there is never any doubt that he is as lethal as any Western star since William S. Hart."

The fans were enthusiastic about Ladd's journey into the West, and *Whispering Smith* proved that Ladd was at home on the range.

Smith (Ladd) shoots it out with the Bartons (Murvyn Vye on ground).

The Great Gatsby
Paramount   (1949)

CREDITS

Director, Elliott Nugent. *Producer*, Richard Maibaum.
Screenplay, Cyril Hume, Richard Maibaum. *From the novel
by* F. Scott Fitzgerald *and the play by* Owen Davis. *Pho-
tography*, John Seitz. *Music*, Robert Emmett Dolan.
Makeup, Perc Westmore. *Costumes*, Edith Head. *Editor*,
Ellsworth Hoagland. *Running time, 91 minutes.*

CAST

Jay Gatsby, ALAN LADD; *Daisy Buchanan*, BETTY
FIELD; *Nick Carraway*, MACDONALD CAREY; *Jordan
Baker*, RUTH HUSSEY; *Tom Buchanan*, BARRY SUL-
LIVAN; *Wilson*, HOWARD DA SILVA; *Myrtle Wilson*,
SHELLEY WINTERS; *Dan Cody*, HENRY HULL; *Ella
Cody*, CAROLE MATHEWS; *Myron Lupus*, ED BE-
GLEY; *Klipspringer*, ELISHA COOK, JR.; *Guest*, NI-
CHOLAS JOY; *Kinsella*, WALTER GREAZA; *Mavrom-
ichaelis*, TITO VUOLO; *Real estate man*, RAY WALKER;
Pamela, DIANE NANCE; *Reba*, JACK LAMBERT; *Golf
Pro*, JACK GARGAN; *Twins*, LYNNE and JEANNE
ROMER

The *Great Gatsby* should have dispelled forever any doubts
critics had concerning Ladd's ability to break out of his
tough-guy mold and be an actor. Yet it is a film often
overlooked in Ladd's long career. This is difficult to
understand, for if ever a role was tailor-made for an actor,
this is it. The parallels between Ladd's life and Gatsby's
are easy enough to draw.

There were three movie versions of *The Great Gatsby*;
the 1926 version starred Warner Baxter and Lois Wilson
and the last version in 1974 starred Robert Redford and
Mia Farrow in a beautiful but tedious flop. Only the
1949 version is worth watching, for it is the only version
that comes close to re-creating what Fitzgerald had in
mind—and even this version has its weaknesses. (Paramount, incidentally, pulled the 1949 *Gatsby* from circulation because of the 1974 release—an act of incon-
sideration, both for Ladd and fans of Ladd.)

The story itself poses the biggest problem. What
works in the novel looks awkward onscreen and because
the focus is on Gatsby, the film must tell you more than
the novel did, more than Fitzgerald wanted you to know.

By creating Nick Carraway as the narrator, Scott Fitzgerald was able to let the reader know only what Nick
knows, thus keeping Gatsby mysterious.

Nick is a literary device. By creating Nick, Fitzgerald
kept the reader out of both Gatsby's and Daisy's heads,
letting them become figures for the imagination.

Still, within that framework, the film comes close to
being great. Even the musical score is superb, lyrical,
playing out the various moods with a haunting roman-
ticism.

The film begins by showing us a Gatsby who is a
gangster and a bootlegger. He and his henchmen drive
to West Egg, where Gatsby has just purchased an enor-
mous old mansion which he sets out to renovate. Only
Klipspringer (Cook), Gatsby's oldest friend, understands. As he watches Jay wander around the empty
rooms he tinkles out "Just a Cottage Small by a Water-
fall" on the piano. Across the bay in East Egg, he tells
Lupus (Begley), lives Daisy Faye (Field), of the Louisville,
Kentucky, Fayes, though she is now Daisy Buchanan.

Gatsby proceeds to throw extravagant, empty parties
to which every freeloader and flapper in the area comes
to drink bootleg booze and dance to hot jazz. Jay himself
looks over these fantastic parties as a ghost might stand
back to observe the living. Then one night Nick (Carey),
Daisy's second cousin, who lives in the small rental cottage on the edge of the estate, shows up at a party and
Gatsby introduces himself at once, disarming Nick by

Wilson (Howard Da Silva) shoots Gatsby while he is talking to Nick (MacDonald Carey) at the pool.

sking, "Now that you have met me, what do you think
f me?" He tells Nick ridiculous lies about himself, but
he lies are so transparent that Nick is more amused than
epelled.

Gatsby's real story is told in a flashback that was in
he book but was missing from the 1974 version (and
s essential if we hope to understand Gatsby at all).

Young, penniless Jimmy Gatts falls in with wealthy
ld reprobate Dan Cody (Hull) and sails around the world
n his yacht, all the while tantalized by Cody's young,
retty wife (Mathews), whom Cody predicts will reject
he handsome boy's advances as long as her elderly hus-
and has the money. "Money is the only thing that
ounts," he counsels Jimmy, giving the boy a set of
alues that will lead eventually to his downfall in West
gg, New York.

Nick learns more of Gatsby from Daisy's friend Jordan
Hussey), who admits she and Daisy knew Gatsby back
n Louisville during the First World War when Jay was
n the army. Daisy and Jay were in love, but Jay had
o go overseas and Daisy grew restless and married
ealthy, socially prominent Tom Buchanan (Sullivan).
poiled, pretty Daisy has not been too happy of late,
wing to Tom's philandering with Myrtle (Winters), the
lond floozy wife of Wilson (da Silva), the man who runs
he garage down the road.

When Gatsby bribes Jordan with a yellow roadster
hat duplicates his own, she sets it up for him to be
eunited with Daisy. The meeting is to take place at
Nick's cottage and in the most touching episode in the
lm, Gatsby, in white flannels and blue blazer, arrives
ith an elaborate tea service to brazenly take over the
ottage. As Nick watches in bemused wonder, the im-
atient lover displays the most pitiable nervous anxiety.
When Daisy drives up, he ducks out the back way and
tands in the rain waiting for the right moment to enter.
Daisy is in mid-sentence when she looks up and their
yes meet—in a moment so moving that it takes one's
reath.

Jay's boyish eagerness to impress Daisy matches her
xcitement in seeing Jay again. Gatsby's dream of ro-
nance inspires Daisy to agree that they will start over
nd she will tell her husband.

But she does not tell Tom. Daisy is incapable of such
decision. Jay is impatient and gets her alone at one of
is crowded parties and insists she not delay further.
Nick tries to make Gatsby see the truth. "She won't do
," he says. "Not Daisy."

The following day Jay comes for her, and the whole
roup is there—Nick, Jordan, Tom, and Daisy. A trip
o town results in a confrontation with Tom. "Look here,
ld sport," Gatsby says, "Daisy doesn't love you. She has
oved me since eleven years ago." Tom is outraged, call-
ng Gatsby a gangster. On the trip back to Long Island,
he distraught Daisy runs over Tom's mistress, who has
un out into the road after a fight with her jealous hus-
and. Daisy fails to stop. Gatsby nobly promises to say
hat he was driving.

lla Cody (Carole Mathews) and Jay are with old Dan Cody (Hull)
hen he dies.

As Jay Gatsby.

*When Daisy tells Tom (Sullivan) she is leaving him for Jay, Tom
tries to humiliate Jay.*

Gatsby buys a mansion in West Egg. (With Ed Begley.)

Tom finds Daisy at home and learns what has happened. "Let him take the blame; he has it coming. We'll all say it was him if we have to—it was his car." Nick is appalled by this callousness and protests. When Tom demands, "Since when were you a friend of Gatsby's?" Nick answers, "Since one minute ago." He leaves and discovers Jay standing outside. He has overheard Daisy's betrayal and seems shattered by it.

The next morning Nick finds Gatsby alone at the mansion, servants departed, sitting by the pool listening to the phone ring and making no move to answer it. Gatsby is calm, telling Nick he is giving up the charade of being a gentleman—to which Nick counters, "But you are a gentleman—the only one I know." Gatsby says he plans to take the blame for the accident because Daisy can't help being Daisy. There is a shot, Gatsby falls into the pool, and the garage man, Wilson, appears with a smoking gun.

Ladd's performance dominates the film, but the whole cast is really top rate. Betty Field has exactly the right fragile voice characterization, though she doesn't quite look the part of Gatsby's obsession. Shelly Winters's role is brief, but she makes her few scenes count. Da Silva, peering through his wire-rimmed glasses with the sadness of the world in his face, seems to echo Gatsby's own dogged devotion to an unworthy illusion. (Da Silva was also in the 1974 version but in a different role.)

No one attends Gatsby's funeral, and Nick, disillu- sioned by his society friends, lays flowers on the grave and finds Jordan waiting. The two plan to return to Nick's hometown in the Midwest.

Voyeur, in *Theatre Arts*, stated: "Among its many virtues, count first Alan Ladd's performance as Gatsby. In the best acting he has ever done, he gives Gatsby the troubled depths and outward appeal that took him to the top."

Said *Good Housekeeping*, "Alan Ladd plays to perfection Jay Gatsby."

And Robert Hatch, in *The New Republic,* said, "As Alan Ladd acts him, a little tough, a little boyish, quite definitely noble, he is a man to pity."

Manny Farber, in *The Nation,* hedged, "An electric, gaudily graceful figure in action movies, here [Ladd] has to stand still and project turbulent feelings, succeeding chiefly in giving the impression of an isinglass baby-face in the process of melting. . . . As a matter of fact, he gives a pretty good impression of Gatsby's depressed, non-public moments."

And Bosley Crowther took his usual swipe at Ladd: "His portrait is quite in accordance with that stock character he usually plays."

The general consensus was that *Gatsby* was very good, and it marked the first time since *This Gun for Hire* that Ladd rated rave reviews. However, this time it was the public that was skeptical. *Gatsby* did not lose money, but the box office was disappointing.

A dying Gatsby makes one last effort to pull himself up.

Jordan (Hussey) and Nick (Carey) witness the renewal of Daisy's and Jay's love.

With Donna Reed

Chicago Deadline
Paramount   (1949)

CREDITS

Director, Lewis Allen. *Producer*, Robert Fellows. *Screenplay*, Warren Duff, *From the novel* One Woman, *by* Tiffany Thayer. *Photography*, John F. Seitz. *Music*, Victor Young. *Editor*, LeRoy Stone. *Running time: 86 minutes.*

CAST

Ed Adams, ALAN LADD; *Rosita Jean D'Ur*, DONNA REED; *Leona*, JUNE HAVOC; *Belle Dorset*, IRENE HERVEY; *Tommy Ditman*, ARTHUR KENNEDY; *Solly Wellman*, BERRY KROEGER; *Anstruder*, HAROLD VERMILYEA; *Blacky Franchot*, SHEPPERD STRUDWICK (JOHN SHEPPERD); *Paul Jean D'Ur*, JOHN BEAL; *Howard*, TOM POWERS; *G. G. Temple*, GAVIN MUIR; *Pig*, DAVE WILLOCK; *Bat*, PAUL LEES; *Jerry Cavanaugh*, ROY ROBERTS; *Hotspur Shaner*, HOWARD FREEMAN; *Hazel*, MARIETTA CANTY; *Pawnshop lady*, CELIA LOVSKY; *Secretary*, CAROLE MATHEWS; *Gribbe*, HARRY ANTRIM; *Sister John*, OTTOLA NESMITH; *Spingler*, DICK KEENE; *Maggie*, LEONA ROBERTS

Originally published in 1933, the Tiffany Thayer novel *One Woman* was surprisingly rougher than this 1949 movie based on it. The novel was a hard-boiled exploration of a reporter's obsession with a story concerning a dead nymphomaniac. Alas, not only was the novel a lot tougher, it was also more interesting than the film. The episodic approach which flows well enough on the page is too fragmented for good continuity on the screen.

The exteriors for *Chicago Deadline* were shot in Chicago and have the sooty, grey look of that city. The picture begins with Ladd as reporter Ed Adams, climbing the stairs of a cheap, southside rooming house. He has come to talk a runaway girl into going home. He inadvertently also finds the body of a dead girl, Rosita, in another room. Curious, he checks around her room and finds an address book, which he pockets.

One by one, Ed and fellow reporter Pig (Willock) call the numbers in the book. Ed must interview or seek out a bank vice-president (Muir), a snarling gangster (Kroeger), the gangster's moll (Hervey), a call girl (Havoc), a sad-eyed hood (Strudwick), a crippled writer (Freeman), a punchy fighter (Lees), the fighter's conniving manager (Roberts), and the dead girl's brother. All are frightened by news of the girl's death. Their names have come up in the investigation, though most claim they never knew her.

Leona (June Havoc) resents Ed's dedication to his job.

(Top) Unaware that Solly (Berry Kroeger) is listening, Ed tries to garner information from Belle (Irene Hervey). (Bottom) Bartender (Jack Gargan) stands by as Ed tries to sober up Leona (Havoc).

In a car park, Pig (Willock) and Ed shoot it out with Solly and his men.

Each step of Ed's inquiry gives him a different picture of Rosita, but the pieces of her life begin to fall together. A runaway, she was widowed before she was out of her teens. During the hard life that followed, she became involved with a small-time hood, then with a ruthless banker who slapped her around. One night the banker had thought he had killed her, and he called in a gangster to get rid of the body. But the girl was alive, and the gangster's henchman, Spingler (Keene), helped her hide. A two-bit fighter becomes enamored of her, and when his manager discovers her past and threatens her, she is forced to disappear again.

When she is found dead of tuberculosis a few months later, the banker who thought he had murdered her, and has been paying blackmail, the gangster-blackmailer who has accepted the money, the fight manager who has lied to his fighter, convincing him Rosita ditched him, and even the sad-eyed hood who really loved Rosita and has never forgiven himself for knuckling under, are all shaken. The gangster begins to dispose of those involved, including on his death list Ed, who knows too much.

Ed shoots it out with Solly in a deserted parking garage. He is wounded, but leaves his hospital bed to attend Rosita's funeral, along with the other principals in Rosita's life.

Ladd is never shown at a typewriter and though he kisses Havoc minutes after he has met her, it means little as he is as elusive a lover as ever, keeping the poor girl waiting all hours, falling asleep on her shoulder in taxis and asking her to the fights, then forgetting to take her home. He is completely wrapped up in his need to know all about Rosita—a touch of *Laura*. Unfortunately, little else about the film matches the fascination of *Laura*.

Bosley Crowther, in the *New York Times*, took a pot shot at Ladd: "Mr. Ladd plays this reporter in the tight-lipped and nonchalant style that those people who cherish the illusion will no doubt idolatrously admire."

Newsweek was nominally more tolerant: "*Chicago Deadline* gives Alan Ladd a chance to put a slightly different twist on his familiar, stony-faced, hard-guy routine. As a Chicago newspaper reporter, he is still so tough even bullets can't stop him. But this time underneath his impregnable exterior lies a great big heart."

Chicago Deadline was remade in 1966 as *Fame Is the Name of the Game*, a TV movie which spawned a short-lived series.

Ed (Ladd) intercepts G. G. Temple (Muir).

He was a charming, sweet man, and he was nine feet tall to those who knew him. In the end he just got tired . . . he just gave up.

WANDA HENDRIX

Captain Carey, U.S.A.
Paramount   (1950)

CREDITS

Director, Mitchell Leisen. *Producer,* Richard Maibaum. *Screenplay,* Robert Thoeren. *Based on the novel* After Midnight, *by* Martha Albrand. *Photography,* John Seitz. *Song,* "Mona Lisa," Jay Livingston, Ray Evans, sung by Nat King Cole. *Editor,* Alma Macrorie. *Running time: 82 minutes.*

CAST

Webster Carey, ALAN LADD; *Giulia de Graffi,* WANDA HENDRIX; *Barone Rocco de Graffi,* FRANCIS LEDERER; *Doctor Lunati,* JOSEPH CALLEIA; *Countess de Cresci,* CELIA LOVSKY; *Count Carlo de Cresci,* RICHARD AVONDE; *Luigi,* FRANK PUGLIA; *Sandro,* LUIS ALBERNI; *Serafina,* ANGELA CLARKE; *Manfredo Acuto,* ROLAND WINTERS; *Frank,* PAUL LEES; *Nancy,* JANE NIGH; *Pietro,* RUSTY (RUSS) TAMBLYN; *Angelina,* VIRGINIA FARMER; *Blind musician,* DAVID LEONARD; *Lucia,* MARIA TAVARES; *Giovanni,* GEORGE J. LEWIS

Captain Carey, U.S.A. was one of the few Ladd films to win an Academy Award—for the best song of 1950. Jukeboxes and radios carried the strains of Nat King Cole's warm and liquid interpretation of "Mona Lisa," a top tune of the hit parade that year.

The film seemed to be an attempt to blend the elements of Ladd's *O.S.S.* thriller with his soldier-of-fortune adventures such as *China, Calcutta,* and *Saigon,* and it is not a mix that works very well.

Webb Carey (Ladd) has returned to the village of Orta near Milan in order to discover who in that village betrayed his O.S.S. team and caused the death of Julie (Hendrix), a member of a noble family who lived in a *palazzo* on an island in a lake. The island is also the hiding place of his team. There is a secret room below the Palazzo de Cresci, long boarded over, where he and

Frank set up their underground radio. Only Julie knew about the room—and the centuries-old paintings hidden there. When Webb, recovered from long convalescence, sees a Bellini painting in a New York gallery window, he returns to discover who else knew about the room and had smuggled out the valuable painting. (Both Frank and Julie had been killed by Nazis.)

The villagers are not happy to see him, and they avoid him on the street, whispering as he passes. He goes to see the aristocratic old countess, Julie's grandmother (Lovsky), and receives a shock when Julie walks in—very much alive—and introduces Barone de Graffi (Lederer) as her husband.

Webb tries to discover who the traitor was who betrayed the hideout in the *palazzo,* for that is the same person responsible for the death of the villagers who were shot after the Nazis found out about the resistance group.

Julie explains to Webb that she married the barone only because she thought Webb was dead and her grandmother had insisted. He suspects the barone, but in the end it proves to be the old contessa. Her grandson, Julie's brother Carlo (Avonde), had been imprisoned during the war, and the contessa asked the barone, an old friend of the family, to make a deal with the Germans—a trade of the O.S.S. men and the village resistance group for her grandson's release. The barone had found the hidden room in the cellar and had smuggled out a painting to bolster family income, but he was only a tool of the contessa. The barone dies, leaving Julie free to be with Webb.

There are simply too many twists and turns here for anyone to follow the plot coherently. The photography is even a little murky, though there is a certain amount of atmosphere projected, particularly when visuals are accompanied by a haunting concertina rendition of "Mona Lisa."

Phillip Hartung, in *The Commonweal,* remarked in his review: "Ladd, hampered somewhat by his handsome but dead pan, must rely more on fisticuffs and dialogue to put over his discontent with the world. *Captain Carey U.S.A.* is little more than a rough and tumble post-war adventure."

Reunited with the young countess, his Julie (Hendrix).

Luigi (Frank Puglia) shows Webb where the townspeople hanged a traitor.

Webb confronts the baron (Lederer), the baroness (Celia Lovsky), and Julie's brother (Richard Avonde).

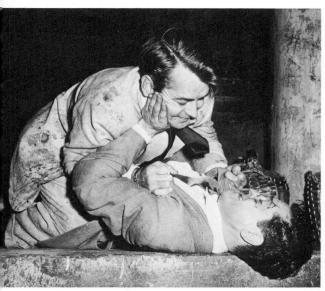

Julie's husband, Baron de Graffi (Lederer), struggles with Webb in the secret cellar.

Serafina (Angela Clarke) helps Webb after he has been hit by a rock.

Branded

Paramount (1951) Technicolor

With Mona Freeman.

CREDITS

Director, Rudolph Maté. *Producer,* Mel Epstein. *Screenplay,* Sydney Boehm, Cyril Hume. *Based on a novel,* Montana Rides, *by* Evan Evans (*aka* Max Brand, Frederick Faust). *Photography,* Charles B. Lang, Jr. *Music,* Roy Webb. *Art directors,* Hans Dreier, Roland Anderson. *Editor,* Alma Macrorie. *Running time: 104 minutes.*

CAST

Choya, ALAN LADD; *Ruth Lavery,* MONA FREEMAN; *Mr. Lavery,* CHARLES BICKFORD; *Leffingwell,* ROBERT KEITH; *Rubriz,* JOSEPH CALLEIA; *Tonio,* PETER HANSEN; *Mrs. Lavery,* SELENA ROYLE; *Ransome,* TOM TULLY; *Tattoo,* JOHN BERKES; *Andy,* GEORGE J. LEWIS; *Hank,* ROBERT KORTMAN; *Jake,* PAT LANE; *Peon,* NATIVIDAD VACIO; *Hernández,* MARTIN GARRALAGA; *Dad Travis,* EDWARD CLARK; *Joe's wife,* JULIA MONTOYA; *Spig,* JOHN BUTLER

The warm welcome of father (Bickford), mother (Royle), and sister (Freeman) makes the conniving Choya ill-at-ease.

Nearly two years were allowed to pass after the success of *Whispering Smith* before Paramount put Ladd back in the saddle. When *Branded* matched its predecessor in popularity, Ladd's regular appearance in westerns was assured.

The opening scenes set the tone for what is to come. Ladd, an itinerant gunman known simply as Choya (a corruption of the Spanish *cholla*, cactus), is making a break from a town where he has killed a man (in self-defense, it is pointed out). Asked by his hostage whether he has any friends, Choya replies in true dime-novel fashion, "My guns."

"Any kin?" the old duffer pursues.

"My horse." And complete with horse and guns, Choya escapes, to search out further adventure. ("If'n he don't look for trouble, trouble finds him!")

Shortly after making his getaway, Choya is approached by the unsavory T. J. Leffingwell (Keith) with an offer to participate in a scheme that could pay more than a million dollars. The Bar-O-M ranch is owned by Richard Lavery, whose only son was kidnapped twenty-five ye[ars] earlier at the age of five. Choya has "the eyes, the rig[ht] age and the nerve" to impersonate the heir to the bigg[est] cattle ranch in Texas.

With the aid of a tattooed birthmark, Choya pass[es] himself off as the lost son and is accepted wholehearted[ly] by the parents (Bickford and Royle) and Ruth (Freeman[,]) the boy's sister. Ruth had responded to his arrival on t[he] ranch as any pretty girl would respond to an intriguin[g,] handsome stranger, but she quickly adjusts to the di[s]covery that he is a relative. As soon as he is welcom[ed] as Richard, Jr., however, something happens to Choy[a.] As a member of a loving family, he experiences feelin[gs] denied him by his own childhood and becomes increa[s]ingly sickened by his part in the deception.

Leading a cattle drive to El Paso, Choya decides [to] abandon his charade and he reveals the hoax to Rut[h] who turns on him with dismay and hostility. The[re] remains only one way to redeem himself and make u[p] for the pain he has caused the Lavery family: He w[ill] nd the real son. At the point of Choya's six-shooter, Leffingwell admits that he was the kidnapper who stole the baby Lavery. But the boy had been taken from him by Matéo Rubriz, a feared Mexican bandit (Calleia), who has raised the boy as his son.

Choya immediately hits the hazardous trail to Rubriz's mountainside hideaway. There he meets Richard Lavery, Jr., (Hansen), who has grown to manhood knowing his identity only as Tonio Rubriz. It takes some tall convincing on Choya's part to have the young man accept the story of his true beginnings. But before Choya can persuade Tonio to return to Texas, a vengeful Leffingwell has intruded and informed Rubriz of Choya's intention of depriving the bandit of his "son." Once again Choya is on the run, but this time he has his quarry with him, as Tonio finds himself abducted for a second time.

With the help of Tonio, who has at last been moved by Choya's devotion to the people he had planned to rob, Choya eludes Rubriz's pursuing army of bandits, and the two young men cross the Rio Grande into Texas. Tonio has been wounded, and Choya must deliver him to the Laverys in a half-conscious state. They are grateful to have the boy back, but they are not pleased to see the double-dealing Choya. But Choya has one last confrontation with Rubriz, who has followed, and manages, at the risk of his life, to bring some kind of harmony to the affair. Tonio will commute between his real and his adopted parents, keeping all satisfied.

Choya is ready to ride into an unknown future—but not alone. Ruth is riding with him, and where Choya goes, she will go—and not as a sister.

All the ingredients in *Branded* are taken directly from the hard-hitting, straight-shooting school of western pulp fiction. Choya, despite his confession to Ruth that he is a "four-flushin' thief," is true-blue horse-opera hero. The cunning Leffingwell has him classified correctly: "You won't hit an older man. You ain't the kind that'll draw first, or shoot a man in the back." Even with the rules thus outlined, Ladd still has a chance to present his standard beguiling bad guy early in the film, barely suppressing a triumphant grin as he feigns bewilderment over the elder Lavery's excited reaction to his birthmark.

The other members of the cast perform dependably; notable are Keith, Bickford, and Calleia. Peter Hansen, here in his movie debut, formed a friendship with Ladd which would result in many appearances in Ladd's Jaguar Productions. Hansen is one of those actors who grow better as they grow older, and he has found his niche in television.

Besides its other values, *Branded* is a visual treat. The credit may be due to director Rudolph Maté's long experience as a cinematographer; his cameras here take full advantage of the Arizona scenery in every location shot. In fact, the movie's one drawback as a western entertainment is a lack of big action highlights. But thanks to a strong story and some enthusiastic performances, *Branded* remains as one of Alan Ladd's top westerns.

Choya shows the tattooed birthmark to Tonio (Hansen).

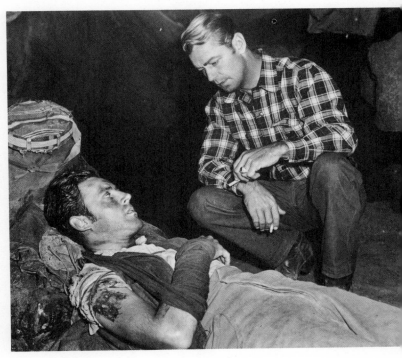

Tonio (Hansen) questions Choya about his family.

Appointment With Danger

Paramount   (1951)

CREDITS

Director, Lewis Allen. *Producer,* Robert Fellows. *Screenplay,* Richard Breen *and* Warren Duff. *Music,* Victor Young. *Photographer,* John Seitz. *Editor,* LeRoy Stone. *Running time: 89 minutes.*

CAST

Al Goddard, ALAN LADD; *Sister Augustine,* PHYLLIS CALVERT; *Earl Boettiger,* PAUL STEWART; *Dodie,* JAN STERLING; *Joe Regas,* JACK WEBB; *Paul Ferrar,* STACY HARRIS; *George Soderquist,* HENRY (HARRY) MORGAN; *David Goodman,* DAVID WOLFE; *Maury Ahearn,* DAN RISS; *Postmaster Taylor,* HARRY AN-TRIM; *Mother Ambrose,* GERALDINE WALL; *Leo Cronin,* GEORGE J. LEWIS; *Gene Gunner,* PAUL LEES

Another of those films completed and then held nearly two years for release, *Appointment with Danger* was above-average Ladd fare, fast moving and full of action. The taut, well-plotted script dealt with the little-known workings of the Postal Inspection Service. On the side of the law (as was to be his habit in the fifties), Ladd plays a tight-lipped, relentless postal inspector assigned to investigate the murder of another officer. The twist here comes in the form of a nun—the only witness to the killing.

Sent to Gary, Indiana, where the murder was committed, Ladd must first find the nun and get her to identify one of the killers (Morgan) from a mug book. Then he must infiltrate the gang, who, it turns out, killed the other officer because he learned of their plans

Al Goddard (Ladd) questions Sister Augustine (Calvert).

"Wanna come up and listen to my bebop records?" invites Dodie.

to rob a big mail shipment of money. Much suspense is generated by Ladd's attempt to convince the gang that he is a postal employee gone corrupt, and he walks a very thin line, coming harrowingly close to discovery.

The gang's resident psycho, Regas (Webb), takes an instant dislike to Goddard (Ladd), and the spite between them threatens to explode into violence at any moment.

Earl (Stewart), the gang's leader, warns Regas, "Somewhere in your blood there's a crazy bug. Get a cure or you'll get us all killed." Which proves prophetic.

A more interesting member of the gang is Dodie (Sterling), Earl's girlfriend. With a wry insouciance, Sterling delivers the standard bad-girl lines impressively, making her disregard for loyalty perfectly plausible. Ladd's encounters with these hardboiled types were usually tempered with a strong dash of sexual insinuation, and this film offers no exception.

Goddard cultivates Dodie, hoping to learn more of the gang's plans, but she has little real interest in what goes on. She invites him to her room to listen to her collection of bebop records and surprises him by becoming completely absorbed in the music and in no mood to discuss Earl's business. Finally she puts her favorite record on the turntable and moves to stand close to Goddard.

"So that's your 'Slow Bus to Memphis,'" he says in his silkiest voice.

"Yeah," she pouts, her look warm as the music pours out seductively "Can I give you a lift?"

"You already have," he purrs, taking her in his arms to dance. Pretty steamy stuff for 1951.

This dalliance with the gang's moll is not taken much further, perhaps because it runs counter to the relationship being developed between Ladd and the nun, Calvert.

The killer the nun identified turns up dead. Joe Regas, the other killer, is obsessed with finding the nun and he nearly fouls up the robbery plan in his zeal to get her. When the robbery is accomplished, with mishaps, the gang meets at the shack and Regas walks in with the nun. In her surprise at seeing Goddard, she inadvertently gives him away, and a gun battle ensues. Police and postal officers close in and save the day.

The problem here is that the scriptwriters want to *tell* us about Ladd's character, rather than show us. He seems entirely manufactured, with little past implied and no future indicated, one of those characters who exist only for the running time of the film. "You need to try a little love," one of the characters says to Goddard, "but you don't even know what love is."

Goddard deadpans, "Sure I do. It's what happens between a man and a .45 that doesn't jam." Still, when Ladd reads such lines, they work a lot better than they should.

The acting is generally good to excellent, with Paul Stewart a standout as the two-faced hotel manager, gracious to his guests, hard-nosed to his gang. Jack Webb's flat-voiced psycho gives real chills. And Harry Morgan, as the stammering, stupid little henchman who gets it from his friends, is plausibly pathetic.

Goodman (Wolfe) assures Goddard the police will work with him

Undercover, Goddard meets Earl (Stewart) and his girl, Dodie (Sterling).

Al questions a shady character (Stacy Harris) in a pool hall.

The violence-crammed climax is riveting and well-staged, with bullets flying and bodies dropping everywhere—and once more a Ladd film came under fire for its unrelenting violence.

Low key and perhaps not really memorable, *Appointment with Danger* was, nevertheless, a good, authentic thriller and one of Ladd's better performances. Regardless of the way the Goddard character was programmed by the script, Ladd put real life into him, making you care what happens to him—essential to any suspense movie. But he had this sort of thing down to second nature by this time, and little critical attention was paid to the film. It could not compare to Ladd's earlier successes.

Red Mountain

Paramount/Hal Wallis (1952) Technicolor

With Lizabeth Scott.

I was an admirer of Alan Ladd. I remember him as an intelligent, gentle, sensitive, shy, and considerate man.

As an actor, I found him quite involved with his craft. His intense concentration was impressive. Scenes were never done for his own self-aggrandizment. They were done with perspective.

LIZABETH SCOTT

CREDITS

Director, William Dieterle. *Producer,* Hal Wallis. *Screen-play,* John Meredith Lucas, George F. Slavin, George W. George. *Based on a story by* George F. Slavin, George W. George. *Photographer,* Charles Lang, Jr. *Music,* Franz Waxman. *Editor,* Warren Low. *Running time: 84 minutes.*

CAST

Brett, ALAN LADD; *Chris,* LIZABETH SCOTT; *Lane Waldron,* ARTHUR KENNEDY; *Quantrell,* JOHN IRELAND; *Skee,* JEFF COREY; *Doctor Terry,* JAMES BELL; *Randall,* BERT FREED; *Benjie,* WALTER SANDE; *Dixon,* NEVILLE BRAND; *Morgan,* CARLETON YOUNG; *Miles,* WHIT BISSELL; *Little Crow,* JAY SIL-VERHEELS; *Marshal Roberts,* FRANCIS McDONALD; *Indian Guard,* HERBERT BELLES; *Indian,* IRON EYES CODY; *Meredyth,* RALPH MOODY; *Calvary Major,* CRANE WHITLEY; *Braden,* DAN WHITE; *Quantrell man,* GEORGE J. LEWIS

Captain William Clarke Quantrill (1837–65) has been a favorite villain for movie-makers using a Civil War setting. The infamous leader of a murderous raid on Lawrence, Kansas, wore the Confederate uniform only to sanction attacks he ordered for the purpose of looting. Thus he can be made the heavy without alienating either northern or southern audiences. Quantrill (here rechris-tened Quantrell) has been portrayed by, among others, Walter Pidgeon, Brian Donlevy (twice), and Leo Gor-don.

In *Red Mountain* this gambler, schoolteacher, and horse thief is depicted as a megalomaniac who intends to become a sort of emperor of the West. Set in the Colorado Territory in 1865, the film plays with the historical facts, which perhaps explains the one-letter change in the man's name. If challenged, Paramount could claim the film was not really about Quantrill.

Ladd plays Brett Sherwood, a captain in the Confed-erate army who has traveled to the Colorado Territory to join the famous Quantrell in a last-ditch effort to prevent a Union victory. On the way he stops in Broken Bow to settle a score with the assayer, a crook who had stolen Brett's claim before the war.

The townspeople find the assayer (White) dead on the floor beside a Confederate-issue shell and are quick to blame Lane Waldron (Kennedy), a former Confederate soldier who has settled in Broken Bow as a private citizen. Sherwood saves Lane from lynching, and they ride out together.

Quantrell (Ireland) and his henchman Dixon (Brand) discover the feverishly ill Lane (Arthur Kennedy) hidden in the cave.

Captured by Lane (Kennedy) and Chris (Scott), Brett is halted on the trail.

At Waldron's mountainside cabin, Lane quickly deduces that his rescuer is the real killer. Knowing the only way to clear himself is to turn in the guilty party, Waldron disregards gratitude in his need to bring Sherwood to justice. His fiancée, Chris (Scott), supports his decision.

Brett breaks free at the first opportunity, and during the ensuing struggle, Lane suffers a broken leg. By now the three are out in the wilderness and Sherwood is hampered with two prisoners he doesn't want but cannot leave. He hides them in a cave, and Lane lapses into a fever. Almost against their wills, Chris and Brett are drawn together, fighting, then embracing.

Then Quantrell (Ireland) and his raiders arrive below in the canyon, and Brett goes to join them. The raiders are wearing Union uniforms from a Union patrol they have slaughtered. Gradually Brett realizes that Quantrell plans to use the South's last gasps as resources for his own gain. With hired Indian warriors and his own "soldiers," he has the strength to conquer the western territories while Union and Confederate forces exhaust themselves on each other. Finally Brett admits to himself that the Confederate cause is dead, but "I'm not going to help a vulture like Quantrell feed on its corpse."

While Lane and Chris hold off Quantrell's men, Brett rides to town for help and also manages to alert a Union cavalry troop, which routs Quantrell's band of scavengers. But Lane has been killed, as has Quantrell. Things are tidied up by Lane's deathbed confession to the murder of the assayer and the news of General Lee's surrender at Appomattox. Brett and Chris are now free to form a union of their own.

Despite a few pretentious moments, *Red Mountain* is, on the whole, a soundly told western yarn. Hal Wallis's production trimmings, which include a solid cast and crew as well as some rugged New Mexico backgrounds, aid considerably.

Ladd has the familiar assignment of a man of action given to serious doubts, and he brings it off in his smoothest style. In his early scenes with Lizabeth Scott, he has a chance to demonstrate once more his impudent approach to the other sex. Captured by Scott and Kennedy as he is about to make camp, he obligingly offers his hospitality: "I'll be glad to share my bedding with the lady," he says, giving Scott a good looking-over. Scott is less comfortable in the sagebrush than her male co-stars, but the erotic tension between her and Ladd serves as a hint of the exceptional team they might have made in a modern urban thriller. Alas, *Red Mountain* was their only co-starring opportunity.

(Top) With Lizabeth Scott.

Brett (Ladd) discovers that the assayer (Dan White) has cheated him.

The Iron Mistress

Warner Bros.   (1952)
Technicolor

CREDITS

Director, Gordon Douglas. *Producer*, Henry Blanke.
Screenplay, James R. Webb, *from the novel by* Paul I.
Wellman. *Photography*, John Seitz. *Music*, Max Steiner.
Art Director, John Beckman. *Costumes*, Marjorie Best.
Editor, Alan Crosland, Jr. *Running time, 110 minutes.*

CAST

Jim Bowie, ALAN LADD; *Judalon*, VIRGINIA MAYO;
Juan Moreno, JOSEPH CALLEIA; *Ursula de Veramendi*,
PHYLLIS KIRK; *Phillipe de Cabanal*, ALF KJELLIN;
Narcisse de Bornay, DOUGLAS DICK; *Jack Sturdevant*,
ANTHONY CARUSO; *Henri Contrecourt*, NED YOUNG;
John James Audubon, GEORGE VOSKOVEC; *Rezin
Bowie*, RICHARD CARLYLE; *General Cuny*, ROBERT
EMHARDT; *Doctor Cuny*, DON BEDDOE; *Andrew
Marschalk*, HAROLD GORDON; *Judge Crain*, JAY
NOVELLO; *Nez Coupe*, NICK DENNIS; *Mrs. Bowie*,
SARAH SELBY; *John Bowie*, DICK PAXTON; *Colonel
Wells*, GEORGE J. LEWIS; *Don Juan de Veramendi*, ED-
WARD COLMANS; *Doctor Maddox*, GORDON NEL-
SON; *Theresa*, DARIA MASSEY

Bowie hires a blacksmith (Wolfe) to fire the knife he has designed.

When Ladd left Paramount in 1951 and signed with
Warner Bros., it was to Warners' (and Ladd's) advantage
to start him on his new contract with a whopper of a
film. Though Paramount had gone sparingly on production budgets during Ladd's entire stay with them,
Warners could not take that chance, considering the sort
of investment they had in his contract. It was decided
a Technicolor epic was needed.

The story of Jim Bowie, frontier legend, seemed a
natural for Ladd. Born in Georgia in 1799, Bowie moved
across the Southwest from Louisiana to Texas, engaged
in smuggling slaves, was an associate of the pirate Jean
Laffite, and was a general hellraiser along the border. He
fought gunfights and knife duels and was involved in
several battles with the Indians. At one time he made
his living by sawing lumber and barging it downstream
to New Orleans—later he and his brother were known
to have engaged in some shady dealing in land specu-
lations and selling illegal land grants. A heroic death at
the Alamo made him part of legend—though it was
rumored he was roaring drunk during the entire siege.
In fact, reliable sources attribute the invention of the
Bowie knife to Jim Bowie's brother, Rezin. The story
would seem to have great potential for Ladd's good–bad
guy iconography.

Jim's prowess with the knife makes him famous in New Orleans.

Bowie cannot convince the lovely, arrogant Judalon (Mayo) to marry him.

Alas, the scriptwriters decided to romanticize Bowie, give him a sappy motive for all his exploits—the love of a beautiful bitch-goddess. They cleaned up his life, and his morals, made him into a naïve country boy who comes to the big city, is disillusioned in love, and finally gets rich and smart and rides off into the Texas sunset. So much for reality.

Jim Bowie (Ladd), young backwoodsman from the bayou country, comes to New Orleans to sell lumber from his family's mill. He meets a painter, James Audubon (Voskovec), who introduces him to a beautiful Creole belle, Judalon de Bornay (Mayo). Jim is imme-

diately infatuated and vows to win her, but he has stro competition in Juan Moreno (Calleia), an ambitious p itician, Phillippe (Kjellin), a playboy, and Henri (Youn, a ruthless duelist. When Judalon shows Jim some i terest, Henri attempts to involve him in a duel, but J emerges the victor.

Jim realizes it is going to take great wealth to w the haughty Judalon, and with her brother Narcis (Dick) as his guide, Jim quickly learns the pastimes so-called gentlemen: gambling and dueling. But wh Narcisse is killed in yet another duel, Bowie goes hor to the bayou. He has sold not only the lumber, but t entire mill, in order to buy a cotton plantation.

The cotton does well, but huge debts pile up. Ji teams up with villainous gambler Sturdevant (Carus and enters a horse against Moreno's favorite in the Du can Cup race. When Jim's horse wins, Moreno becom a deadly enemy.

Wealthy at last, Jim seeks Judalon—and learns s has married Phillippe. Threatened by Phillippe, Ji designs a knife for his own protection and has it ma to his specifications. The knife is forged from a bit meteorite (so myths are born) and, as the smithy te Jim, "Has a bit of heaven in it—or a bit of hell." Whe Moreno makes an attempt on his life, Jim uses the kni to slay the political boss.

Meanwhile, Phillippe is losing heavily at the gamir tables and Judalon begs Jim to help her husband on t promise that she will leave the man and marry Jim. I a confrontation with the crooked gambler Sturdevan Bowie is wounded and left for dead; however, he is lat found and nursed to health by lovely Ursula de Ver mendi (Kirk).

On a business trip Jim runs into Judalon and h husband for the last time. This encounter on a riverbo explodes into a series of violent incidents when Jim di covers Sturdevant is on board and lying in wait for hir Both Phillippe and Sturdevant are killed. Jim turns awa from the self-centered Judalon, seeing for the first tim that he has been nothing to her but an errand boy. H returns to Texas and the vice-governor's daughter, Ur sula.

Director Gordon Douglas was one of Warners' mor versatile directors, and he excelled in the fields of actio and suspense, talents he brought to bear in *The Iro Mistress.* Highlights include a knife-versus-rapier clas in a darkened room, the vicious knife fight between Lad and Caruso, and a fog-enshrouded pistol duel that turn into a full-scale battle. All this is effectively capture by John Seitz's Technicolor photography, which, wit the lavish costumes and sets, makes the film a pleasur to watch even when the story is at its most banal.

Douglas was to team with Ladd on three more films *McConnell Story, Santiago,* and *The Big Land.* Like mos of Ladd's co-workers, Douglas remembers Ladd as "on of the nicest guys I've ever known," though as an acto he considered that Ladd was not "a homerun hitter," bu always "hit the ball as hard as Alan Ladd could hit."

Thunder in the East

Paramount   (1953)

As Steve Gibbs.

A French girl (Calvet) tries to finagle a ride in Steve's plane.

Steve finds he cannot make a deal with Singh (Boyer).

CREDITS

Director, Charles Vidor. *Producer,* Everett Riskin. *Screen play,* Jo Swerling. *Adaptation,* George Tabori, Frederick Hazlitt Brennan. *From a novel* Rage of the Vulture, *by* Alan Moorehead. *Photography,* Lee Garmes, Everett Douglas. *Music,* Hugo Friedhofer. *Running time, 97 minutes.*

CAST

Steve Gibbs, ALAN LADD: *Joan Willoughby,* DEBORAH KERR; *Singh,* CHARLES BOYER; *Lizette Damon,* CORINNE CALVET; *Doctor Willoughby,* CECIL KELLAWAY; *Moti Lal,* MARK CAVELL; *Nitra Puta,* JOHN ABBOTT; *Newab Khan,* PHILIP BOURNEUF; *General Harrison,* JOHN WILLIAMS; *Maharajah,* CHARLIE LUNG: *Doctor Paling,* LEONARD CAREY; *Norton,* NELSON WELCH; *Miss Huggins,* QUEENIE LEONARD; *Bartender,* GEORGE J. LEWIS; *Servant,* ARAM KATCHER; *Hotel Clerk,* JOHN DAVIDSON; *Mr. Darcy^hompson,* TREVOR WARD; *Harpoole,* BRUCE PAYNE; *Mrs. Harrison,* MAEVE MacMURROUGH; *Mrs. Corbett,* MARGARET BREWSTER; *Mr. Corbett,* ARTHUR GOULD PORTER

In the first of four Ladd starring vehicles to be released in 1953, Alan Ladd is once more presented as the aggressive Yank pursuing his own business in the middle of the Orient—but here the resemblance to such films as *Calcutta* and *Saigon* ends.

Thunder In The East has as its backdrop the violence and turmoil of India in its first years of independence from Britain. In fact, although the plot and characters are fictitious, the U.S. State Department apparently felt the material politically inflammatory, and at the department's request, Paramount withheld the 1951 film from release until early 1953. The film was not released at all in India and Pakistan.

The story opens with Steve Gibbs (Ladd) landing his plane in the war-torn province of Ghandahar. The recent withdrawal of British troops has left the isolated community vulnerable to such guerrilla leaders as Nawab Khan (Bourneuf), and Ghandahar lies directly in the path of his marauding army. Gibbs, whose plane is loaded with arms and ammunition, plans to make some quick deals and fast bucks.

But Ghandahar's Prime Minister Singh (Boyer) is a devout pacifist who believes he can reach a civilized agreement with Khan. When Singh refuses to buy Gibbs's cargo, Gibbs suggests that Khan himself might be interested and Singh immediately orders the plane's cargo confiscated.

Though blind, Joan (Kerr) proves to be an enchanting tour guide.

Gibbs meets some of the local British citizens. Among
[th]em is Joan Willoughby (Kerr), the lovely, gentle,
[k]ind daughter of a parson (Kellaway).

The British residents are living in the past, the prime
[m]inister is in a world of his own, and the maharajah
[(L]ung) is a fool. Gibbs has no patience for any of them.
[H]e dallies with a pretty French refugee, Lizette (Calvet),
[b]ut she is interested in him only as a means of trans-
[p]ortation out of Ghandahar. Gibbs's real interest centers
[i]n the courageous and beautiful Miss Willoughby, and
[s]he returns his interest—until he offers to fly the other
[E]nglish residents out for a substantial fee. Horrified,
[J]oan opts to stay behind. By now, however, Khan's men
[h]ave reached the city, and no one can get out. Steve's
[p]lane is surrounded by guards.

Singh makes a last attempt to reason with the brigand
[b]ut becomes convinced of the futility of his negotiations
[w]hen Khan tortures him and cuts off the prime minister's
[h]and. Singh is unable to comprehend such viciousness,
[a]nd his faith in his principles is badly shaken. Still he
[w]ill not release Steve's guns. When the bombardment
[b]egins the few Britishers remaining in Ghadahar move
[in]to the palace and prepare for the siege. Steve and Joan
[c]annot remain estranged in such a crisis, and they ask
[t]hat Joan's father marry them.

When the guerrillas storm the palace, the refugees
[a]re helpless to fight back, but Singh holds out against
[t]heir pleas to give them the guns. Then Singh sees a
[y]oung peasant boy die, and he capitulates. Shoulder to
[s]houlder, Singh and Steve face the charging horde of
[g]uerrillas with chattering machine guns.

In Gibbs, Ladd had a more believable version of his
forties cynic, the unfeeling profiteer. Ironically, the very
accuracy of his performance may have alienated the fans.
The more realistic setting serves to strip the glamour
from the cool, self-sufficient loner and reveal his flaws.

Charles Boyer is marvelous, showing us a saintly man
who has witnessed and endured great suffering but who
has a mission and a belief that is higher, more significant
than any needs or desires of his own. It is therefore
impossible to believe that this noble man would start
mowing people down with a machine gun.

The film seemed to be saying that force must be met
with force, that peace is a nice idea but unworkable.
Given the circumstances depicted, it is a persuasive
message, but perhaps not one an intelligent audience can
accept in good conscience. This same message seemed
to run through many of Ladd's films, in varying degree,
and this matter of violence-as-an-answer was as big a
concern to parents and critics then as it is now, with
television.

Maybe it was the depressing mood, or the critical
drubbing the film received for its unbelievable resolu-
tion, or the vague and unfinished ending (Ladd fans liked
their movies to wind up with exclamation points, not
question marks)—whatever the cause, *Thunder in the East*
made little impression in Paramount's ledger books.

Steve attempts to meet the Maharajah (Lung).

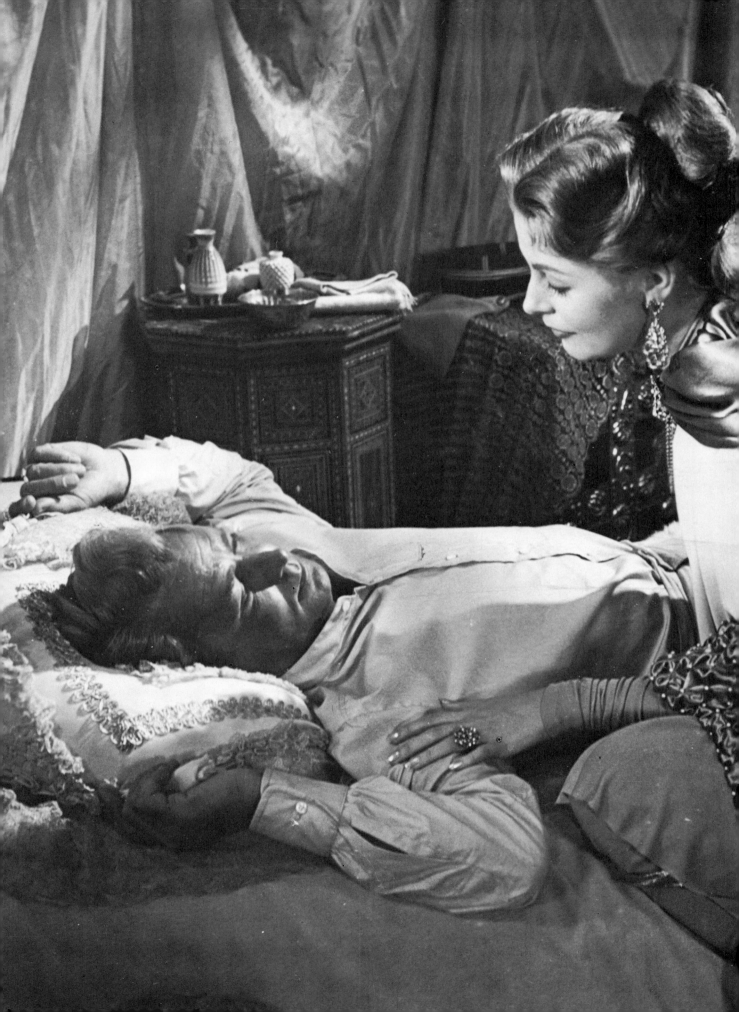

The Desert Legion

Universal   (1953)
Technicolor

CREDITS

Director, Joseph Pevney. *Producer*, Ted Richmond. *Screenplay*, Irving Wallace, Lewis Meltzer. *From the novel* The Demon Caravan, *by* George Arthur Surdez. *Photography*, John Seitz. *Editor*, Frank Gross. *Music*, Frank Skinner. *Choreography*, Asoka. *Running time, 86 minutes.*

CAST

Paul Lartal, ALAN LADD; *Crito*, RICHARD CONTE; *Morjana*, ARLENE DAHL; *Private Plevko*, AKIM TAMIROFF; *Si Khalil*, OSCAR BEREGI; *Major Vasil*, LEON ASKIN; *Lieutenant Messaoud*, ANTHONY CARUSO; *Corporal Schmidt*, IVAN TRIESAULT; *Kumbaba*, DON BLACKMAN; *Alyoun*, DAVE SHARPE; *Tabban*, TED HECHT; *Lieutenant Lopez*, GEORGE J. LEWIS; *Dancers*, SUJATA and ASOKA; *General*, HENRI LETONDAL; *Lieutenant Doudelet*, PETER COE; *Villager*, PAT LANE; *Handmaiden*, ELSA EDSMAN

The Desert Legion was a mixture of *Lost Horizon* and all those lush, romantic desert fantasies that were the special product of Universal Studios in the 1940s. Maria Montez was conspicuous by her absence. *The Desert Legion* was as close to outright fantasy as Ladd had yet come in his career.

Following a band of Omar Ben Calif's villainous raiders into the foothills of the mysterious Iraouen Mountains, Captain Paul Lartal (Ladd) realizes too late that he has led his men into a trap. A bullet nicks his forehead, and his last image is of his men being slaughtered by raiders' gunfire. The image that greets him upon awakening is much more pleasant, if a little startling: A beautiful redheaded maiden is bending over him and he is lying on silken cushions in an elegant desert tent. Before he can question the lady, who says she is Princess Morjana (Dahl), he again lapses into unconsciousness.

After being ambushed, Paul awakens to a vision (Dahl).

Next he finds himself back at his home base, the legion's Fort Tabelbala, where he has been carried on the back of a camel. When he tries to tell his tale, the high command is a mite skeptical and reluctant to allow Lartal to go off to the mountains in search of the elusive Omar Ben Calif.

When a note comes from Princess Morjana requesting his help, Lartal and his faithful friend bumbling Private Plevko (Tamiroff) go AWOL from the fort and follow the bearer of the note into the mountains to a lush hidden city, Madara. There he is greeted by Khalil, an ex-legionnaire who deserted to help build Madara and who rules it but is afraid because the power-mad Crito Damou (Conte) is determined to marry Khalil's daughter Morjana and take over Madara.

Khalil has summoned Lartal because he has heard of his valor and he has chosen the legionnaire to marry his daughter and become the heir to the throne—a proposition hardly objectionable to Lartal. But duty calls, and Paul feels he must first do what he has set out to do— get Omar.

Events convince Paul that he is on the right track when he finds evidence that the men who attacked his troop are there in Madara. Paul's and Khalil's suspicions lead to the same conclusion: that Crito Damou is in reality none other than that scourge of the desert Omar Ben Calif! Revealed, Omar-Crito fights a duel with Lartal, and Paul wins. But when he is taking Crito his prisoner, Crito's men come to the rescue and take Madara by force. With the aid of Khalil, Lartal escapes in time

Ladd, Don Blackman, Arlene Dahl and Anthony Caruso.

to rally Khalil's faithful followers and regain the city. He then leads Khalil's men to save Major Vasil (Askin) and his legion troops, who are riding into a trap.

Khalil gives his life in the ensuing battle, and Lartal finally kills Crito in a hand-to-hand struggle. He then turns down honors from the legion to return to Madara, marry Morjana, and rule the utopian city in peace.

Here it is action that counts. Highlights include some literal cliffhanging, as well as the bare-chested spear-throwing contest between Ladd and Conte. Conte is no more at home in this kind of setting than is Ladd—both are immutable modern-urban types, and Conte had traces of New York in his voice, no matter what part he was playing. Still, he makes an attractive, if hissable, villain.

Arlene Dahl, who seemed to be born for Technicolor, does it full justice, although she is given little else to do. As the obligatory comic relief, Akim Tamiroff has the same problem without the photographic advantage.

The press was generally willing to go along with the fun, with comments ranging from "reasonably lively family fare" to "a romantic delight from start to finish." *Time* magazine, always ready to condemn a Ladd film, called it "a tepid melodrama . . . as patently unreal as a mirage."

The problem was that *The Desert Legion* was a throwback, and the audiences of 1953 were not really interested in what amounted to a rather silly exercise in action fantasy. But the film made a reasonable profit.

THE YEARS OF CHANGE: 1953-64

ertainly Paramount didn't plan *Shane* as a farewell gift
a defecting star. To be released early from his contract
Paramount, Ladd signed a deal to give them two more
ctures at $100,000 a picture. (There was a deal for a
iird picture, but Ladd paid Paramount $135,000 to get
it of doing it.) By happy chance, *Shane* was the first
the deal.

Apparently, George Stevens asked particularly to have
dd as his star in *Shane*, and all during the long
immer's shooting, as the budget ran over, Paramount
ervously worried that the whole thing would turn out
be just another standard Ladd film, though with
eorge Stevens at the helm, they should have known
etter.

For Alan, working with a director like Stevens was
revelation. And Stevens found Ladd to be a good, solid
rofessional, a man of great sensitivity and willingness
give. Stevens brought out all that was fine about Ladd
e actor.

Ladd's entire family went along on location. That
cluded young Alan, Jr., who was now living with the
idds and was in his glory on the *Shane* set because his
nbition even then was to become a producer. He
atched everything with an eagle eye. Van Heflin
rought wife Fran to Wyoming also, and the Ladds and
le Heflins became fast friends.

But the release of *Shane* was far in the future—Par-
mount held it back until 1953 and served it up as a
ide-screen production, though it had been shot to fit
le old screens. In the meantime, Ladd finished the other
blor film on the two-picture deal, *Botany Bay*, a sea-
ring epic with James Mason.

Warner Bros. welcomed Ladd with red-carpet enthu-
asm, but he was shy and uncomfortable in the new
irroundings. It helped that his co-star in his first picture
lere was an old friend, Virginia Mayo. When Ladd
ked someone, he could be fiercely loyal. Anthony Ca-
iso, for instance, started with Ladd in *Lucky Jordan* and
'as in dozens of Ladd films, even after Ladd left the
aramount lot. George J. Lewis was another staple of
add's films. As long as Ladd worked, these two had
bs. Virginia Mayo says that Ladd "liked having people

around him that he knew well because of a shyness that
prevented him from making new friends. So he had a
sort of stock company of players, people who were in a
lot of his films with him."

From the big-budgeted, Technicolor *Iron Mistress*,
Ladd went over to Universal for a foreign legion thing
called *The Desert Legion*. He later stated that he did it
only for the money—Universal agreed to pay him a
chunk of the profits over a span of several years.

At this point Ladd made what some consider the
mistake of his life—he signed with Warwick Productions
to do three films abroad. The money was, again, too
good to pass up, and the tax break was no small incentive.
The entire family—Sue, Carol Lee, Alan, Jr., Alana,
David, and a teacher, Jean Martin—sailed to England
in the late summer of 1952. Alan had hurt his hand
while making *The Iron Mistress*, and he was feeling tired
and depressed. His beloved boxer dog, Jezebel, had been
poisoned just before they were to leave and Sue had the
difficult task of telling him of the dog's death after they
were on shipboard.

A second shock came when the family stepped off the
boat, to be met by a hostile press. The British had always
been avid Ladd fans, and Alan hadn't expected anything
but friendliness. It turned out they resented an American
playing the role of a Red Beret hero in the film he was
to do, *Paratrooper*. They were sick of having their wars
on screen fought by Americans and felt the role should
have gone to someone like Richard Todd, who had been
a real Red Beret soldier. For all the sniping in the press,
the fans were enthusiastic and greeted him with the usual
mob scenes.

The Ladds took up residence in a nice cottage in Went-
worth, Surrey, not far from Shepperton Studios. Work
on *Paratrooper* went well enough, though the script was
nothing special. When that film was finished, Alan began work on *Hell Below Zero*, another undistinguished
adventure film.

By summer the Ladd entourage was in Canada filming
Saskatchewan, a Mounted Police adventure. Co-star Shelley Winters complained to the press about having to
stand in ditches in her scenes with Ladd, and the first

he pinnacle of Ladd's career—the classic western Shane.

Ladd's portrayal of a Red Beret upset the British press, who felt an American in the part was inappropriate.

With Marilyn Monroe at the Photoplay *Awards.*

barrage of cruel jokes about his small stature began t[o] make the rounds.

Alan fell off a bed while playing with the childre[n] and fractured his ankle badly enough to have to wear [a] cast, which delayed the start of his next picture f[or] Warwick. The accidents were piling up—he already ha[d] an infected finger—and somewhere in this period th[e] drinking began to be evident.

The older children, Laddie and Carol Lee, had t[o] return to school in California, but Alana and David along with Jean Martin, returned to England with Su[e] and Alan, while Alan prepared to make the last pictur[e] on the deal, *The Black Knight*. This film was a piece o[f] hokum about knights and maidens in distress, directe[d] by Alan's old friend from *Wild Harvest*, Tay Garnett[.] *The Black Knight* was supposed to be shot in Spain, bu[t] there was an outbreak of typhoid there. Alan was no[t] permitted to enter Spain, and many of the action scene[s] were shot with a double and the second unit crew. Th[e] script looked doubtful. The finished picture was worse[.] Not one of Ladd's foreign ventures was a credit to hi[s] career.

Meanwhile, back in the United States, *Shane* ha[d] opened in New York to the finest reviews any Ladd fil[m] had ever received. Alan had to read about it in the papers[.] He found it frustrating to be so far away from all th[e] excitement the picture was creating. It must have bee[n] even more frustrating to realize that after this great jewe[l] of a picture was a hit, being acclaimed as an instan[t] classic, such klinkers as *Paratrooper, Saskatchewan, Hel[l] Below Zero*, and, particularly, *The Black Knight* wer[e] waiting in the wings. One cannot help but speculate— if Paramount had released *Shane* the year it was made[,] would Ladd have even signed such work-a-day deals a[s] the one with Warwick or the percentage thing with Universal?

The Ladds returned to the United States in time for Alan to be present at the annual Photoplay Gold Meda[l] Award banquet, where he and Marilyn Monroe received the awards as the most popular movie stars in the world. He continued to win popularity awards for the next couple of years, until that surfeit of bad pictures caught up with him. His last for Paramount, *Botany Bay*, though beautifully photographed, didn't turn out to be much of a film either.

All these so-so films had a neutralizing effect on the impact *Shane* might have had on Ladd the actor. And it didn't help that Paramount, unhappy that Ladd had deserted them for Warners, would not even push for an Academy Award nomination for Ladd for *Shane*. They instead backed Bill Holden, a long-time Paramount star. Holden won.

Ladd made *Drum Beat*, a western produced under his own production company; then he was offered a role in a new George Stevens production, an epic to be made from Edna Ferber's *Giant*. The picture would be first-class all the way, budgeted at a then-generous five million dollars. Alan was extremely anxious to work with Stevens again. He badly needed to work with a director like Stevens, someone who understood his own special qualities and how to use them. Stevens was equally anxious to have Alan for another picture. The only problem was that Stevens had in mind for Alan the Jett Rink role, a role that had the most dramatic possibilities but was not the romantic lead. Alan saw himself as Bick, the picture's hero. He faced the same dilemma Bill Holden had faced when offered the second lead in *Shane*. With Rock Hudson and Elizabeth Taylor in the cast, Ladd would have trouble grabbing off much attention.

Giant was prestige, the sort of picture he most needed at that point in his career. Sue, who had made so many of his career decisions for him, was dubious. She felt the Rink role was a supporting role and advised him to turn it down. She loved him dearly, but she saw him as a great romantic star. To take a secondary role would be like admitting he wasn't the big matinee idol any more. In actuality, the Rink role might well have developed into the strongest part in the picture, but as played by James Dean, an actor much too young for the part, it was strictly a puzzle and a disappointment.

Even after years in the business, Alan still got the jitters every time he began a new project. He was not drinking on the job, but alcohol was taking its toll, eating away at his looks and his well-being. He was susceptible to illness and accidents, a man over forty who was feeling all the letdown middle age can bring. He had a great deal of money and a huge mansion in Holmby Hills, and the fan clubs still flourished. But a restlessness had settled over him.

Alan, always the butt of his own jokes, was in fine form on the set of *The McConnell Story*, kidding his own fear of flying while playing the fearless jet flying ace. After his usual jitters were calmed, he began to enjoy making the film with co-star June Allyson. Soon rumors began drifting off the set about a romance between the two—the first time magazines had printed such rumors about Ladd. Sue, busy with the lavish preparations for Carol Lee's forthcoming wedding to Richard Anderson, could hardly have ignored the "fire where there is smoke" gossip.

Lloyd Nolan has said, "The great tragedy in Alan's life, I think, was that he had no real passion for anything. If he had had even a passion for women . . . well, he had one flurry with a star, but that petered out. He didn't have a great desire to read or travel or to build things or to write. He was very sad in many ways. You've got to have a drive in this life."

A strong sense of gratitude and closeness had kept Alan's interest at home, but with Sue rushing around, being mother of the bride, Alan was at loose ends. Sue later told the press, "Alan was feeling neglected—and he had a right to feel that way." Whatever was going on, the rumors were getting louder.

Carol Lee's wedding was one of the most extravagant in Hollywood in years, with Alan in a dress suit leading his stepdaughter down the aisle. Photographers recorded the whole affair, including the reception in the Ladd garden. (Unfortunately, the marriage lasted less than a year.)

A week or so after the wedding, Alan packed up and

Van Heflin and Ladd on location in Wyoming.

Alan dances with stepdaughter Carol Lee at her wedding to Richard Anderson.

Setting up a Shane *scene with director Stevens and star Ladd.*

Lonnie and David join Sue and Alan for a meal in the outdoor commissary on the Shane *location.*

moved out of the Holmby Hill mansion. Then in two or three days they were back together, with Sue doing most of the talking, as usual, and the fan magazines printing "reconciliation" stories. It was the first and last time the marriage was in rift, but the trouble seemed to have a lasting effect on Alan. The drinking grew steadily worse as each year passed, and his once-handsome face aged rapidly. By the time he made *Hell on Frisco Bay* in 1955, he looked ill, and his once-graceful movements were stiff and seemed almost painful.

His Jaguar company produced *Cry in the Night*, employing his old friend and mentor Frank Tuttle as director. Tuttle also did *Hell on Frisco Bay* for the company. A diabetic, Tuttle had been in poor health for years, and work had not been easy for him. His final film as a director was *Island of Lost Women* for Jaguar/Warners in 1959. Tuttle also had some problems during HUAC's Hollywood witchhunt in 1947, but Ladd was his good friend and kept it that way, never forgetting it was Tuttle who had first had enough faith in him to hire him for *This Gun for Hire*.

Two more so-so pictures were completed; then Alan was called in to replace Robert Mitchum in a color production to be made in Greece. This would seem a natural thing, since Mitchum's style was close to Ladd's. However, the film in question was not suited to either actor's style. Mitchum turned it down because he had a contract conflict; Ladd apparently took the job because the money was good.

On the Shane *location, Alan talks with his teenaged son, Laddie, Jr.*

175

Dining with Sue.

The usual star turn—putting his name in cement in the courtyard of Grauman's Chinese Theatre.

Once he was in Greece and had met his co-star, sexy Sophia Loren, he was absolutely miserable. Obviously he was miscast as a professor of archaeology, and Sophia, with her big eyes, big lips, big *everything*, was simply overpowering for a man Ladd's size. Sophia was in the process of being turned into an international star, and everyone's attention was focused on her. Ladd, by now regretting the whole thing, showed some temperament for the first time, and he did not make his usual good impression on the film crew. Sophia did not help by making cute remarks about the fact that she had to stand in ditches in all their scenes together. His size was not the least funny to Ladd. Loren and Mitchum might have made some lazy sparks fly, but Ladd and Loren were an indifferent pair indeed.

Because of some panoramic color photography, a dreamy, hummable theme melody, and some spectacular shots of Sophia emerging dripping wet from the sea, the picture did well at the box office, and the critics were tolerant. They scarcely noticed Ladd.

Dependent as ever on Sue, Alan continued to slide downhill at an alarming pace. Only one picture made during the last years of the 1950s was worthy—the simple and touching western *The Proud Rebel*, which co-starred Olivia de Havilland and Ladd's youngest, David Ladd, who had made his debut in his father's production of *The Big Land*. If Laddie, Jr., was production-struck, David was movie-struck. Both loved to hang around and watch their father work. Ladd was a strict father, in some ways too strict, and he was not given to showing his emotions freely, but he loved his sons, and young David wanted to be as much like his dad as possible.

When *The Proud Rebel* was released, David was suddenly in demand as a child star and made several films, among them *Misty* and *Dog of Flanders*, the latter filmed in the Netherlands. Only his education slowed him down. It was decided he should study and finish school instead of act. Later, when he tried to take up where he left off, David found grown-up parts were harder to land.

The Proud Rebel failed to make the impact it deserved, and Ladd's next few films were generally poor to awful. Some were now playing bottom of the bill. When the critics took note of him at all, it was with pens dipped in vitriol. Though many film stars were turning to television, Alan was not really comfortable with the new medium. He had done three *G.E. Theatre* shows in the mid-fifties, and there had been some talk of a series, but it came to nothing.

By the end of the decade, Alan Ladd was a shell of his former handsome self. His face was bloated and aged, his hairline had receded, and his beautiful low voice had thickened and become slurred. There were rumors coming off the sets that Ladd was difficult, something he could never have been accused of in the old days.

Times had changed, and audiences had changed. In the forties Ladd was a comforting strength, he was interested in minding his own business, but woe be to those heavies whose schemes intruded on his own. He personified our patriotic vision of ourselves: This terrible war wasn't our mess, but forced into it, we would clean

(Left) Ladd and Clifton Webb discuss a scene during the filming of Boy on a Dolphin in Greece.

(Above) The Ladds and Beret on their rented yacht during the filming of Boy on a Dolphin.

it up. It was a time of action, not introspection. Most Americans were moral and honest and minded the rules and therefore took a vicarious pleasure in Ladd's amoral, self-serving, likable tough guy. His lack of concern over what others expected of him and his lazy defiance of the established rules of behavior were secretly envied, if not admired. Above all, Alan Ladd was cool. Nothing, not even the most vicious thug, could ruffle his self-possession.

Toward the end of the forties and at the beginning of the fifties, world issues were less clear cut. Many veterans had trouble adjusting to the shaky peace, and the cold war brought great uneasiness. Ladd's cool, arrogant, one-two-three efficiency was now out of tune. The new tough guys, as exemplified by Burt Lancaster, Kirk Douglas, and Richard Widmark, were more often the victims of circumstance rather than its masters, and all of them, regardless of which side of the law they represented, were racked by neuroses. It was the time of the psychological drama. Ladd's appeal lay mainly in escapism. It was necessary to broaden that appeal.

Then came Shane. Finally united with a sensitive director and an honest character to play, Ladd delivered a beautifully balanced portrayal. He was still a loner, but one saddened by his alienation from society, rather than one who is defiant. Stevens discovered Ladd's subtle ability to project a man in turmoil, a man suffering with conflicting emotions. Outwardly Shane was as self-sufficient as any Ladd role, but inwardly he was a deeply troubled man. Shane was made right on the threshold of the so-called adult western era, and it combined the simplicity of the traditional Western and the style of the new sociologically concerned drama.

Unfortunately, Ladd next became a free lance, more

A rare shot of the three Ladd men: Alan, David, and Alan, Jr.

or less, and seemed intent on choosing his film roles on the basis of economic, rather than artistic, rewards. The Ladd roles in most of his subsequent films (including his own Jaguar productions) seemed to alternate between tired attempts to imitate the magic of *Shane* and nondescript hero chores in action vehicles of steadily decreasing worth.

When he left for Italy to film a sword-and-sandals epic, it was obvious he was grasping at straws. The trip to Italy was a disaster. Most of the time the foreign crew was driving Alan crazy with their lack of professional efficiency, and finally, when he wasn't being paid, Alan walked off the picture. He returned and finished it, but even that may have been a mistake. The film, a costume spectacular about Horatio called *Horatio* or *Duel of Champions*—and in Italy, *Orazi e Guriazi*—was never put into general release. After opening in a small New York theater, it quietly disappeared.

Warners had put the lid on Jaguar Productions, finding it a financial liability. There was no need for Alan to go on working—he was a very rich man and owned much real estate, including a house and a hardware store in Palm Springs, two ranches, some office buildings, and some oil wells. Sue had an interior decorator's license to fall back on—a need that was hardly likely to arise since she had a shrewd business head and had invested wisely. Alan made a crack in a 1957 *Saturday Evening Post* interview: "I'm working myself to death so that the guy Sue marries afterwards won't be in financial want."

But there wasn't a chance Sue would marry again after he was gone. From the day they had fallen in love, she had lived her life through him and through their children. Jean Martin remembers Sue's saying, "I could spend the rest of my days cooped up in one room with my children and not mind a bit." It was Sue who had compassion for Alan, Jr., when Alan had problems with the relationship between a father who felt guilty for having left a baby son and the son who had been raised by another. That relationship was not easily resolved, even when Laddie reached manhood.

Ladd's first wife, Midge, died in 1957. Laddie wanted to make it in the film industry and was working as an agent. He married a young woman he had met in college, an attractive dental technician named Patty. The Ladds supplied the wedding.

In 1962, Alan did a picture with Rod Steiger called *13 West Street*. It wasn't a bad thriller, but the time had passed when a routine film could make money on the strength of Ladd's name alone.

The career seemed to have run out on him. There was a new crop of younger leading men receiving the kind of attention he used to command. Alan turned to close friends Bill Bendix and Van Heflin for companionship and understanding. Possibly he was still haunted by the insanity of his mother's last act and some bitter childhood memories he still harbored. He needed help and could not accept it. He took to going around to his different properties, his ranch, and his Palm Springs house.

One night in November 1962, Sue received word that Alan had been found unconscious, lying in his own blood on the ranch-house floor, a bullet wound near his heart. He was rushed to Woodland Park Hospital and was operated on. The bullet had penetrated his left lung and was embedded in his back muscles. Somehow he pulled through. Various stories were given to the press—that he had been cleaning a gun, that he had heard a prowler and, grabbing up a gun, stumbled in the dark—but most people who knew him and had seen the sad weariness in him were not inclined to think it entirely an accident, premeditated or not.

Back in 1940 a young director named Edward Dmytryk had directed Alan Ladd in a Monogram movie, *Her First Romance*. By the 1960s Dmytryk was one of Hollywood's leading directors and had been given the assignment of directing a blockbuster color film for Paramount. Producer Martin Rakin suggested Dmytryk use his old friend Alan Ladd in the film. Thus it was that Alan Ladd came back to the studio where his fame had started.

The part wasn't the lead—that went to George Peppard, one of the new breed of film actors. Ladd accepted that with his typical modesty, but he knew he was now a character actor, and the knowledge did not sit easily. He had just turned fifty and had lost a bit of weight, but he looked drawn, tired, and much older than his years.

The Carpetbaggers, by Harold Robbins, was a highly colored success, gaining some notoriety for its steamy sex and the fact that it was a very thinly veiled fantasy about millionaire Howard Hughes. The critics were kinder to Ladd than they were to the picture; nevertheless, to the true, dedicated Ladd fan, sitting through *The Carpetbaggers* is a painful experience. Ladd had made bad pictures in the past, but this was his first trashy film. He had far more class than the picture had—and he deserved a better farewell.

Late in January 1964, after *The Carpetbaggers* was completed but before it was released, Alan went alone for a few days rest to the house in Palm Springs. He liked to spend time at the Ladd Hardware store, and for some years friends traveling through Palm Springs could generally find him there. This time, though, he kept to himself.

On January 29 Sue received a call that Alan had been found dead in his bed by the Ladds' butler, Wendell Tyler. The death certificate states there was an autopsy and cause of death was a cerebral edema, a reaction to a combination of depressant (most likely sleeping pills) and ethanol. Once more there were rumors of suicide, but it seems probable that in the end it was an accident of combining drink and sedatives. Ladd was fifty-one.

All his children turned out well—unusual in a town like Hollywood. Both Carol Lee and Alana married decent, successful men. David, who divorced Louise Hendricks and later married TV star Cheryl Ladd, has tried hard to carry on his acting career, though the marriage

Alana and David comfort Sue at Ladd's funeral.

failed, and the career does not seem to be working out. A sensible, likable man, David will probably survive both. Laddie, Jr., made good on his earliest ambitions by working his way up from agent to the presidency of 20th Century-Fox, an incredible achievment. Recently he left Fox and announced he was forming an independent company. He is an attractive, pleasant man, unlike the colorful cutthroats of the old film industry. He and Patty, as well as Carol Lee and her husband, John Veitch, an executive at Paramount, made the Ladds grandparents in the late 1950s.

Sue still lives in the North Maple Drive house, and the children visit her frequently. She runs the hardware store and other various investments, and though her health hasn't been good lately, she keeps busy.

It is difficult to find anyone who knew Alan Ladd and disliked him. He appears to have been well loved by a strong family and a number of loyal and caring friends. And he left the world a legacy of three or four classic performances and several notable ones. It is sad, therefore, to think that Alan Ladd may have been the one person who never learned to like and appreciate Alan Ladd.

David and his wife, Cheryl Ladd.

Shane

Paramount (1953)
Technicolor

CREDITS

Director, George Stevens. *Producer*, George Stevens. *Associate Director*, Fred Guiol. *Associate Producer*, Ivan Moffat. *Screenplay*, A. B. Guthrie. *Based on the novel by* Jack Schaefer. *Additional dialogue*, Jack Sher. *Photography*, Loyal Griggs. *Music*, Victor Young. *Art direction*, Hal Pereira, Walter Tyler. *Editor*, William Hornbeck, Tom McAdoo. *Technicolor color consultant*, Richard Mueller. *Running time, 118 minutes*.

CAST

Shane, ALAN LADD; *Marian Starrett*, JEAN ARTHUR; *Joe Starrett*, VAN HEFLIN; *Joey Starrett*, BRANDON DE WILDE; *Jack Wilson*, WALTER JACK PALANCE; *Chris Callaway*, BEN JOHNSON; *Fred Lewis*, EDGAR BUCHANAN; *Rufe Ryker*, EMILE MEYER; *Frank Torrey*, ELISHA COOK, JR.; *Shipstead*, DOUGLAS SPENCER; *Morgan Ryker*, JOHN DIERKES; *Mrs. Torrey*, ELLEN CORBY; *Grafton*, PAUL McVEY; *Atkey*, JOHN MILLER; *Mrs. Shipstead*, EDITH EVANSON; *Ernie Wright*, LEONARD STRONG; *Johnson*, RAY SPIKER; *Ed Howells*, MARTIN MASON; *Mrs. Howells*, NANCY KULP; *Mrs. Lewis*, HELEN BROWN; *Pete*, HOWARD J. NEGLEY; *Ryker man*, GEORGE J. LEWIS; other Ryker men, CHESTER W. HANNAN, BILL CARTLEDGE, STEVE RAINES

Though the subject matter in *Shane* was out of the familiar traditions of popular westerns—the old conflict between cattlemen and homesteaders—there was nothing familiar in the way the material was handled. Veteran director George Stevens did his best work when he had a story about basic human realities, about ordinary people and their emotions.

The character of Shane is no less than that classical folk figure of the knight-errant, the strong, mysterious stranger with a past who rides in, saves the day, and rides out again. There has to be a certain sense of im-

Shane and Starrett (Heflin) struggle to remove a stump from the yard.

"His slenderness could fool you at first. But when you saw him close in action, you saw that he was solid, compact, that there was no waste weight on his frame, just as there was no waste effort in his smooth flowing motion."

Jack Schaefer, *Shane*

Leaving the saloon, Shane is challenged by Chris (Johnson).

mortality about him, something larger than life, something innocent and worldly at the same time. Stevens's choice of Alan Ladd for this role would seem inevitable, for Ladd, with his golden good looks, his calm authority, and his almost magical magnetism, is the modern embodiment of the Lochinvar figure.

In the summer of 1951, Stevens packed up the entire cast and crew of *Shane* and moved them out to Jackson Hole, Wyoming, a spot that is almost mythical itself. Rising like gray-blue ghosts behind the valleys are the peaks of the Grand Tetons, about as awesome a backdrop as a movie could hope to have. Filming at that altitude made a difference; the effect of color is richer, more vivid, and the clouds, which seem to sit on the shoulders of the hills, cast rolling shadows across the land.

Out in the open flatland, Stevens had his work crew build a starkly realistic frontier town. There is no gloss

added; the mud in the street is real and so are all the artifacts in the general store. One can almost smell the wood chips burning in the mountain air, feel the coolness of the heavy cloud cover. Also built to realistic specifications were the cabins of the homesteaders. Again, nothing was glamorized—the Starrett kitchen was outfitted with authentic items that would have been used in 1889. Everywhere one sees indications of the hard, barren life led by the homesteaders.

The story is told in a series of stark, clean movements, with the music, the rhythm of the speeches, and the pacing of action building a mixture of reality and fable into unforgettable scenes of beauty. First we see the rim of the mountains and a lone rider coming over the trail from the left. The camera cuts to a small homestead that lies in the valley, and we see a raw-boned farmer, Joe Starrett (Heflin), toiling doggedly to remove an old

ump from his yard. His young son, Joey (de Wilde),
tracking a deer with his play rifle. From the cabin
mes a spiral of cook-smoke and the faint voice of a
oman singing.

The focus of the film is on the small boy, and it is
rough him that we see the events of the plot. Joey
oks up and sees, framed between the antlers of the
ately deer, a figure on horseback riding toward the
rm. When the stranger reins in, Joey's blue eyes widen
awe. Dressed all in buckskin and packing a pearl-
andled revolver in a studded holster, the man is like
alien from another world. His eyes meet Joey's and
says, "You were watching me for quite a spell, son.
like a man who watches what goes on around him.
an like that will make his mark." The seed of Joey's
ero-worship is sown.

The stranger is polite enough, but when Joey cocks
s rifle, both he and big Joe are startled at the stranger's
ghtning-fast reaction as he whirls, gun drawn. Ob-
iously this is a man alert to trouble. But Joe also rec-
gnizes a good man when he sees one and, much to his
on's delight, asks the stranger to stay. "Call me Shane,"
he stranger says, and Joe asks no more questions.

Mrs. Starrett (Arthur) serves what Shane calls "an
legant dinner" and in exchange Shane goes outside and
egins to hack away at the old stump. In one of the most
xhilarating scenes in the film, the friendship between
he two men is cemented as together they swing axes in
he common task of beating nature.

But there is trouble on the horizon. Rancher Rufe
Ryker (Meyer) wants all the range land so he can run his
attle freely, and he has been trying to bully the settlers
off their claims. When Shane resists getting involved in
fray with one of Ryker's cowboys, the homesteaders
uspect him of being a coward. Though Joey has said,
"Pa doesn't want you to fight his battles for him—just
elp with the work," Shane knows he cannot avoid a
howdown.

Shane seeks out Chris (Johnson), the cowboy who
aunted him, and there begins one of the most slam-
bang, rousing, bloody fights ever put on film. When
Shane downs Chris, Ryker tries vainly to buy him away
rom Starrett, then resorts to insult: "That's a mighty
pretty wife Starrett's got," insinuates the old man, and
at once the fight flares again with all of Ryker's men
ganging up on Shane before Joe wades in to fight alongside Shane. The camerawork is magnificent, rolling up
on Starrett's avenging face, on the hurtling bodies as
they crash across the room. Between them Joe and Shane
beat the whole pack.

Ryker is outraged at the defeat and sends to Cheyenne
for a gunfighter, vowing that "next time the air will be
filled with gunsmoke!"

The Starretts' tenth wedding anniversary falls on the
Fourth of July, giving the settlers cause for a double
celebration. By this time Shane has given in to Joey's
pleas to teach him to shoot and, in one of the key scenes
of the film, reveals his skill with a deadly weapon. The
film, unlike most westerns, makes a point of showing

Confronted by Ryker's men, Shane decides to stand and fight.

he gunslinger as the outsider, the exception, and the
eaceful farmer as the rule. When Marian objects to
oey's learning about guns, Shane tells her with a hint
f regret and apology, "A gun is a tool—no better and
o worse than the man using it," as if he knows carrying
gun is not an easy thing to defend.

While the homesteaders laugh and feast, Joe notices
hane dancing with Marian and senses the attraction
etween them. The settlers' celebration coincides with
e grim arrival of the Cheyenne gunman, a man so evil
at the saloon dog slinks out when he enters the room.
Wilson (Palance) wastes no time in selecting his first
ictim: farmer Stonewall Torrey (Cook), a hot-headed
x-confederate whose feisty temper makes him an easy
arget for legal murder. Tottering there in the mud as
hunder rumbles and black clouds cast heavy shadows,
orrey stands up to the snake-faced Wilson and loses.
His body slams backward at the impact of Wilson's
ullet, and the horrified Shipstead must carry his corpse
ack to the other homesteaders.

Life is not cheap in this film. We clearly feel the
ftermath of death in the attitudes of the mourners lined
p on cemetery hill. The widow nearly collapses, and
ven Torrey's mongrel dog whimpers at the grave. While
ne man plays a lonely taps on his harmonica, the camera
moves up and back to show us the figures on the hill,
n the background the town standing isolated on the
lain, and farther away the faint purple shapes of the
nountains.

But Ryker isn't through. He knows it is Starrett who
s holding the other settlers together, and he sends word
or Starrett to come to town and "talk." Joe is determined
o go, but Shane knows Joe is no match for Ryker's hired
un. As the camera shoots between the frantic, kicking
ooves of frightened horses, Joe and Shane struggle in
desperate fight to determine who will go to town.
inally Shane ends the contest by knocking Joe cold with
he butt of his gun. Then he saddles up his horse.

The unspoken love between Shane and Marian almost
omes out in the open as she asks softly, "Are you doing
his for me, Shane?" He answers just as softly, "For
ou—and Joe and little Joe." Shane has too much respect
or his friend to take his wife, and he knows he must
eave, no matter what happens in town with Wilson. As
e rides out over hills and across the river, Shane is
naware that young Joey and Torrey's dog are racing
fter him.

It is nearly dark as Shane steps into the saloon. He
s once more in his buckskins and wearing his gunbelt.
He leans almost leisurely against the bar, eyeing the two
ccupants of the room, Ryker and Wilson. "I've heard
hings about you," he says to Wilson.

hane astonishes young Joey with his sharpshooting.

Marian (Arthur) and Shane.

*Jack Wilson (Palance) guns down the Reb (Cook) in the muddy
street. John Dierkes at right.*

185

Director George Stevens checks his star's makeup.

"What have you heard, Shane?" Wilson asks, rising with an icy little smile.

Shane delivers the provocation: "I've heard you're a low-down Yankee liar."

Bullets fly. Wilson collapses against the table as Shane whirls to outdraw Ryker. A look of infinite sadness crosses Shane's face as he inspects what he has done.

Joey and the dog have been watching under the door, and now Joey cries, "Was that him, Shane? Was that Wilson?"

"Yes, that was Wilson," Shane answers. "He was fast—fast on the draw."

He knows little Joe is admiring him for the wrong reasons, and he tells him he must move on. "A man has to be what he is. You can't break the mold. There's no living with a killing; it's a brand that sticks." His eyes fill with sad affection for the boy. "Go home now and tell your mother there are no more guns in the valley."

Joey cannot bear to part with the man he has come to idolize and as Shane rides out into the twilight meadow he calls after him, tears streaking down his face. "Shane—come back, Shane!" cries Joey and in that famous cry is all the anguish of a young heart that is breaking. These closing scenes remain among the most haunting memories in the history of cinema.

Each mood is supported and enhanced by Victor Young's superb musical score. Certain characters have special themes; there are a Shane theme, a Marian theme, a Ryker theme. Also used to advantage are authentic melodies of the period. At the Fourth of July celebration the settlers dance to an old tune we used to call "Put Your Little Foot" at square dances back in the west. A form of this melody underlines the moments of silent longing between Shane and Marian.

The story seems very simple, but as William Boyd points out in *The Great Movies*, "Only the most sophisticated filmmaker could have achieved the studied simplicity of *Shane*. Only a man in total control of his medium could have created so perfect a primitive folk tale."

The film opened in 1953 to almost unanimous critical acclaim, and Alan Ladd received his best personal notices since *This Gun for Hire*. "Ladd, in a performance of which I would not have believed him capable, makes the child's worship and affection wholly real and justified.... He becomes not the Wild West caricature but a very real man wrestling with the problems of a past he cannot escape," wrote Al Hine in *Holiday*.

The Commonweal agreed that Ladd "gives the best performance of his career," and *Variety* accurately noted that "Ladd's performance takes on dimensions not heretofore noticeable in his screen work, possibly because he has seldom had such an honest character to portray."

Even perennial Ladd-knocker Bosley Crowther of the *New York Times* grudgingly admitted that Ladd, "though slightly swashbuckling as a gunfighter wishing to retire, does well enough by the character." There were a few dissenters, of course. "Ultimately the superman heroics of Mr. Ladd strike a jarringly unreal note," carped *America*. And Arthur Knight in *Saturday Review* qualified his generally positive feelings thus: "As Shane, Alan Ladd has one of his best roles and gives what is surely his most rewarding performance. Tight-lipped, laconic, assured, he repeats a characterization that has become standard with him. But this time his good bad man is credible; it is as if the character Ladd has created so often on the screen has at last been traced back to its authentic origins." This is to confuse style with content, for *Shane* was a much more complex character than any of Ladd's roles since the murderous, confused Raven in *This Gun for Hire*.

George Stevens and Alan Ladd became fast friends during the filming of *Shane*, and that friendship was formed of mutual admiration. The respected director's confidence in his star was an immeasurable boon to the insecure Ladd. Ladd said later that he "learned more about acting from that man in a few months than I had in my entire life up until then. Stevens is the best in the business." Ladd responded to ex-cameraman Stevens' direction with complete cooperation. Stevens described Ladd's work as "One of the classic performances of the screen," and he would hear no criticism of his choice of Ladd for *Shane*.

Each member of the troupe seems the perfect embodiment of his or her character. But impressive as the individual characterizations are, it is the ensemble playing that is at the core of *Shane*'s success. Much has been made of the unspoken attraction between Marian and Shane, but equal attention should be given to the empathy between the gunfighter and the solid farmer, one of the best depictions of male friendship in American films. The interplay among the various other characters is carried off with the same conviction, and it is the

On the hillside, the homesteaders gather for the funeral.

honest human relations which really separate *Shane* from countless other westerns with similar plotlines. We come to know Torrey and so we feel his needless death; we are against Ryker, though we are made to understand his point of view and to sympathize with it. The contrast between good and evil is simple and easy to see in the figures of Shane and Wilson, but in the fight between cattlemen and homesteaders, the issues of right and

wrong are more complex.

The breathtaking views of the Grand Tetons won photographer Loyal Griggs the Academy Award for best color cinematography. The award has a certain irony attached. By 1953, when *Shane* was released, CinemaScope had been introduced, and Paramount was anxious to go with the new trend. Thus, some prints were trimmed top and bottom to fit the new wide screens, distorting Griggs's original handiwork. Other Oscar nominations went to Stevens, de Wilde, and Palance, and to Guthrie for best screenplay, and to the film for best picture, but all were swept away by Columbia's blockbuster *From Here to Eternity*. Studio politics were blamed for Ladd's not being nominated—after all, he was defecting to Warners and Paramount had a loyal star, William Holden, up for *Stalag 17*. It was a painful oversight for Ladd—a nomination could have made it clear to him that he was a star worthy of better roles.

Shane reaped by far the biggest return of any Ladd starrer, a solid nine million dollars, at a time when six million dollars was considered a gratifying success. A western with a difference, *Shane* would influence and shape the western genre for many years to come.

"Take care of your mother," Shane tells Joey in his farewell.

Botany Bay

Paramount   (1953)
Technicolor

With Patricia Medina.

CREDITS

Director, John Farrow. *Producer,* Joseph Sistrom. *Scree]*
play, Jonathan Latimer. *From the novel by* Charles No]
dhoff, James Norman Hall. *Photographer,* John F. Seit]
Music, Franz Waxman. *Special Photographic effects,* Gord]
Jennings, Wallace Kelly. *Process Photography,* Farci]
Edouart. *Editor,* Alma Macrorie. *Running time, 93 mi]*
utes.

CAST

Hugh Tallant, ALAN LADD; *Captain Gilbert,* JAME]
MASON; *Sally Monroe,* PATRICIA MEDINA; *Govern]*
Phillips, SIR CEDRIC HARDWICKE; *Reverend Thynn]*
MURRAY MATHESON; *Nellie Garth,* DOROTH]
PATTEN; *Nat Garth,* JOHN HARDY; *Ned Inchin]*
HUGH PRYSE; *Nick Sabb,* MALCOLM LEE BEGG]
Moll Cudlip, ANITA BOLSTER; *Tom Oakly,* JONA]
THAN HARRIS; *Jenkins,* ALEC HARFORD; *Soence]*
NOEL DRAYTON; *Guard,* BRANDEN TOOMEY]
Green, BEN WRIGHT; *Doctor,* BRUCE PAYNE; *Sail]*
HARRY MARTIN; *Boatswain's mate,* PATRIC]
AHERNE

As early as 1942 Paramount had writers working on a]
adaptation of Nordhoff and Hall's sea adventure, *Bota]*
Bay. The project was revived in 1946 and shelved agai]
possibly because the writers were stymied by a sem]
documentary novel, encompassing as it does an enti]
generation. Finally, in the 1953 version, most of th]
book's narrative was scuttled and the resulting screenpl]
was Ladd's last picture on his Paramount contract.

Botany Bay concentrates on the arduous sea journe]
of a handful of British prisoners to an island penal colon]
and particularly on the conflict between prisoner Lad]
and a sadistic sea captain, played by James Mason.

The saga opens in London's Newgate Gaol in 1787]
Because of overcrowded conditions, the government h]
decided to transport many of the occupants of this an]
other prisons to a newly discovered land, New Sout]
Wales. Although they have no idea what lies ahead, th]
prisoners can feel only relief at the chance to leave th]
filth of Newgate.

Among those to be moved is Hugh Tallant (Ladd]
an American who came to England to study medicin]

out fell prey to an unscrupulous agent, who pocketed Hugh's inheritance. When Tallant took matters into his own hands, he was caught retrieving his own legacy, which the agent then swore he stole. Unable to convince the court that the money was actually his own, he was judged guilty of highway robbery.

On board the transport ship *Charlotte*, Tallant meets crafty Nick Sabb (Beggs), who by means of bribes has secured relatively luxurious quarters. Sabb learns that Tallant has been pardoned, thanks to recently uncovered evidence, but Captain Paul Gilbert (Mason) has no intention of losing a good wind in order to return a pardoned prisoner—and in any case, Tallant, with his medical training, might prove useful. Tallant attempts an escape and is severely punished.

Despite his callousness toward most of the prisoners, the captain is rather attentive to one—the lovely Sally Monroe (Medina). When the former actress-entertainer indicates a preference for fellow inmate Tallant, Tallant's chances for a comfortable trip become even slimmer. And Tallant, though he finds Sally sexy, is not fond of her morals.

After many hardships, the *Charlotte* puts in at Botany Bay in New South Wales. There the understanding Governor Phillip (Hardwicke) listens to Tallant's case and persuades him to stay and practice medicine in the new settlement. But the malicious Gilbert, having forced Tallant to travel halfway around the world, now demands that the prisoner be returned to England to face charges of mutiny.

Knowing Gilbert would never allow him to reach England alive, Tallant once again plans escape but is betrayed and taken by Gilbert. Then a sudden encounter with some frightened local tribesmen leaves Gilbert dead and Tallant free to go.

A discovery of plague among the crew members of an incoming ship keeps Tallant on the island treating the sick and trying to keep the disease from spreading. At last Governor Phillip grants Tallant full pardon and freedom to return home, but Hugh decides instead to make the colony his home, with the fair Sally as his bride.

Director Farrow kept things moving—the film includes a wild free-for-all involving the women prisoners, assorted knife fights, and various tortures for Ladd, including a much-publicized keelhauling. But this just isn't the sort of picture in which Alan Ladd could shine. He always seemed slightly out of place in historical melodramas, though he tries hard and does an acceptable job as the sympathetic prisoner.

The notices and reviews on *Botany Bay* were the usual for-and-against assortment, but the more malicious critics seemed to take great glee in proclaiming Ladd's descent from the heights he had attained in *Shane*, as if a good performance from Ladd were an affront to them. *Time* reported that the star "carries himself as if he were wearing a dinner jacket under his rags," and John McGarten in the *New Yorker* referred to Ladd's "effortless

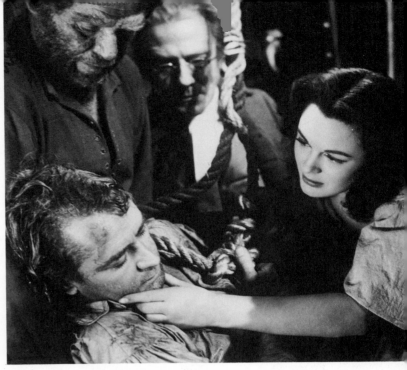

Sally (Medina) and the Reverend Thynne (Murray Matheson) try to revive Hugh.

Hugh's escape is thwarted by the scheming Captain Gilbert (Mason).

refusal to have anything to do with the art of acting."

Such needless ridicule surely contributed to Ladd's weary sense of resignation as the fifties wore on.

Canada (Ladd) and Major Snow (Genn) hold the line.

Paratrooper (The Red Beret)

Warwick/Columbia   (1953)   Technicolor

CREDITS

Director, Terence Young. *Producers,* Irving Allen, Alber R. Broccoli. *Screenplay,* Richard Maibaum, Frank Nu gent. *Story by* Hilary St. George Sanders, *from his boo* The Red Beret. *Photography,* John Wilcox. *Music,* Joh Addison. *Editor,* Gordon Pilkington. *Running time, 8 minutes.*

CAST

Canada, ALAN LADD; *Major Snow,* LEO GENN; *Penn Gardner,* SUSAN STEPHEN; *Regimental Sergeant Major* HARRY ANDREWS; *Taffy,* DONALD HOUSTON *General Whiting,* ANTHONY BUSHELL; *Flash,* PAT RICK DOONAN; *Breton,* STANLEY BAKER; *Pinky* LANA MORRIS; *Rupert,* TIM TURNER; *Dawes,* MI CHAEL KELLY; *Pole,* ANTON DIFFRING; *Alf* THOMAS HEATHCOTE; *Rossi,* CARL DUERING *Sergeant Box,* JOHN BOXER

Alan Ladd was at the peak of his box-office value in 195: when he signed to do the Warwick Company's first three productions. His movies put Warwick on its fiscal feet (Warwick continued to be profitable for the remainde of the decade, after which the co-founders split up and went on to more success—Broccoli as co-producer of the phenomenally popular James Bond series and Allen stay ing at Columbia to echo his ex-partner with the Matt Helm series.) Regardless of how advantageous the dea was for Warwick, Ladd found his try at European movie making a disaster. The release of Ladd's Warwick entries, soon after Paramount released the highly acclaimed *Shane,* effectively put Ladd back to square one with the critics.

Paratrooper (released in England as *The Red Beret*) opens in a British training camp in 1940. Steve MacKendrick, known as Canada (Ladd), is a member of the latest group of young recruits in the British army who have volun teered for parachute duty, a highly dangerous service. Obviously the Canadian knows more of airplanes and fighting than do his classmates, but he makes it clear that any discussion of his past is off limits.

The unit's new commanding officer, Major Snow (Genn), also notices Canada's experience and leadership qualities and decides to trace MacKendrick's record, though Canada tells Snow he wants no part of an officer's commission. "I'm a private—I take orders. Let somebody else give 'em."

Meanwhile, MacKendrick has noticed pretty Penny

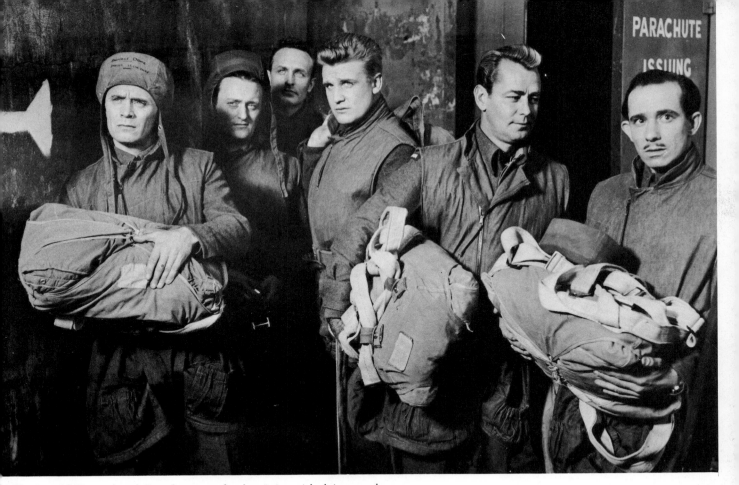

Taffy (Donald Houston) and Canada prepare for the mission with their comrades.

Gardner (Stephen), an English lass doing her bit for the war effort by packing parachutes. The attraction is mutual, although Canada's evasion of innocent questions and his inexplicably hostile reactions to slights on the United States cause the romance some rough spots.

In combat, the major finds MacKendrick exhibiting qualities of leadership, and by now the major's inquiries have shed some light on the Canadian's behavior. Actually a native of Los Angeles, MacKendrick had been an officer in the U.S. army. As pilot of a test flight, he had ordered his co-pilot and close friend to jump when they lost control. MacKendrick was able to land the plane safely, but his friend's chute failed to open. Shattered by guilt, MacKendrick resigned his commission and bolted to Montreal, where he enlisted with the British. Now he wants only to help fight the war as a common soldier and never again risk making a life-or-death command.

Naturally that inevitable day comes when he must assume command—there is no way out. During a raid to recapture an airfield in North Africa, the men find themselves trapped in the middle of a mine field with the Nazis closing in. With Major Snow wounded, it is up to MacKendrick. Using a bazooka to clear a path in the mines, MacKendrick successfully leads the men through, though the regimental sergeant major (Andrews) dies. At last Canada understands that the power of authority to save lives outweighs the dangers of responsibility. Back at base, Penny is waiting—and MacKendrick will try his best to become an officer in Red Berets.

Paratrooper was received with general indifference by American critics but was the cause of some controversy in the British press due to the casting of an American star as the hero of an honored British regiment. However, the film proved scarcely important enough for such an uproar of protest.

Ladd's playing of a familiar role was competent, but the chip on his shoulder does seem a bit heavy. It is too easy to compare *Paratrooper* with *Beyond Glory*, in which he portrayed another soldier disturbed by battlefield guilt—and it didn't work much better in *Paratrooper* than it had in *Glory*.

With Susan Stephen

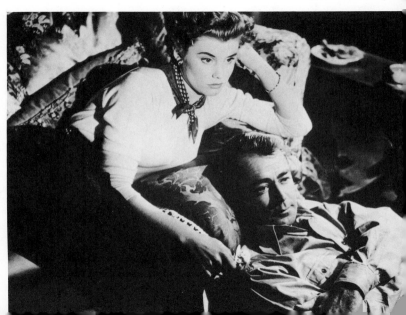

Duncan's meeting with Erik (Baker) is full of tension. Judy (Tetzel) stares in silence.

Hell Below Zero
Warwick/Columbia   (1954)   Technicolor

CREDITS

Director, Mark Robson. *Producers*, Albert R. Broccoli, Irving Allen. *Screenplay*, Alec Coppel, Max Trell. *From the novel* The White South, by Hammond Innes (Ralph Hammond-Innes). *Adaptation*, Richard Maibaum. *Photography*, John Wilcox. *Music*, Clifton Parker. *Editor*, John Guthridge. *Running time*, 90 minutes.

CAST

Duncan Craig, ALAN LADD; *Judie Nordhall*, JOAN TETZEL; *Bland*, BASIL SYDNEY; *Erik Bland*, STANLEY BAKER; *Captain McPhee*, JOSEPH TOMELTY; *Doctor Howe*, NIALL MACGINNIS; *Gerda Peterson*, JILL BENNETT; *Miller*, PETER DYNELEY; *Kathleen*, SUSAN RAYNE; *Sandeborg*, PHILO HAUSER; *Larsen*, IVAN CRAIG; *Manders*, PADDY RYAN; *Ulvik*, EDWARD HARDWICKE; *Martens*, JOHN WITTY

lmed at Pinewood Studios, *Hell Below Zero* is at its st when illustrating lessons in whaling and at its worst the first twenty minutes or so, when the setting up the plot is so slow and contrived as to nearly kill terest before it can begin. Duncan Craig (Ladd) has ade a ten-thousand-dollar investment as a silent partner an African mine, only to find he has been swindled. e goes to Capetown to investigate and on the plane sits xt to a lovely girl who immediately kindles his interest. owever, she does not react to his attempts to flatter d impress her. She has other matters on her mind.

Duncan learns that Judie (Tetzel) is on her way to ard a whaling ship in search of her father, who is issing. When he discovers there is no chance for him recover his ten thousand from his crooked partner, uncan decides to look up Judie and ask her to dinner. e arrives at the Bland-Nordahl Whaling Company, to nd that Judie has no interest at all in dinner with him— he has just had word that her father is dead.

Duncan withdraws, but he can't give up. On the flip f a coin, he decides to sign up as part of the crew of he ship she will be on. He lands the job of first mate f the *Kista Dan*. The ship is off in search of the factory hip, the head boat in the whaling fleet where the whales re processed.

Judie's father's partner, Mr. Bland (Sydney), thinks er father's death was suicide, but Judie is not convinced. hen the drunken ship's doctor (MacGinnis) implies to Duncan that Bland's son Erik (Baker) may be involved, nd he informs Duncan that Erik is Judie's fiancé.

Heading into the Antarctic, the weather cold and ough, the principals on the heaving *Kista Dan* have ecome as cool with each other as the winds that buffet hem. When a storm strikes and Captain McPhee is hurt, Duncan must take over the ship. While battling the torm he learns from Judie that the doctor's gossip was ut-of-date—she had broken with Erik before boarding he *Kista Dan*. This news puts her in Duncan's arms.

When they join the factory ship, they are met by Erik, and he and Duncan become instant enemies. Dun-can is still trying to investigate Nordahl's death and getting nowhere; then the sighting of whales pushes everything else out of mind. Duncan is assigned to the catcher ship *Southern Trace*, and Erik takes over the *Kista Dan*.

The captain of the *Southern Trace* is a woman, Gerda Petersen (Bennett), a whiz with a harpoon gun and a ship's wheel. An ice jam stops the *Southern Trace*, and the *Kista Dan* rams her. With both ships sinking, all hands must abandon and make camp on the ice floe. By now it is clear that Erik murdered Nordahl and is out to kill Duncan as well; he nearly does as the two men track each other over the ice and snow with bullets flying. After a ghastly struggle, Erik topples into freezing waters, a greedy man who wanted his share of the part-nership and Judie as well. As the factory ship comes to the rescue, Judie declares herself to be Duncan's.

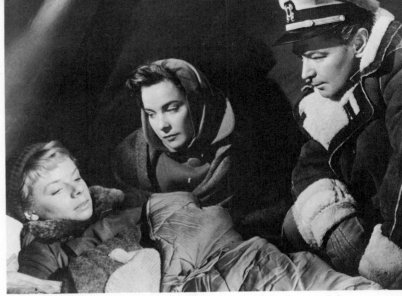

Marooned on the ice floe, Judie and Duncan try to help the wounded Gerda (Bennett).

Pretty stage and radio star Joan Tetzel was a nice enough leading lady for Ladd, but pint-sized dynamo Jill Bennett had the more interesting role as a whaling-ship captain who could handle a harpoon as well as any man. And it was always a pleasure to watch Stanley Baker, one of the few actors who could make three-di-mensional characters out of one-dimensional villains. Ladd's performance was competent enough but hardly enthusiastic.

Variety called Ladd's efforts "a typically virile perfor-mance." In a review in the *New York Times*, Howard Thompson wrote, "As a blandly confident American ad-venturer, Mr. Ladd signs up as first mate of a British whaler to follow Miss Tetzel to the frozen South. . . . The plot has been turned throughout to show Mr. Ladd as an invincible man among men."

195

O'Rourke stops Grace (Winters) from dealing out her own justice.

Saskatchewan

Universal (1954) Technicolor

CREDITS

Director, Raoul Walsh. *Producer*, Aaron Rosenberg. *Screenplay and story*, Gil Doud. *Photography*, John Seitz. *Editor*, Frank Gross. *Running time: 87 minutes.*

CAST

O'Rourke, ALAN LADD; *Grace*, SHELLEY WINTERS; *Benton*, ROBERT DOUGLAS; *Batouche*, J. CARROLL NAISH; *Smith*, HUGH O'BRIAN; *Scanlon*, RICHARD LONG; *Cajou*, JAY SILVERHEELS; *Chief Dark Cloud*, ANTONIO MORENO; *Banks*, LOWELL GILMORE; *Spotted Eagle*, ANTHONY CARUSO; *Keller*, FRANK CHASE; *Merrill*, HENRY WILLS; *Brill*, ROBERT D. HERRON; *Cook*, JOHN CASON

Any difference between *Saskatchewan* and a thousand other westerns lies entirely in the red jackets and the lush green backgrounds of actual Canadian locations. Ladd plays Inspector Sergeant Thomas O'Rourke, who with his Indian blood brother, Cajou (Silverheels), returning from a long winter's trapping in the north country. O'Rourke will resume his duties at the mounted police fort in Saskatchewan, while Cajou is heading home to the Cree village where both men were raised.

Along the way they find the burning remains of a small wagon train. The lone survivor is Grace Marke (Winters), whom O'Rourke takes along to the fort, though she is oddly reluctant. She claims that an Indian raid destroyed the wagon train. When they reach the fort, O'Rourke learns that though the only local Indians are the peaceful Cree, Sioux warriors, fresh from a bloody victory over the American Seventh Cavalry, have been moving into Canada and hope to incite the Cree to join them against the whites.

As a precautionary measure, the Mounties are disarming the Cree, and O'Rourke realizes that this action will only serve to push the friendly tribes into the Sioux alliance. His arguments are in vain—the new commanding officer, Benton (Douglas), is a novice in dealing with Indians and a stubborn hardhead as well.

An even less pleasant surprise awaits Grace. Marshal Smith of Montana (O'Brian) is at the fort with a warrant for her arrest on a charge of murder. Then word comes from Fort Walsh, an outpost near the border, that the Sioux are preparing for a full-scale assault. Benton and O'Rourke must leave with arms and reinforcements; that means the marshal and his prisoner will have an escort. This is lucky for Grace, since the lawman seems more interested in dragging her off into the trees than in seeing her brought to justice. Grace, of course, has eyes only for O'Rourke.

When Benton's lack of experience proves dangerous, O'Rourke rebels, and the men follow him. Instead of traveling in the hazardous open, O'Rourke leads the party over rugged backwoods paths. Along the way Marshal Smith shows his ugly side by attempting to persuade the troops to leave a wounded Mountie, Scanlon (Long), and later he makes sexual advances to an unwilling Grace. He and O'Rourke fight, and Smith confesses that he trumped up the charges against Grace in a blackmailing ploy to force her to be his mistress. When Smith grabs a pistol to shoot the unarmed O'Rourke, Benton downs him with a shot.

The group's safe arrival at the fort, after facing so many dangers, is marred by the arrest of O'Rourke and his men for their mutinous actions on the trail. Commander Banks (Gilmore) plans to meet the Sioux, even though most of his reinforcements are in the brig awaiting courts-martial. O'Rourke's pleas for good sense fall on deaf ears.

Benton, Gilmore, and the men are surrounded before O'Rourke, having escaped with the help of Cajou, rounds up the Crees, arms them, and leads them into the fray. The massacre is prevented, and the warring Sioux are driven back across the border. Gratefully Benton drops the court-martial charges.

The film has scenery and action and little else. Though similar in subject, it lacks both the sincerity of Ladd's subsequent *Drum Beat* and the flamboyant fantasy of director Raoul Walsh's earlier *They Died with Their Boots On*.

Nor can the cast do much with the uninspired script. Bosley Crowther might be forgiven for describing Ladd in *Saskatchewan* as "wrapped in the obvious assurance of his own infallibility" and stating, "Gil Doud has so written his script that everything Mr. Ladd forecasts turns out to be absolutely so. [Ladd] handles things with such utter competence that there is no cause for terror or concern. In short, the suspense is non-existent. That's what comes of being infallible."

O'Rourke provides an escort for the marshal (O'Brien) and his prisoner (Winters) while his commanding officer (Douglas) and Batouche (Naish) ride along.

With Marshal Smith (Hugh O'Brian).

O'Rourke (Ladd) and his friend Cajou (Silverheels) return from a trapping expedition.

*King Arthur (Anthony Bushell) gives his blessing to the marriage
of John and Linet (Patricia Medina).*

The Black Knight

Warwick/Columbia   (1954)
Technicolor

CREDITS

Director, Tay Garnett. *Producers,* Albert R. Broccoli, Irving Allen. *Screenplay,* Alec Coppel. *Photography,* John Wilcox. *Music,* John Addison. Editor, John Addison. Editor, Gordon Pilkington. *Running time, 85 minutes.*

CAST

John, ALAN LADD; *Linet,* PATRICIA MEDINA; *Sir Palamides,* PETER CUSHING; *Earl of Yeonil,* HARRY ANDREWS; *Sir Ontzlake,* ANDRE MORELL; *Major Domo,* LAURENCE NAISMITH; *King Mark,* PATRICK TROUGHTON; *King Arthur,* ANTHONY BUSHELL; *Abbot,* RONALD ADAM; *James,* JOHN LAURIE; *Sir Hal,* BASIL APPLEBY; *Lady Ontzlake,* OLWEN BROOKES; *Queen Guinevere,* JEAN LODGE; *Bernard,* BILL BRANDON; *Countess Yeonil,* PAULINE JAMESON; *Apprentice,* TOMMY MOORE; *Woodcutter,* JOHN KELLY; *Troubadour,* ELTON HAYES

There are pictures that are terrible and pictures that are so terrible that they are fun. *The Black Knight* falls into the second category. As unintentional comedy it is moderately enjoyable.

The tale unfolds on the estate of the earl of Yeonil, where love has bloomed between the blacksmith, John (Ladd), and the earl's daughter Linet (Medina). Although he is fond of the young blacksmith, the earl (Andrews) realizes the impossibility of any union between his highborn daughter and a commoner, and he reluctantly orders John off his lands as soon as he learns of the romance.

Clearly the only way John can win the hand of the fair Linet is to join the nobility. Encouraged by the sympathetic Sir Ontzlake (Morell), who has himself risen from beginnings on the wrong side of the moat, John ets out to meet the lofty standards required of a knight f the Round Table.

He has picked the right time, for the helmeted heroes' anks are in need of additions since the countryside has een beset by savage Viking raids, one of which claims he life of Linet's mother and inflicts grievous injury pon the earl. John, in pursuit of an invader, is mistakenly thought by his lady love to be running away and s branded a coward.

But Ontzlake is suspicious of the source of the attacks are they really Vikings?) and asks John to accept this njust reputation of coward in order to perform deeds f valor in disguise. Somehow he feels this will help the air prove that the responsibility for the raids actually es with two very unsavory visitors, King Mark of Cornwall (Troughton) and his Saracen companion, Sir Palamdes (Cushing).

Ontzlake then sets about to train the young smithy o be a real knight, to John's awed admiration: "O champion of the oppressed, greatest in combat of all knights!" Try to imagine Ladd reading lines like that in his flat American accent!) We see him taking jousting lessons nd hacking with a broadsword, falling on his face, but lways scrambling up to try again.

In his personally designed armor, John's imagination ruly takes flight; using his smith's skills he makes himelf a lightweight suit and a winged chicken helmet perhaps in keeping with his coward's brand). Sir Ontzake is impressed. "Put on your black armor and let us seek adventure," he says. So they do. With John as an ironclad Lone Ranger, they ride around the forest picking jousts with strangers and otherwise doing deeds of the sort to prove John worthy of knighthood while, incidentally, getting the goods on the bad guys.

The court is abuzz with stories of the mysterious Black Knight. The cunning Palamides turns the gossip to his advantage by implyinq that the Black Knight hides his face because he is the so-called Viking raider in disguise. "A friend has no cause to hide his face," Palamides observes astutely, and King Arthur buys it.

An attack on the new monastery (the villain's motivation is anti-Christian, you see), where John and Linet are separated in the furious melee, results in John's overhearing plans for a Druid's festival at Stonehenge. He manages to escape from the burning abbey just in time to see Linet being carried away as a captive.

Now comes the ceremony at Stonehenge. Reconstructed to look as they supposedly looked before they became a ruins, the great arches enclose one of the silliest pagan rites of sacrifice ever devised by a movie choreographer and a misguided costume designer. Girls run around in gauzy veils looking like members of a modern dance troupe who missed the bus. There is much moaninq and ahhhing from a hidden chorus. The Druid priest stands by his altar, sword drawn over the writhing Linet, who is tied to the stone. Ringed around are poles from which swing wicker cages, and in each cage is a monk. All of this is just too deliciously funny to be scary, even when the wicker cages are set afire.

As John the smithy-knight.

Sir Ontzlake (Andre Morell) counsels John on how to be a knight.

Into the circle rides John in his chicken hat, sword swinging, slashing the ropes that hold the basket cages aloft (if the fire doesn't kill the monks, the fall will). The last basket falls square on the priest and crushes him.

John is hopelessly outnumbered, and just as it looks as if his fight is doomed, in rides the Camelot cavalry to the rescue. The heathens are wiped out, and Linet is saved. King Arthur, riding at the head of his band of aroused extras, decrees loudly, "Destroy this place!" And that is how Stonehenge got to be ruins.

Naturally, John is able to rid the kingdom of both King Mark and his evil ally, Sir Palamides, before winning knighthood and the fair Linet.

In the midst of all this, Ladd looks, as critic Moira Walsh pointed out in *America* magazine, "completely non-medieval and non-British and uncomfortably aware of it." Nor are the rest of the cast, despite more credible dialects, much better off.

The Black Knight made money, but it was worth zero to Ladd as an actor.

Drum Beat

Jaguar/Warner Bros. (1954)
WarnerColor
CinemaScope

MacKay (Ladd) returns on the stage with Nancy (Dalton) and a chatty passenger (Isabel Jewell).

CREDITS

Director, Delmer Daves. *Original story and screenplay*, Delmer Daves. *Music*, Victor Young. *Photography*, J. Peverell Marley. *Editor*, Clarence Kolster. *Running time, 111 minutes.*

CAST

Johnny MacKay, ALAN LADD; *Nancy Meek*, AUDREY DALTON; *Toby*, MARISA PAVAN; *Bill Satterwhite*, ROBERT KEITH; *Scarface Charlie*, RUDOLFO ACOSTA; *Captain Jack*, CHARLES BRONSON; *General Canby*, WARNER ANDERSON; *Crackel*, ELISHA COOK, JR.; *Manok*, ANTHONY CARUSO; *Doctor Thomas*, RICHARD GAINES; *President Grant*, HAYDEN RORKE; *Modoc Jim*, FRANK DE KOVA; *Bogus Charlie*, PERRY LOPEZ; *Lily White*, ISABEL JEWELL; *Mrs. Grant*, PEGGY CONVERSE; *O'Brien*, PAT LAWLESS; *Mr. Dyar*, FRANK FERGUSON; *Captain Alonzo Clark*, GEORGE J. LEWIS; *Lieutenant Goodsall*, PETER HANSEN; *General Gilliam*, WILLIS BOUCHEY; *Scotty*, STROTHER MARTIN; *Jesse Grant*, EDGAR STEHLI; *Colonel Meek*, RICHARD CUTTING

In 1951, with his move to Warner Bros., Ladd Enterprises was set up to produce some of the star's films, as well as television and radio projects. Warners would act as distributor. When the Ladd Unit, now named Jaguar Productions by Ladd and Delmer Daves, finally put its first film before the cameras in 1954, the film's source was an original story by director Daves, whose initial Hollywood success had been as a writer. Daves was descended from pioneer stock and took pride in the realism of his western films. In 1950 he had directed *Broken Arrow*, a milestone in the history of Hollywood's treatment of the Native American (Indian). *Drum Beat* trod the same path, dealing soberly with the white–Native American relations during the settlement of the frontier. The film was a personal favorite of Daves, who felt it was more authentic than most westerns he directed in that decade. It was also Ladd's best film since *Shane*.

General Gilliam (Willis Bouchey) asks for MacKay's help.

As hardened Indian fighter Johnny MacKay (Ladd) is enroute by stagecoach to negotiate a peace with the California Modoc tribe, he is ambushed by a Modoc scouting party led by renegade Captain Jack (Bronson). MacKay has been to the White House to see President Grant (Rourke) and has been assigned to put his guns away and deal with the Native Americans through sweet reason. However, he must use his guns to rout the ambush before continuing to Fort Klamath.

Part of his assignment was to escort the lovely Nancy Meek (Dalton) to the home of her aunt and uncle, and though the pretty Washington socialite knows little of frontier matters, a romance develops between the rough westerner and the fragile eastern girl. This does not please Toby (Pavan), sister of the friendly Modoc chief, Manok (Caruso). Toby has loved Johnny ever since he saved her life.

Captain Jack is more troublesome than ever and the President asks that Johnny try to arrange a separate peace with the renegade. MacKay ignores Toby's warnings of Jack's treachery, and she and her brother decide they must accompany him on his dangerous mission.

A surprise attack staged by Jack proves bloody, and gentle Toby dies trying to save Johnny by shielding him with her body. Her death is the final outrage. MacKay, whose party has been strengthened by some newly arrived volunteers, sets out after the renegade band.

When he catches up with Jack at his hideout, the two engage in fierce hand-to-hand combat, using guns, knives, and fists and tumbling into the sweeping current of the river. MacKay is able to capture the murderous Indian alive while his men round up the other renegades.

With Jack arrested, the peace negotiations can once more be opened. And Johnny can settle down with his Nancy.

Ironically, *Drum Beat*'s major flaw is Dave's earnestly written script. Characters frequently engage in eloquent discussions on the relative merits of war and peace and on waging war to obtain peace, sounding at times like a debating society rather than real people whose lives depend on the events depicted. When Bronson declares with finality, "I'm tired of talk, I talk no more!" it is

General Gilliam (Bouchey) and General Canby (Anderson) plan tactics with MacKay.

Captain Jack, right, with guard (Norman Willis) and Oliver Blake.

MacKay finally confronts the ruthless Captain Jack (Bronson).

difficult not to identify with him and welcome the sound of gunfire.

Drum Beat is more successful in its handling of the various representatives of the Modoc culture; each is given an individuality denied Native Americans in the less-enlightened days of horse operas. Charles Bronson, in his first film after ridding himself of the surname Buchinsky, had the most colorful character in the film as the glory-hungry Captain Jack, and he plays it to the hilt. Bronson's only Ladd film gave him a definite boost up from the bit roles and minor heavies he had been playing since 1951. The rest of the cast, including several who would become Jaguar Films regulars, Anthony Caruso, Peter Hansen, George Lewis and Perry Lopez, all do good jobs in smaller roles.

As star of his first film under his own independent banner, Ladd gives himself a softer character than most of his Paramount vehicles had offered. With an unac-

customed amount of respect toward the other characters and an appealing shyness in his romantic interludes with Dalton, Ladd probably comes as close as he ever did to playing himself. Once on the battlefield, of course, he is as strong and heroic as ever. If Ladd's playing is less sensitive and more spelled out than it was in *Shane*, he still seems realistically confused and frustrated by the clash between his peaceful mission and his practical desire to be in on the fight. Ladd and *Drum Beat* received generally good reviews.

Filmed in Arizona in color and CinemaScope, *Drum Beat* was an auspicious debut for Jaguar Productions. Alas, it did not set the standard.

The McConnell Story

Warner Bros.   (1955)
WarnerColor
CinemaScope

Mac is given a hero's welcome home.

CREDITS

Director, Gordon Douglas. *Producer*, Henry Blanke. *Screenplay*, Ted Sherdeman, Sam Rolfe. *From a story by* Ted Sherdeman. *Photography*, John Seitz. *Music*, Max Steiner. *Editor*, Owen Marks. *Technical advisors*, William L. Orris, colonel, U.S.A.F., *and* Manuel "Pete" Fernandez, captain, U.S.A.F. *Running time, 106 minutes.*

CAST

Mac McConnell, ALAN LADD; *"Butch" McConnell*, JUNE ALLYSON; *Ty Whitman*, JAMES WHITMORE; *Sergeant Sykes*, FRANK FAYLEN; *Bob*, ROBERT ELLIS; *Mom*, SARAH SELBY; *Newton Bass*, WILLIS BOUCHEY; *Red*, PERRY LOPEZ; *First MP*, GREGORY WALCOTT; *Second MP*, JOHN PICKARD; *Pilot Instructor*, DABBS GREER; *Medical Corps Instructor*, EDWARD PLATT; *Blonde*, VERA MARSHE

During the Korean War, air force Captain Joseph C. McConnell, Jr., became the first American jet pilot to shoot down fifteen enemy aircraft. He came home a hero, America's first triple jet ace. A few months after his return, Warner Bros. acquired the screen rights to his story and the studio writers set about to put together a script.

The real-life hero, described as "a quiet-spoken, mild-mannered father of three," had hoped to return to the front for a second tour of duty, but his request had been denied with the explanation that he was "more valuable alive than dead." Then, on August 25, 1954, shortly before Alan Ladd and June Allyson were set to go before the cameras, Captain McConnell was killed in the line of duty when an F-86H Sabre Jet he was test piloting went out of control and crashed.

The McConnell Story (retitled *Tiger in the Sky* in British release) introduces Ladd as Private Joseph McConnell, U.S. army. The year is 1942; the place, Fitchburg, Massachusetts. We follow Mac through his assignment to the Medical Corps, his private flying lessons (designed to get him into the air corps), his whirlwind courtship of local girl, Pearl Brown (Allyson), whom he nicknames Butch, and their transfer to Texas. No sooner have they settled there, than Mac is transferred to Washington for pilot's training. Pregnant, Pearl returns home to Massachusetts to await the birth of their daughter. Mac finishes his course but receives a disappointing assignment as navigator aboard a bomber, where he spends the duration of World War Two.

Ty (Whitmore) gets Mac to join his new training program for jet flying.

Butch knows she must let Mac be free to fly, though it means she lives with constant fear.

205

Butch (Allyson) and Mac finally have their own home.

Mac (Ladd) mixes it up with his sergeant (Faylen).

A friend of Mac's from Washington, Ty Whitman (Whitmore), is now in command of a training program for pilots of a new form of aircraft—jets. Mac is anxious to join this program, and Ty tells Butch, "If there ever was a man who was meant to fly, he's it." Reluctantly she gives her blessing, and they continue to hop from base to base. By the time they reach George Air Force Base, which promises to be Mac's permanent station, they have three children, and Mac buys land in bordering Apple Valley, where he plans to build the house Butch longs to have.

The plans are set aside by the outbreak of war in Korea. Mac goes as a fighter pilot and is under the command of Ty, who is now a major. With his exceptional flying skills, Mac soon downs enough MIGs to be hailed as the first triple jet ace. Finally he is sent home, along with another top ace (mentioned in the script only as "the top ace of the Fourth Fighter Wing" but in reality Captain Manuel Fernandez, who was to serve as technical advisor on this picture.)

Mac is to be flight instructor at George Air Force Base. Reunited with Butch, he is overwhelmed to find that his neighbors in Apple Valley, in appreciation of his service record, have built the McConnells a new house. Now they have the stable family life they have always wanted. Then along comes Ty, and his offer of a position test piloting new Sabre Jets is too tempting for Mac to turn down.

Sick of being the dutiful wife waiting at home for tragic news, Butch cries. However, she knows she cannot ground a man like Mac, so she sets aside her misgivings and unselfishly gives him her love and her blessings.

His love for his wife stronger than ever, Joe McConnell returns to the sky—and his date with destiny.

If all this sounds a little saccharin—it is. Most of the Hollywood biography clichés are present—the hero's dedication above and beyond the call of duty, his mission and his dream, his loving, self-sacrificing wife who understands her husband's greater responsibilities. But newspaper briefs on the real McConnells give every indication that they were indeed (at least in public moments) as they were presented here.

It is probably the unabashed patriotism that really tips the scales of *The McConnell Story* toward the bathetic. The film opens with an introduction by air force General Otto P. Wayland, who informs us stirringly that we are able to pray in the church of our choice and stroll freely down Main Street, U.S.A., thanks to the sacrifice of men like Captain McConnell. James Whitmore is made to sound like the voice of Uncle Sam most of the time and at the end, when he shows Mac's widow the jet her husband died to perfect, he tells her, "We need this plane, Butch. You need it, and your kids need it. If that pilot can fly that plane, then Mac will have won." And in the final shot June is shown smiling into the sky as the Sabre soars away, apparently secure in the knowledge of her husband's victory.

Yet the film was handled with an obvious sincerity that still makes it watchable. A picture which all too obviously belongs to 1955, *The McConnell Story* was counted a success.

Marcia (Dru) gives Steve (Ladd) the key to her apartment.

Hell On Frisco Bay

Jaguar/Warner Bros. (1956) WarnerColor
CinemaScope

CREDITS

Director, Frank Tuttle. *Associate producer*, George C. Be
tholon. *Screenplay*, Sydney Boehm, Martin Rackin. *Fro
the* Collier's magazine serial "The Darkest Hour," l
William P. McGivern. *Photography*, John Seitz. *Mus*
Max Steiner. *Editor*, Folmer Blangsted. *Running time*, §
minutes.

CAST

Steve Rollins, ALAN LADD; *Victor Amato*, EDWARD (
ROBINSON; *Marcia Rollins*, JOANNE DRU; *[*
Bianco*, WILLIAM DEMAREST; *Joe Lye*, PAUL STE*
ART; *Mario Amato*, PERRY LOPEZ; *Kay Stanley*, F*
WRAY; *Anna Amato*, RENATA VANNI; *Lou Fiaschet*
NESTOR PAIVA; *Hammy*, STANLEY ADAMS; *Lie*
tenant Neville, WILLIS BOUCHEY; *Detective Conno*
PETER HANSEN; *Sebastian Pasmonick*, ANTHON
CARUSO; *Monsignor LaRocca*, GEORGE J. LEWI
Bessy, TINA CARVER; *Brodie Evans*, RODNEY (RO
TAYLOR; *Landlady*, MAE MARSH; *George Pasmonic*
PETER VOTRIAN; *Girl in Nightclub*, JAYNE MAN
FIELD

With Joanne Dru.

shortly before he began work on *The McConnell Story*, it was announced Alan Ladd would star in *O Promised Land* for independent producer Edmund Grainger, to be directed by old Paramount hand George Marshall. The film was never made. Instead, Ladd stayed at Warners to prepare the second of his Jaguar Productions, *The Darkest Hour*, a crime story by William P. McGivern.

For Ladd, *Hell on Frisco Bay* (as the film was released) would mark a return from the wide-open spaces to the tough urban environment that had been the scene of his earlier successes. The producers wisely chose another veteran of the genre, Edward G. Robinson, as head gangster, and Robinson responded with a performance as fiery as any of his thirties portrayals.

Brought in to direct was Frank Tuttle, who hadn't directed Ladd since *Lucky Jordan* in 1942. *Hell on Frisco Bay* was Tuttle's first directorial job since 1951, and his next and final two films would also be for Jaguar Productions.

Ladd is back in his trench coat as Steve Rollins, a former police detective, leaving San Quentin, where he has just finished serving five years on a phony manslaughter rap. Word had reached him in prison that there was a witness on the outside who knew the identity of the real murderer and who was willing to talk. But Rollins's inquiries lead nowhere—the witness turns up dead. Rollins has little doubt who is responsible for silencing the witness, but he must get proof. To do this he is willing to give up his friends and cold shoulder his pretty wife (Dru).

Victor Amato (Robinson), whose organization is gaining control over the docks, is not averse to squeezing poor fishermen or threatening dock workers. Aided by his lieutenant, Joe Lye (Stewart), who despises him, Amato eliminates anyone who gets in his way. His involvement in Rollins's bad luck is obvious.

The relationship between Amato and Lye is one of the more interesting aspects of the film. Goaded, insulted, taunted, Lye falls into a hopeless stammer before his tormentor, unable to answer back because Amato continually blackmails him with past jobs he has done. The worm tries to turn when Amato propositions Lye's girl, a former actress (Wray), but Lye is not strong enough to defeat Amato.

Rollins's investigation is stymied by Amato's ability to seal people's lips, but then he finds a weak link in Amato's cocky young nephew, Mario (Lopez). Mario is Amato's messenger boy, and Rollins's less than gentle questioning provides information that ties Amato to the murder of the unfortunate witness.

Furious at this betrayal, Amato orders Lye to kill Mario. This done, Lye informs his boss that they will be partners from now on or else Lye will talk. Amato kills him.

Steve packs up without an explanation.

Steve catches up with a two-bit tough (Rod Taylor) when he threatens Bessy (Tina Carver).

209

Amato (Robinson) and Steve have it out as Joe (Stewart) tries to cool tempers.

Feeling that his empire is crumbling around him, Amato decides to head for a South American vacation. Rollins turns Amato's wife against her husband by telling her Amato killed their nephew. A last ugly confrontation with Amato solves nothing, and when Amato makes his run for it, Rollins and the police (whom Rollins has finally convinced) are there to stop him, cutting across the bay in speedboats in an exciting climactic chase.

Ladd's own performance is overshadowed by his co-star's, though he was clearly familiar with his character's type. He looks uncomfortably accurate as a man who had spent five years in a cell; the physical corrosion of age is accompanied by the beginnings of a grim weariness that would gradually invade his later work. Those flashes of mocking vitality and of dangerous calm which marked his early work, are missing and missed. Still, he has his moments of hard authority and sardonic humor.

Hell on Frisco Bay was not highly regarded but has since gained a minor reputation as an enjoyable throwback—a fifties film with all the verve of its thirties counterparts. And Ladd did well enough to cause a twinge of regret that he chose not to revive his streetwise tough guy more often in his last decade of stardom.

Gun runners Paul Fix, Ladd, Frank de Kova and Lloyd Nolan

Santiago

Warner Bros.   (1956)   WarnerColor

CREDITS

Director, Gordon Douglas. *Producer*, Martin Rackin. *Screenplay*, Martin Rackin, John Twist. *From a novel by* Martin Rackin. *Photography*, John Seitz. *Music*, David Buttolph. *Editor*, Owen Marks. *Running time, 92 minutes.*

CAST

Cash Adams, ALAN LADD. *Isabella*, ROSANNA PODESTA; *Clay Pike*, LLOYD NOLAN; *Sidewheel*, CHILL WILLS; *Trasker*, PAUL FIX; *Digger*, L. Q. JONES; *Jingo*, FRANK DE KOVA; *Pablo*, GEORGE J. LEWIS; *Lobo*, ROYAL DANO; *Sam*, DON BLACKMAN; *Juanito*, FRANCISCO RUÍZ; *Dutch*, CLEGG HOYT; *José Marti*, ERNEST SARRACINO; *Governess*, NATALIE MASTERS; *Keiffer*, WILLARD WILLINGHAM; *Ferguson*, RUSS M. SAUNDERS; *Lorenzo*, EDWARD COLMANS; *Domínguez*, RICO ALANIZ

Taken on its own terms, *Santiago* is an enjoyable Ladd film and one of those lusty adventure items that had long ago become a staple of Ladd's career.

Based on the novel *The Great Courage*, by Martin Rackin, who is also the producer, the film presents Ladd in the now-familiar role of a self-serving tough guy who experiences enough excitement, romance, and mayhem to cause anyone to have a change of heart. It isn't the storyline that makes *Santiago* fun entertainment, however—it is the performances of Ladd and Lloyd Nolan. Between them they keep things moving at a rollicking pace.

It is 1898, and the people of Cuba are in the midst of a valiant struggle to win independence from Spain. For weapons they turn to American gun runners. Enter "Cash" Adams (Ladd), a former U.S. army captain gone sour over a dishonorable discharge, who has brought his contraband guns to Florida to sell to the Cuban emis-

Cash finds himself defending a lady's honor.

Jonas makes a movie of Nevada's past—starring Nevada.

saries. Along the way, Adams's cargo was attacked by hijackers, whom he was able to fend off, but in Tampa he learns his customers are willing to deal only on a C.O.D. basis—he must get the guns to Cuba to collect his money. Disgusted, Adams ups the ante, and the Cubans are in no position to argue.

The vessel upon which he is to travel is the *Vicksburg*, a former Mississippi paddleboat, which has seen better days and which is captained by a drunkard named "Sidewheel" Jones (Wills). This is discouraging enough, but Cash also finds an old nemesis, Clay Pike (Nolan) aboard. Pike sold guns to the Apaches during Adams' cavalry days and is now ready to make a fast buck in Cuba. Adams has no trouble figuring out that it was Clay who tried to hijack his own guns. Their encounters are decidedly hostile.

Both Pike and Adams are surprised to learn that there is a tantalizing lady named doña Isabella (Podesta) aboard. Dubbed Cuba's Joan of Arc, she is returning from a fund-raising trip to America, and she has little interest in matters outside the Cuban struggle. Whereas before Captain Jones had to keep Cash's and Pike's hands off only each other's throats, now he must see that those idle hands stay off doña Isabella.

Pike cannot contain himself; he makes a rather coarse pass at Isabella, and Cash calls him on it. Since Pike has noticed that Cash isn't unaware of the lady's charms, the argument explodes into an ungentlemanly fight, which the captain must halt.

Adams claims that he has been "vaccinated against sentiment" and that "lovers die broke," but he readily agrees to Sidewheel's suggestion that he act as unofficial bodyguard for Isabella. With Pike around it is obvious that she needs one, and after Cash defends her, she is warmer toward him and colder toward Pike.

The journey to Santiago is strewn with hazards. Being with doña Isabella, Cash finds her idealism has begun to crack his cynical defenses. Then it is discovered the boat has a stowaway, Isabella's young brother Juanito (Ruíz), who is filled with desire to become a soldier. At Santiago the guns must be lugged overland, and Cash easily takes command. Encounters in the jungle with Spanish troops leave several dead, including young Juanito, and Cash is genuinely saddened. Pooling forces, Pike and Adams break through the Spanish blockade, only to discover that the Cubans have suffered a costly defeat. The survivors in hiding need the guns more than ever, but payment is doubtful. Pike naturally decides to sell his guns to the ones with the money—the Spaniards. But Cash, head over heels in love with Isabella, is determined her Cuban friends will have the guns.

When the smoke clears, Pike is dead. Adams, with Isabella at his side, is ready to begin a new life.

Hardly the freshest of plots, but director Douglas keeps the action going with fist fights, dynamite blasts, and some crackling dialogue between Ladd and Nolan. These two are supposed to be deadly adversaries, but

ney have a comradely antipathy that is carried on with
happy insults. Nolan, as the rotten-clean-through villain, is so appealing that you are quite sorry to see him
die at the end. Nolan, who does not remember *Santiago*
as anything special, does admit he had a good time
playing an unwashed, lecherous scoundrel. And Ladd
certainly fit snugly into the role of the mercenary with
a heart of gold.

Variety's critic, more willing than most to accept a
movie simply as entertainment, found the star's performance "excellent." But *Catholic World* stated, "Acting,
even in the broadest definition of the term, is unheard
of in this juvenile thriller."

Bosley Crowther was surprisingly tolerant: "There are
a couple of amusing compensations scattered in and
around the general bunkum. . . . One is the shameless
hee-haw acting of Chill Wills . . . and, finally, there are
several lively run-ins between Mr. Nolan and Mr. Ladd,
whose encounters, both physical and verbal, have a nice
corned-beef flavor about them. . . . [*Santiago*] has its
moments of fun."

*(Right) Clay (Nolan) and Cash both decide to help Isabella (Po-
sta).*

Cash and Clay fight side by side through the jungle.

The Big Land

Jaguar/Warner Bros.   (1957)
WarnerColor

Chad manages to save Jagger (O'Brien) from hanging, but they ar[e n]ot welcome anywhere.

CREDITS

Director, Gordon Douglas. *Associate Producer*, Georg[e] Bertholon. *Screenplay*, David Dortort, Martin Rac[kin.] *Screen story by* David Dortort. *From the novel* Buffalo G[rass] *by* Frank Gruber. *Photographer*, John Seitz. *Music*, D[avid] Buttolph. *Song "I Leaned on a Man" by* Wayne Sha[nklin] *and* Leonard Rosenman. *Editor*, Thomas Reilly. *Run[ning] time, 92 minutes.*

CAST

Chad Morgan, ALAN LADD; *Helen Jagger*, VIRGIN[IA] MAYO; *Joe Jagger*, EDMOND O'BRIEN; *Brog*, [AN-] THONY CARUSO; *Kate Johnson*, JULIE BISHOP; [*Jorg* ?] *Johnson*, JOHN QUALEN; *Draper*, DON CAST[LE;] *David Johnson*, DAVID LADD; *Olaf Johnson*, JA[CK] WRATHER, JR.; *Dawson*, GEORGE J. LEWIS; [*?*,] JAMES ANDERSON; *Billy*, DON KELLY; *McCullo[ch*,] CHARLES WATTS; *Smoky*, JOHN McKEE; *Ben*, JA[MES] SEAY; *Brog Gang Member*, GAYLE KELLOGG; *Mana[ger* ?] STEVE DARRELL; *Man*, STACY KEACH, SR.; [*?-*] *gan*, JOHN DOUCETTE; *Texas Rider*, LES JOHNS[ON;] *Bartender*, PAUL BRYAR

With George J. Lewis, featured in many Ladd films

By the second half of the 1950s, Alan Ladd had given up trying to please the critics. "Maybe I can't act," he told an interviewer in 1957, "but I know the gimmicks. I've studied movies all my life, and I know what's good for me. I can't play black or gray; I can't be a villain or anything too close to it. I have to play white." Ladd's resignation had apparently led him to forget the part and the performance that had earned him stardom fifteen years earlier. His reliance on "gimmicks" by this point could only speed his sad decline.

The first two Jaguar productions in which he had starred had been competent bread-and-butter pictures. The third, *The Big Land*, was a cynical attempt to cash in on its star's presumably presold qualities. Frank Gruber's novel *Buffalo Grass*, whose hero was an ex-soldier who wants to kill no more, had little to recommend it.

In *The Big Land*, this poor second cousin to *Shane* is called Chad Morgan (Ladd). Morgan has led a group of fellow Texans on a cattle drive to Missouri, where they have heard there is a railroad for shipping. Upon their arrival, the cowboys learn that there is only one beef buyer, and he is paying no more than $1.50 a head, instead of the $10 they had anticipated. Naturally, by such opportunistic behavior Brog (Caruso), the buyer, is asking for an inglorious death from an outraged cowpoke's six-shooter. The only man qualified to face him, however, is Morgan. But Morgan has seen enough of killing in the late war, and he sells out. Disgusted by his cowardice, the men return to Texas without him.

That night Chad finds shelter in a stable already occupied by a wanderer named Jagger (O'Brien), an educated man turned drunkard, who is hiding out. When Jagger is almost lynched, Chad saves him, and the two ride out of Missouri together. At the ranch of a farmer, Sven Johnson (Qualan), Chad learns there is a need in the area for a railroad. Through a friend of Jagger's, a railroad builder named Draper (Castle), Chad is able to get a promise of a new railroad spur, provided a town is built to meet the spur.

Jagger, whose promising career as an architect has been defeated by alcohol, turns out to have a lovely sister named Helen (Mayo), who is immediately drawn to Chad, as he is to her. They encourage Jagger to design the new town, the funds and labor to be supplied by local farmers, who need the spur to get their wheat to market. And Morgan is sure he can persuade the Texans to lead their cattle drives to the new spur, which will assure the railroad of plenty of business.

Jagger, his drunken life given new meaning by the task at hand, sets to work while Morgan heads for Texas to organize the cattlemen.

But things have been going too well. The grand opening of the new settlement to outside cattle buyers is invaded by Brog and his men, who discourage the competition with guns and murder. Brog guns down Jagger

Chad fights back.

I thoroughly enjoyed working with Alan—he was the kindest man that ever lived. His work was vastly underrated by some people. I think he was the most sensitive, tender actor I ever worked with! And the beauty of his face! Fabulous.

VIRGINIA MAYO

On the trail with Edmond O'Brien

Chad proposes a new spur line to Ben (James Seay), Draper (Don Castle), and Sven (John Qualan).

Chad meets Jagger's sister Helen (Mayo).

when Jagger makes a pitiful attempt to stand up to him, and by the time Morgan and his Texas friends return, Brog has pretty well taken over and wrecked the nearly completed town by causing a cattle stampede.

Morgan has no alternative. He must strap on the old shootin' iron and finish off Brog and his henchman before settling down to marry Helen and rebuild the new town.

The Big Land offers scant evidence of real acting prowess on anyone's part. Bosley Crowther of the *New York Times* wrote that Ladd "presents a pasteboard cutout of the cowboy performance he gave in *Shane*." For once it was impossible to argue with Crowther. Stated *Time*, " 'Thuh East needs beef!' That's what the man says but regrettably, as in most of his independent productions, Actor Alan Ladd is able to deliver almost nothing but corn."

As an alcoholic, O'Brien is forced to alternate between supposedly humorous lines that sound like rejects from the *W. C. Fields Joke Book*, and melodramatic cases of the shakes. Virginia Mayo gives the film its few moments of sensitivity in the scene where she takes out on Morgan her grief over her brother's death, but her character is as ill-defined as the rest. Anthony Caruso brings more punch to his role as the heavy, but as Moira Walsh pointed out in *America*, Brog is merely "a stock bad man . . . as ubiquitous as he is unmotivated."

Despite a premiere in Kansas City, *The Big Land* failed to make *Variety*'s annual list of top-grossing films—a first for a Ladd vehicle.

Boy on a Dolphin

20th Century-Fox   (1957)
DeLuxe Color
CinemaScope

Phaedra (Loren) seeks out Doctor Calder (Ladd) to tell him of her find.

CREDITS

Director, Jean Negulesco. *Producer*, Samuel G. Engel. *Screenplay*, Ivan Moffat, Dwight Taylor. *From the novel by* David Divine. *Photography*, Milton Krasner. *Music*, Hugo Friedhofer. *Song "Boy on a Dolphin" based on "Tinafto", music by* Takes Morakis. *Greek text*, J. Fermanglou, *American lyric*, Paul F. Webster, *adapted by* Hugo Friedhofer. *Orchestrations*, Edward B. Powell. *Greek folk dances and song society "Panegyris" directed by* Dora Stratou. *Special effects*, Ray Kellogg. *Editor*, William Mace. *Running time, 103 minutes.*

CAST

James Calder, ALAN LADD; *Victor Parmalee*, CLIFTO WEBB; *Phaedra*, SOPHIA LOREN; *Government m* ALEXIS MINOTIS; *Rhif*, JORGE MISTRAL; *D Hawkins*, LAURENCE NAISMITH; *Niko*, PIE GIAGNONI; *Miss Dill*, GERTRUDE FLYNN; *Will B. Baldwin*, CHARLES FAWCETT; *Mrs. Bald* CHARLOTTE TERRABUST; *Miss Baldwin*, M GARET STAHL; *Chief of Police*, ORESTES RALLIS

220

One of Fox's biggest hits of 1954 had been *Three Coins in the Fountain*, which blended a light romantic narrative with some very impressive CinemaScoped–DeLuxe Colored views of the glories of Rome, where the film was shot on location. A strong ingredient of the film's success was a lilting title song, which made all the jukeboxes that summer. Naturally Fox was eager to take the best elements of *Coins* and try for another such hit.

Repeating from *Coins* would be director Jean Negusco, cameraman Milton Krasner, and actor Clifton Webb. According to John Belton's *Robert Mitchum*, Mitchum was originally assigned the male lead. When the production was delayed, Mitchum got tied up in another picture. Fox needed a big star in a hurry and was willing to pay well for him. (Estimates of Ladd's salary range from $275,000 to $290,000, a hefty sum by 1956 standards.) Ladd signed the lucrative contract while winding up *The Big Land* and within a month was on location in Greece. His co-star would be the little-known Sophia Loren.

Alan's initial encounter with Sophia left him dismayed. His complex about his height had intensified with the passage of time and the gradual dwindling of box office receipts. Sophia was not only taller than Ladd, but she also had other attributes that would gain her the exclusive attention of the audience.

Ladd's apprehensions were justified by the finished *Boy on a Dolphin*. The title refers to a statue, a boy of old riding a bronze dolphin. The priceless artifact had lain at the bottom of the Aegean Sea for two thousand years when discovered by Phaedra (Loren), a peasant sponge diver working the sea with her lover (accompanied by a lush musical score).

News of the treasure reaches the interested ears of Doctor Jim Calder (Ladd) and Victor Parmalee (Webb). The two have been acquainted since the post–World War II years. Calder, then a captain in the U.S. army, had devoted his efforts to restoring works of art to their home countries, while Parmalee strove with equal zeal to add them to his personal collection. Calder's archaeological expertise now benefits a Greek museum, but little else has changed. Parmalee is still trying to grab off national treasures for himself. This latest prize is still hidden in the deep blue Aegean, and neither man wastes any time in courting the person who knows where—the luscious but uneducated Phaedra.

Despite the immediate attraction between Phaedra and Jim, the American's bid for the statue cannot match Parmalee's, and Phaedra is a poor girl who owns only one pair of shoes and whose ambitions are to buy some comforts and to send her young brother Niko (Giagnoni) to school. Parmalee instructs Phaedra to lead Calder on a wild-goose chase, diving everywhere but where the statue waits. Only when Calder has given up can Parmalee risk taking the statue from Greek waters.

After two wasted weeks of scouring the Aegean depths, Calder is indeed ready to quit. Then Niko tells him of the rich man whose yacht waits patiently in a

Over drinks at a local café, Phaedra is a charming companion.

nearby bay. Calder now realizes that he has been played for a fool and has let his emotions get in the way of his job. With the aid of a metal detector, and without Phaedra, he becomes more determined to keep the boy on a dolphin out of Parmalee's grasp.

Phaedra, meanwhile, has decided to let her heart rule her more practical nature. She rushes back to Jim to tell him the statue's whereabouts. When the two go down to recover it, they find it gone—taken by Parmalee and

Phaedra's jealous fishing boyfriend Rhif (Mistral).

Calder and Phaedra, along with plucky little Niko are able to block Parmalee's escape run, with the valuable assistance of a Greek-government authority. At this official's suggestion, Parmalee resignedly leaves Greek waters empty-handed. The Greek people have their treasure and Jim has Phaedra.

The film was a buildup for lush Sophia, who had yet to make a movie in America and was trying to gain an international reputation. This was her first American production release. When Sophia lifted her skirt, tucked it between her legs, and pinned it to her belt in back, then dived into the blue-green water, she emerged moments later as what *Time* called the "Finest vision since Botticelli painted Aphrodite on her shell." Not even the Greek scenery could compete with Loren.

Boy on a Dolphin was a solid financial success, better than Ladd had had in some time. But he was uncomfortably aware that he was merely box-office insurance in a film whose real emphasis lay elsewhere. His part was ill-fitting, and his romantic scenes have little passion.

Ladd showed more vitality in his scenes with Webb, and their encounters have an engaging cat-and-mouse quality. Webb, of course, was in his element as the supercilious Parmalee. Once back home in Hollywood, he would use his acerbic wit to complain of Ladd's behavior on the *Dolphin* location.

All in all, Ladd's Greek adventure had been a mistake—at least for Ladd.

950-13

The Deep Six

Jaguar/Warner Bros.   (1958)

WarnerColor

CREDITS

Director, Rudolph Maté. *Producer*, Martin Rackin. *Associate Producer*, George Bertholon. *Screenplay*, John Twist, Martin Rackin, Harry Brown. *Based on the novel by* Martin Dibner. *Photography*, John Seitz. *Music*, David Buttolph. *Editor*, Roland Gross. *Running time, 110 minutes.*

CAST

Alec Austen, ALAN LADD; *Susan Cahill*, DIANNE FOSTER; *Frenchy Shapiro*, WILLIAM BENDIX; *Lieutenant Commander Edge*, KEENAN WYNN; *Commander Meredith*, JAMES WHITMORE; *Lieutenant Blanchard*, EF-REM ZIMBALIST, JR.; *Claire Innes*, BARBARA EILER; *Paul Clemson*, WALTER REED; *Lieutenant Dooley*, PETER HANSEN; *Lieutenant Junior Grade Swanson*, RICHARD CRANE; *"Ski" Krakowski*, JOEY BISHOP; *Slobodjian*, ROSS BAGDASARIAN (DAVID SEVILLE); *Mrs. Austen*, JEANNETTE NOLAN; *Collins*, MORRIS MILLER; *Al Mendoza*, PERRY LOPEZ; *Pilot*, WARREN DOUGLAS; *Pappa Tatos*, NESTOR PAIVA; *Eddie Loomis*, ROBERT WHITESIDES; *Ensign David Clough*, ROBERT CLARKE; *Ann*, CAROL LEE LADD; *Elsie*, ANN DORAN; *Steve*, JERRY MATHERS; *Waiter*, FRANZ ROEHN; and THE OFFICERS AND MEN OF THE U.S.S. STEPHEN POTTER

Alec must say goodbye to Susan (Foster) when he is inducted into the navy.

Alec finds it difficult to fit in with the other men (Joey Bishop, Perry Lopez, and others).

The Deep Six opens with a title thanking the U.S. na[vy] for its cooperation "without which this picture wou[ld] not have been possible." Obviously the navy's coopera[ra]tion would have been impossible had the producers a[t]tempted a faithful adaptation of the 1953 novel on whi[ch] the film is based. The book has an unsavory assortme[nt] of cowards, incompetents, degenerates, and bullies w[ho] make up the motley crew of the World War II crui[ser] *Atlantis*. In order to make the script palatable to th[e] authorities whose approval meant so much to the finish[ed] product, the writers had to abandon most of their sour[ce] material.

As cleaned up for the screen, the soft, spoiled capta[in] of the novel has become fatherly James Whitmore, t[he] alcoholic ship's doctor turns into understanding Efre[m] Zimbalist, Jr., and the grimy, at times bloodthirs[ty] crewmen have been deloused to the point where th[ey] resemble a pack of seagoing boy scouts.

The one rotten apple remaining in the bunch is Lie[u]tenant Commander Mike Edge (Wynn), a hardnose[d] officer with a fanatical hatred for the enemy and an a[p]petite for morphine.

Having smoothed over the navy's rough spots, t[he] film concentrates on the conflict between hero Auste[n] (Ladd's) Quaker upbringing and his position as a warti[me] naval officer. This character is, of course, right in li[ne] with Ladd's 1950s image—unquestionably courageo[us] but hesitant to fight.

Ladd's Austen is an artist with a Madison Avenue a[d] agency, who has just fallen in love with Susan Cah[n] (Foster) and is looking forward to settling down. How[w]ever, he was in naval ROTC in college and has been [in] the reserves, and now that war has broken out in t[he] Pacific, he has been notified to report. Susan, sensi[ng] his own divisions, cannot promise to marry him.

As a gunnery officer aboard the U.S.S. *Poe*, Alec ge[ts] acquainted with the crew, most particularly with Frenc[hy] Shapiro (Bendix), a tough, burly enlisted man who h[as] a heart of pure much. The one man to give Alec troub[le] is Lieutenant Commander Edge, who discovers Ale[c's] Quaker background and never fails to needle him abo[ut] it, predicting that religion will get in the way of Auste[n's] duties as a fighting man.

Edge's prophecy proves true when Alec refrains fro[m] firing on an unidentified plane—but then Alec win[ds] up a hero when the plane turns out to be American. B[ut] Alec confesses he had not recognized the plane's markin[gs] and had simply been unable to give the order to fire.

From here he must prove his mettle to himself an[d] his shipmates. When Austen courageously removes a[n] unexploded bomb from belowdecks, he regains the crew[s] approval. Later he participates in a waterfront braw[l] showing himself to be one of the boys (a dubious di[s]tinction). Frenchy is his one close friend through all thi[s] Besides wondering if his girl will still be waiting whe[n] he gets home, Austen still has no idea how he will behav[e] under fire.

With Lieutenant Dooley (Hansen) and Lieutenant Commander Edge (Wynn), Alec questions an enemy survivor.

He soon finds out when he volunteers to lead a hazardous mission to rescue some U.S. flyers who are boxed in on a Japanese-held island. In the ensuing action Austen leads his few men through a heavy battle, and yet only when his friend Frenchy is shot and crying out for help can Alec bring himself to fire at the advancing enemy. His misgivings wiped out by outrage and anger, he downs them all—but it is too late for Frenchy. The flyers are saved and make it back to the ship, dragging Alec, who has passed out from his own wounds.

Later, reunited with Susan, Alec seems to have made some sort of peace with himself.

Perhaps if the irony of Frenchy's death had been stressed more heavily, *The Deep Six* would have elicited a more sympathetic response from critics. As it was, it was simply shrugged off as another hack war movie.

Mary C. Hatch wrote in *Library Journal*: "On such a theme, a great film could have been developed, but the present one is purely routine, and it is the small side incidents involving the enlisted crew that give the picture such vitality as it has, rather than the main plot. Alan Ladd, as the Quaker officer, makes a handsome lieutenant, but at no time does he convince one that he is a man at war with his own conscience." Howard H. Thompson in the *New York Times* stated, "Unfortunately, having stated its case—the hero's mental conflict—this Warners release then sidesteps the issue, almost to the finale. The loose, rambling result brims with clichés, at the expense of dramatic unity and, finally, conviction. The key to the strong, provocative war drama that *The Deep Six* might have been, with less compromise, lies in the admirably casual but tight-lipped performance by Mr. Ladd. *The Deep Six* is okay—just a little too scared to venture too far below the surface."

Father and son in real life and in the film. David and Alan Ladd with Olivia de Havilland.

The Proud Rebel

Formosa Production/Buena Vista   (1958)
Technicolor

CREDITS

Director, Michael Curtiz. *Producer*, Samuel Goldwyn, Jr. *Screenplay*, Joe Petracca, Lillie Hayward. *From the story "Journal of Linnet Moore," by* James Edward Grant. *Photography*, Ted McCord. *Music*, Jerome Moross. *Art director*, McClure Capps. *Editor*, Aaron Stell. *Running time, 103 minutes.*

CAST

John Chandler, ALAN LADD; *Linnett Moore*, OLIVIA de HAVILLAND; *Harry Burleigh*, DEAN JAGGER; *David Chandler*, DAVID LADD; *Doctor Enos Davis*, CECIL KELLAWAY; *Jeb Burleigh*, DEAN STANTON; *Tom Burleigh*, THOMAS PITTMAN; *Judge Morley*, HENRY HULL; *Gorman*, ELI MINTZ; *Birm Bates*, JAMES WESTERFIELD; *Traveling Salesman*, JOHN CARRADINE; *Lance*, KING (the dog)

The casting for *The Proud Rebel* was an inspiration. Ladd, who had never had much of an actor's ego, was happy to give his son David scene after scene. And David, who adored his father, did his best to imitate his father's professionalism. He even went to a class to learn sign language in order to prepare for the role of the young mute. The work between father and son has a restrained poignancy that never gives way to the maudlin. As the indigent father wandering around desperately seeking a doctor to cure his stricken son, Ladd's eyes and demeanor give a fine indication of a man burdened with a heavy heart and motivated by despair. He is marvelously gentle with the boy; yet you have no doubt he is capable of killing to protect the boy. With a finely tuned, all-of-a-piece script, an accomplished director, Michael Curtiz, and a sensitive, respected actress like Olivia de Havilland for a co-star, the film had a great deal going for it.

Filmed in the high plateau region near Kanab, Utah (which doubles for Illinois), the movie opens with proud but poor John Chandler (Ladd) taking his mute young son David (David Ladd) to Aberdeen to seek the advice of a doctor there. Following along behind the horse is David's dog, Lance, a working sheep dog turned pet.

Doc Davis (Kellaway) gives David an examination and then learns from the father that the boy was stricken mute during the Civil War when the Union cannons shelled the Chandler home, causing a fire, which killed his mother, John's wife. The boy has not spoken since the tragedy, but the doctor can find no physical reason. Doc advises that "there's a man in Minnesota—with a Doctor Mayo. An operation and treatment might help—but I couldn't try that kind of surgery."

John comes out of the doc's office to find that the dog, which means so much to the boy, has been stolen by two toughs, the sons of a local sheep farmer. In retrieving the dog, John gets into a one-sided fight, and David, unable to scream, runs for help. He finds a kindly woman, Linnett Moore (de Havilland), who wants to help but cannot understand until she sees John dumped in a heap in the alley and soaked in whiskey. When the marshal picks him up, the sheep men, Jeb (Stanton) and Tom (Pittman) Burleigh, tell enough lies to have John arrested.

In the course of the trial, John is sentenced to jail and pleads to remain with his son. Linnett, touched by the boy's plight, offers to let John work off his fine of thirty dollars at her rundown ranch.

Linnett is a widow with two hundred good acres, but she is unable to handle the place alone. John does chores and plowing and even has to fend off the wild Burleigh boys, who try to stampede their sheep over Linnett's land. Lance's part in this last crisis is observed by a sheep buyer, Bates (Westerfield), who offers a handsome price for the talented dog. But John cannot sell David's dearest friend, though he desperately needs three hundred dollars to send the boy to the Minnesota doctor.

The Burleighs continue to plague John and Linnett,

De Havilland, David, Ladd. (Bottom) James Westerfield, de Havilland, Ladd.

and the two draw closer together, giving David the sense of a real family. Then cruel boys in town taunt David and provoke him to fight, and John makes up his mind—he must sell Lance and get David to the doctor.

Linnett accompanies David and returns with a heavy heart—the operation has failed to restore the boy's speech, and David is outraged at his father for selling the dog. When John attempts to get the dog back, he learns that Bates has lost the dog in a poker game—to the cruel Burleighs. Lance will work only for John or David, however, so Burleigh has taken to beating the animal.

The man's brutality enrages John, and he straps on his gun, ignoring Linnett's attempts to stop him. Unknown to John, David follows him, and when the boy sees his father being stalked by gun-toting Jeb and Tom, he strains to cry a warning—and the words come: *"Look Out!"* The warning is enough. John starts shooting and Jeb and father Harry wind up dead. Tom gives up.

Exhausted, John and David return to the Moore ranch, where they find Linnett waiting for them both with open arms and a warm, open heart.

At last Ladd had a film that rated some glowing reviews. A. H. Weiler in the *New York Times* wrote, "A genuinely sentimental but often moving melodrama. . . . Alan Ladd, who is not noted for explosive portrayals, is restrained but exceptionally expressive as the father. Mr. Ladd's 11-year-old son, David Ladd, contributes an astonishingly professional and sympathetic stint as his son . . . not only extremely likable but also projects movingly and with surprising naturalness and fidelity the helplessness of the mute."

Phillip Hartung in *The Commonweal* seconded that opinion: "Perhaps Alan Ladd was able to add tenderness to his usual stoic portrayal because his own son, David, plays the role of the mute boy, or perhaps some of David's touching portrayal rubs off on the father. In any case, they make a fine team."

For reasons not fully understood, this well-made film was not an overwhelming success, though it made a respectable showing ($1,500,000 at the box office). But for young David the film meant being in instant demand as a child star, and he was the only one to really prosper after making *The Proud Rebel*.

De Havilland and Ladd.

Doc (Kellaway) says goodbye to David (David Ladd) as Linett (deHavilland) takes the boy off to Minnesota for treatment.

229

The Badlanders

Arcola/MGM   (1958)

MetroColor

CinemaScope

Ladd with Ernest Borgnine, and Katy Jurado.

CREDITS

Director, Delmer Daves. *Producer*, Aaron Rosenber
Screenplay, Richard Collins. *From the novel* The Asph
Jungle, *by* W. R. Burnett. *Photography*, John Seitz; *E
itors*, William H. Webb, James Balotto. *Running tin
85 minutes.*

CAST

Peter Van Hoek, ALAN LADD; *John McBain*, ERNES
BORGNINE; *Anita*, KATY JURADO; *Ada Winto*
CLAIRE KELLY; *Lounsberry*, KENT SMITH; *Vincen*
NEHEMIAH PERSOFF; *Sample*, ROBERT EM
HARDT; *Comanche*, ANTHONY CARUSO; *Lesli*
ADAM WILLIAMS; *Warden*, FORD RAINEY; *Le*
JOHN DAY; *Marshal*, KARL SWENSON; *Jeff*, PAU
BAXLEY; *Pepe*, ROBERTO CONTRERAS

The Badlanders, Ladd's only starring film for MGM, wa
a western remake of MGM's modern crime classic *Tl
Asphalt Jungle*. John Huston's 1950 thriller, the grand
daddy of heist films, detailed the planning and executio
of a million-dollar jewel robbery. *The Badlanders* stick
close to the original's plotline, with Ladd replacing Sar
Jaffe as the mastermind and Ernest Borgnine taking ove
for Sterling Hayden as the strong-arm member of th
team.

Peter Van Hoek (Ladd), known as the Dutchman, i
counting the days until the end of his term on a chai
gang at the Yuma Territorial Prison. Once an exper
mining engineer in Prescott, Van Hoek had been cheated
out of his share of a gold mine when the mine's owner
Cyril Lounsberry (Smith), had him jailed on false thef
charges. The Dutchman has outlined a strategy for se
curing his quota of the gold but requires the services o
one of his fellow prisoners whose release is also imminent.
The burly John McBain (Borgnine) is another victim o
Lounsberry's chicanery, having had his farm swindled
away from him. His violent reaction to that swindle is
the cause of his being in prison. Now he wants only to
pick up the pieces of his ruined life, and yet he cannot
resist the Dutchman's talk of a partnership in a hundred-
thousand-dollar gold steal and revenge for his unjust
imprisonment.

Ladd, Borgnine.

Prisoners Van Hoek (Ladd) and McBain (Borgnine) appear before the prison board.

Dutchman knows of a rich offshoot from the principal vein of the Lounsberry Lisbon mine, a secret he has kept to himself, and he plans to reopen it. He figures he can bring two-hundred-thousand-dollars in ore from the abandoned shaft, and he is willing to sell it for half its worth—to Lounsberry, who is unaware the stolen gold will be taken from his own property.

Lounsberry is under the thumb of a wealthy wife, and once he possesses the Dutchman's stolen gold, he plans to run off to Europe with his girlfriend, Ada Winton (Kelly). Unknown to Lounsberry, the luscious Winton is bestowing her favors on a fascinating new tenant of the hotel where she is kept—the newly released Peter Van Hoek.

McBain, too, has found time for female diversion, but on a more serious level. Anita (Jurado) has fallen into a life of prostitution only because it is the only means of survival for a Mexican woman in Prescott. After meeting the kindly, respectful McBain, Anita resolves to

change her life, and together the two hope to forget their tarnished pasts.

But business must come first. Together with Vincente (Persoff), an old co-worker of Van Hoek's who can barely support his family on Lounsberry wages, the ex-convicts enter the mine in darkness and set explosives. The Dutchman's calculations prove correct—the dynamite reveals the gold.

McBain and Van Hoek have underestimated Lounsberry, however. Covering them with the help of a gun held by a corrupt lawman (Williams), Lounsberry prepares to steal their weighty cargo of gold when they deliver it. McBain attacks the henchman, and Lounsberry can only stand and gape as Van Hoek, McBain, and all the gold slip from his greedy grasp.

McBain is left in the loving care of Anita, and after dividing the gold, Van Hoek leaves town on the morning stage, taking the willing Ada Winton with him and making poetic justice complete.

With a cynical attitude rare in westerns (especially
1958) *The Badlanders* works surprisingly well. Reunit
with director Delmer Daves, the star delivers one of h
more compelling performances of this later stage of h
career. Although the character lost some of its ecce
tricity in the translation to western lead, Ladd still h
a meatier part than those offered by his more convention
heroes and seems more relaxed as the clever, sympathe
robber than as a deadly do-gooder. Ladd also seems mc
comfortable with his lighthearted love interest, the sau
flirtation with Claire Kelly contrasting nicely with t
touching romantic scenes between Borgnine and Jurad
(The year following the film's release, Borgnine and Ju
ado began a marriage that lasted until 1964.)

The Badlanders was greeted with some of the sar
critical reactions given its predecessor: praised by sor
for its nimble execution, condemned by others for gl
rifying its less-than-saintly protagonists. The film d
not begin to enjoy the same prominence as the sour
film, *The Asphalt Jungle*. Indeed, few guessed it was
remake.

Adam Williams, Ladd, Robert Emhardt.

The Man in the Net

Mirisch-Jaguar/United Artists   (1959)

CREDITS

Director, Michael Curtiz. *Producer*, Walter Mirisch. *Screenplay*, Reginald Rose. *Based on the novel* Man in a Net, *by* Patrick Quentin. *Photography*, John Seitz. *Music*, Hans J. Salter. *Editor*, Harold La Velle. *Running time, 96 minutes.*

CAST

John Hamilton, ALAN LADD; *Linda Hamilton*, CAROLYN JONES; *Vickie Carey*, DIANE BREWSTER; *Brad Carey*, JOHN LUPTON; *Steve Ritter*, CHARLES McGRAW; *Gordon Moreland*, TOM HELMORE; *Roz Moreland*, BETTY LOU HOLLAND; *Mr. Carey*, JOHN ALEXANDER; *Captain Green*, EDWARD BINNS; *Mrs. Carey*, KATHRYN GIVNEY; *Emily Jones*, BARBARA BEAIRD; *Angel Jones*, SUSAN GORDON; *Timmie Moreland*, CHARLES HERBERT; *Buck Ritter*, MIKE McGREEVY; *Leroy*, STEVEN PERRY; *Alonzo*, ALVIN CHILDRESS; *Charles Rains*, DOUGLAS EVANS; *Mrs. Jones*, NATALIE MASTERSON; *State Trooper*, PAT MILLER

As artist John Hamilton.

Little more than a year after founding their own company, the Mirisch Brothers were well on the way toward becoming one of the more important independent production outfits in Hollywood. Their ambitious schedule for 1959 included a mystery novel, *Man in a Net*, by Patrick Quentin, the story of a man falsely accused of his wife's murder who must evade his pursuers until he can track down the real killer.

Any similarity between this and Ladd's 1946 hit *The Blue Dahlia* ends there. Obviously made on the cheap, *The Man in the Net* shows a tired, dispirited Ladd as an ordinary man fighting to escape a web of prejudice and circumstantial evidence. This melodrama of survival suited Ladd's physical appearance better than his usual fifties guise of brash adventurer, but an inadequate script and a sluggish performance by Ladd make it pretty unconvincing stuff.

The movie was filmed in New England and set in a small suburban community whose quiet exterior conceals hidden emotions and secret vices à la *Peyton Place*. Aspiring artist John Hamilton (Ladd) likes to watch the village children play and to try to capture their innocent charm on canvas. The easy affection between the painter and his subjects is shared most closely with the oldest, Emily (Beaird), who is sensitive enough to sense that

23

With Susan Gordon.

Linda (Jones) argues that John should return to his job in New York City.

John's adult relationships are not so amiable. John, h sleek, pretty wife, and his paintings are all subjects f town gossip—and John has become something of a r cluse to avoid such scrutiny.

The reason for his isolation is wife Linda (Jones), dipsomaniac with a mental problem who hates living the bucolic farm setting. She wants John to return his lucrative former position with a slick New Yor advertising firm, but John knows that the pressures Linda's hectic big-city lifestyle caused her alcoholism an a past nervous breakdown. Their squabbles make on wonder how two such mismatched types ever got to gether. Linda is a pathological liar and John has manage to cover up her erratic behavior, as well as her drinking from prying neighborly eyes, but she is always threat ening to break loose. At the end of his rope, John goe to New York to see a doctor, a psychiatrist friend wh may be able to help her.

When he returns he finds the house turned upside down, his paintings all slashed, and Linda missing. I looks very much like foul play, and he knows his forme seclusion is working against him. When the evidenc piles up against him, he has no one to turn to, and th angry townspeople set out to hunt him down.

Surprisingly, he does have friends after all—the chil dren. Emily sees him fleeing through the woods, and she leads him to a secret cave and then enlists the ai of all her young friends. They intend to search for th truth behind Linda's disappearance—the whole mystery becomes a game to them. With the children's help, John is able to learn the identity of the real killer and clea himself.

Ironically, at the same time that *The Man in the Ne* was playing the lower half of double bills, Paramoun was collecting top dollar on a national rerelease of *Shane*. This could only have made more conspicuous the shabby quality of the star's latest vehicle. If there is any con solation, it is that few people saw *The Man in the Net.*

The artist finds his paintings ruined.

With Frankie Avalon, Jeanne Crain, and Gilbert Roland.

Guns of the Timberland
Jaguar/Warner Bros.   (1960)   Technicolor

CREDITS

Director, Robert D. Webb. *Producer,* Aaron Spelling. *Associate Producer,* George C. Bertholon. *Screenplay,* Joseph Petracca, Aaron Spelling. *Based on the novel by* Louis L'Amour. *Photography,* John Seitz. *Music,* David Buttolph. *Songs,* "Gee Whiz Willikers Golly Gee," "The Faithful Kind," by Mack David and Jerry Livingston, "Cry Timber," by Sy Miller. *Sound,* Francis M. Stahl. *Art Director,* John Beckman. *Editor,* Tom McAdoo. *Running time, 91 minutes.*

CAST

Jim Hadley, ALAN LADD; *Laura Riley,* JEANNE CRAIN; *Monty Welker,* GILBERT ROLAND; *Bert Harvey,* FRANKIE AVALON; *Clay Bell,* LYLE BETTGER; *Blackie,* NOAH BEERY, JR.; *Aunt Sarah,* VERNA FELTON; *Jane Peterson,* ALANA LADD; *Sheriff Taylor,* REGIS TOOMEY; *Vince,* JOHNNY SEVEN; *Amos Stearnes,* GEORGE SELK; *Bill Burroughs,* PAUL E. BURNS; *Judd,* GEORGE J. LEWIS; *Logger,* HENRY KULKY

Guns of the Timberland was probably the worst film Alan Ladd ever made.

Ladd is cast as Jim Hadley, who, with his crew of lumberjacks, is looking for a new forest to cut. But Hadley and crew soon find that they will have to fight for their next load of wood. Inhabitants of the valley town of Deep Wells, led by Laura Riley (Crain), realize that without the natural protection provided by the surrounding woodlands, their ranches and homes would be buried by mudslides during the first heavy rains.

Although the obligatory spark of romance lights up between Hadley and Riley (as the lady rancher is called) the two remain at cross purposes. The efforts of the townspeople to force the intruders to move on begin with denials of horses and supplies and escalate to the dynamiting of the logging road. Hadley, bracing himself for a fight, still insists on legal means to reach the lumber. But his hotheaded partner, Monty Welker (Roland), favors a more direct approach.

The fast friendship between the two loggers is strained to the breaking point when Monty decides to open the road by the same method that closed it: dynamite. This causes a fire, and when Riley's young ward Bert (Avalon) is caught in the blast and left near death, Jim knows it is time to pull up stakes: "We came here to cut down trees, not kids." Before he can leave to seek a less-guarded forest, Jim is forced into a final gunfight by the now hysterical Monty, who dies asking his partner's forgiveness. Jim's heavy heart as he boards the train out of town is lightened somewhat when the lumbermen are joined by Laura, who is leaving her ranch behind for a future in the woods as Mrs. Jim Hadley.

The dissipation in Ladd's appearance by this point in his career made obvious his increasing dependency on alcohol. His puffy, waxen face projects only exhaustion, which is matched by his listless performance.

Nor does anyone else in the cast emerge from this sad business with any dignity. Presumably brought in to boost the box office was singer Frankie Avalon in his film debut. The teen idol's musical numbers are among the more ludicrous moments in an already sorry film. As Avalon's love interest, Alana Ladd is cute but makes no great impression as an actress.

"Ron" in *Variety* was as kind as possible in reviewing Ladd's fumbling performance, noting simply that the star "has looked better, and he's had better roles than this." Most other reviewers chose to ignore the film completely. Audiences did the same, and *Guns of the Timberland* ended Alan Ladd's tenure at Warner Bros. on a depressing note.

Frankie Avalon with Alana and Alan.

Towler (Poitier), Cotton (Darren), and Kincaid (Ladd) keep watch on the hill.

All the Young Men

Hall Bartlett-Jaguar/Columbia   (1960)

CREDITS

Director, Producer, Screenplay, Hall Bartlett. *Photography,* Daniel Fapp. *Music,* George Duning. *Art Director,* Carl Anderson. *Assistant Director,* Lee Lukather. *Editor,* Al Clark. *Running time, 86 minutes.*

CAST

Kincaid, ALAN LADD; *Towler,* SIDNEY POITIER; *Cotton,* JAMES DARREN; *Wade,* GLENN CORBETT; *Crane,* MORT SAHL; *Maya,* ANA ST. CLAIR; *Bracken,* PAUL RICHARDS; *Casey,* DICK DAVALOS; *Dean,* LEE KINSOLVING; *Jackson,* JOE GALLISON; *Lazitech,* PAUL BAXLEY; *Torgil,* INGEMAR JOHANSSON; *Lieutenant,* CHARLES QUINLIVAN; *Cho,* MICHAEL DAVIS; *Hunter,* MARIO ALCALDE; *Korean woman,* MARIA TSIEN

After his exit from Warner Bros., Alan Ladd began the final, freelance phase of his movie career with a picture for Columbia that promised to deal in a realistic way with the important problem of racial prejudice and its effect on men at war.

All the Young Men falls far short of its professed goal. The setting is somewhere near Wonsan, Korea, in the winter of 1951. A marine platoon has been sent to take over a certain farmhouse overlooking a pass that the advancing Third Battalion must cross. The marines are not alone in realizing the importance of this area—it is filled with Chinese soldiers waiting for the American troops.

After a brief, murderous ambush, only eleven of the original thirty-five marines are alive. One of the casualties is the platoon's lieutenant, who lives long enough to pass on his command to the ranking survivor, Sergeant

Towler momentarily loses control.

With Sidney Poitier and Paul Richards.

Towler (Poitier). The decision is a shock to the rest of the men and Towler as well, all of whom feel the command should have gone to the group's only professional soldier, the experienced Kincaid (Ladd). Even though Kincaid had recently lost his master sergeant's stripes, the men have more faith in his leadership than in that of Towler who is a newcomer—and a black.

Towler knows the men's acceptance rests solely with Kincaid and tries to enlist his support. But the veteran, allowing his concern for his men to cloud his judgment, sees Towler as a martinet, a "black man with an ax to grind." Towler, though, realizes the fate of their small band is unimportant weighed against the lives of a thousand others.

All bitterness between the two men disappears when they must work together to destroy an approaching Chinese tank. The newfound unity between the former antagonists becomes physical when Kincaid, whose leg requires amputation after being crushed in the tank tread, receives the necessary blood transfusion from Towler.

Even as the two recuperate from the operation, Towler orders the rest of the platoon to retreat from the oncoming enemy forces. As Towler and Kincaid prepare to face the final assault together, an additional battle noise greets their ears: the welcome roar of fire from the U.S. Third Battalion.

Despite Ladd's top billing, Sidney Poitier is obviously the star, a fact that was reportedly cold comfort to Poitier. Burdened at the time with the responsibility of representing an entire race on movie screens, Poitier put aside his low opinion of the material to act with reasonable conviction in his deliberate style. Ladd, unfortunately, merely gives a monotonous recital of his stereotyped dialogue. By this time Ladd was probably incapable of bringing the Kincaid character to life even in a decent film, and here he seems the opposite of the reliable soldier, behaving more out of jealousy than any real concern for his men.

Time magazine claimed that former heavyweight champ Johansson's "two basic expressions (faintly amused and faintly serious) beat Actor Ladd's range by one." Arthur Knight, in *Saturday Review*, may have been more objective: "It is not merely that the acting is one-dimensional; so is the basic conception of the roles."

Despite its numerous faults, the film opened to better receipts than Ladd's other recent vehicles. There could be no mistaking the reason, however—the growing box-office appeal of up-and-coming star Sidney Poitier.

With Wade (Corbett), Maya (St. Clair), Cotton (Darren), and Bracken (Richards) looking on, Kincaid gets a life-saving transfusion from Towler.

One Foot in Hell

20th Century-Fox (1960)
DeLuxe Color
CinemaScope

CREDITS

Director, James B. Clark. *Producer,* Sydney Boehm. *Screenplay,* Aaron Spelling, Sydney Boehm, *based on a story by* Aaron Spelling. *Music,* Dominic Frontiere. *Photography,* William C. Mellor. *Assistant Director,* Arthur Lueker. *Art Directors,* Duncan Cramer, Leland Fuller. *Editor,* Eda Warren. *Running time, 90 minutes.*

CAST

Mitch Barrett, ALAN LADD; *Dan Keats,* DON MURRAY; *Harry Ivers,* DAN O'HERLIHY; *Julie Reynolds,* DOLORES MICHAELS; *Stu Christian,* BARRY COE; *Doc Seltzer,* LARRY GATES; *Sheriff Olson,* KARL SWENSON; *Sam Giller,* JOHN ALEXANDER; *Ellie Barrett,* RACHEL STEPHENS; *George Caldwell,* HENRY NORELL; *Mark Dobbs,* HARRY CARTER; *Nellie,* ANN MORRISS

One Foot in Hell was based on a television play Aaron Spelling had written with Martin Manulis and John Frankenheimer, which had seen duty as a *Playhouse 90* episode in 1957, featuring Sterling Hayden and Spelling's wife at the time, Carolyn Jones. It was a project better suited to the small screen. The film opens with Mitch Barrett (Ladd) desperately urging his team of horses toward the welcome sight of Blue Springs, Arizona. In the wagon is Mitch's ailing, pregnant wife, Ellie (Stephens), and Blue Springs is the first sign of civilization after a long journey. The town, which had seemed a godsend, soon turns into a nightmare for the Barretts as Mitch seeks help for his wife.

Thanks to a hostile, distrustful reception from the local hotel manager (Norell), the storekeeper (Alexander), and the town's sheriff (Swenson), Mitch is unable to save either Ellie or their unborn child. After burying his wife in this hated town, Mitch prepares to move on. But when the shamed townspeople offer him a job by way of retribution (and as sop to their collective conscience) Mitch accepts—not out of gratitude for their hypocrisy, but rather to carry out a vow of revenge.

And Mitch knows how to hate. As deputy sheriff, he soon becomes a respected member of the community. No one doubts his story when he reports the sheriff's death in a skirmish with outlaws, and Mitch is the

Mitch Barrett (Ladd) cannot get help from the storekeeper (Alexander).

Mitch is sworn in as the sheriff of Blue Springs.

unanimous choice as replacement. As Blue Springs' sheriff, Mitch is able to form his plan in earnest, hiring drunken ex-Confederate Dan Keats (Murray), dandified but deadly gambler Harry Ivers (O'Herlihy), and cold-blooded traveling gunman Stu Christian (Coe) to help exact his vengeance. Completing the unsavory group is Julie Reynolds (Michaels), a saloon floozie who will pose as Mitch's new wife.

While the couple are supposedly on their honeymoon, Mitch is actually outlining plans for a bank robbery to be pulled by Christian and Ivers, guided by diagrams drawn by artist Keats. The two bring off the heist smoothly, pausing long enough to visit the men who had originally "welcomed" the Barretts into town and who now pay with their lives for their earlier lack of compassion.

Both robbers head for their prearranged hideouts while Mitch decoys the posse. But the sheriff has no notion of splitting the loot, and he leads his men straight to the fugitives, killing them both. Next, to cover his tracks, Mitch plans the same fate for Julie and a sober Dan, who have by now struck up a tender romance of their own and no longer care about the robbery. In desperation Julie faces Mitch and offers to replace his dead wife if he will spare Dan, but this only enrages Mitch. Dan takes advantage of the deranged man's hysteria to jump him, and in the ensuing struggle Mitch is killed. Julie and Dan are free to forget their soiled pasts and try for a future together.

Variety gave *One Foot in Hell* a surprisingly good review, praising "a gripping, powerful piece of Western storytelling" and rating Ladd's performance "an intense, interesting one." But the *New York Times'* evaluation, by Howard Thompson, of the film as a "soured, corny mishmash" was apparently shared by most moviegoers, who steered clear of the few theaters where *One Foot in Hell* was shown.

As Horatio, Ladd fights the enemy.

Duel of Champions (Horatio)

Lux Film–Tiberia Film/Medallion   (1961)
Eastman Color   Totalscope

CREDITS

Directors, Terence Young, Ferdinando Baldi. *Producer*, Angelo Ferrara. *Screenplay*, Carlo Lizzani, Ennio De Concini, Giuliano Montaldo. *Story*, Luciano Vincensoni. *Photography*, Amerigo Gengarelli. *Music*, Angelo Francesco Lavagnino. *Art director*, Giulio Bongini. *Costumes*, Mario Girosi. *Editor*, Renzo Lucidi. *Running time, 93 minutes.*

CAST

Horatio, ALAN LADD; *Marcia*, FRANCA BETTOJA; *Curazio*, FRANCO FABRIZI; *King of Rome*, ROBERT KEITH; *Elio*, LUCIANO MARIN; *Marcus*, JACQUES SERNAS; *King of Alba*, ANDREA AURELI; *Caio*, MINO DORO; *Warrior of Alba*, OSVALDO RUGGERI; *Horatia*, JACQUELINE DERVAL; *Warrior of Alba*, PIERO PALMERI; *Grand Priest*, UMBERTO RAHO; *Sabinus*, ALFREDO VARELLI; *Scilla*, ALANA LADD

Early in 1961, Alan Ladd signed for the starring role in something to be called *Orazi e Curiazi*, filmed in Italy. Ladd's usual discomfort with unfamiliar surroundings was aggravated in this case by the failure of Tiberia Films to deliver his agreed-upon salary, and in the middle of filming the producers found themselves without a star. Ladd refused to report to work until a new investor, another Italian company called Lux Films, bought into the project and guaranteed his paycheck. Then shooting in Italy and Yugoslavia resumed and dragged to a close. The final result was scarcely worth the effort.

The film's story and setting are as foreign to Alan Ladd as were the locations. Ancient Rome, before it became a great empire, is the scene of continual warfare between the Roamns and the people of neighboring Alba. The people of Rome and Alba, weary of the pestilence and famine brought on by seven years of war, are eager for peace. The kings of both cities, Lucius of Rome (Keith) and Nezio of Alba (Aureli), agree in principle to ending the strife but differ over which city shall rule. The kings visit a high priestess and place the question in the hands of the gods, who submit an impartial edict: Each city is to choose three brothers as its champions, and whichever side can claim the survivors of their duel to the death will be the winner.

Alba has three skilled warriors in the house of Curiazi. The only Romans who can match them are Marcus (Sernas), Elio (Marin), and their older brother, Orazio (Ladd), the great Roman hero who has renounced Rome and le[ft] for the Tiberian mountains. Marcus rides to the hills b[ut] is unable to persuade his brother to return, althoug[h] Princess Marcia (Bettoja) is more successful.

The ritual begins. Marcus and then Elio are slain. Orazio judges the odds and gallops off toward the neare[st] forest. Ready to take charge, the Albans are reminde[d] that all three brothers on one side must die before t[he] other side can claim victory. The three Alban warrio[rs] set off into the forest in pursuit, but once there reali[ze] they are not the hunters, but the prey. Stalking the[m] one by one, Orazio emerges a new champion.

Now that a just peace has been won, the Roma[n] conqueror becomes a citizen of Alba to ensure that the[ ] peoples will be truly joined. Joining Orazio as he rid[es] off into the east is the luscious princess Marcia.

Orazi e Curiazi is typical of its breed, but the st[ep] from cheap American pictures to a cheap foreign pictu[re] is definitely down. And Ladd's presence does little [to] grace the film. Apparently he had forgotten the lesso[n] taught by *The Black Knight*—that whatever his skills [as] an actor, he was simply not capable of the classical d[e] livery required by a swashbuckling costume role.

Lux Films tried to find a U.S. distributor for *Duel [of] Champions*, but there were no takers. The property l[ay] dormant until 1964, when the minor-league Medallio[n] Pictures announced it for spring release. After a very fe[w] bookings, the film vanished from theaters—a blessi[ng] for Ladd.

13 West Street
Ladd Enterprises/Columbia   (1962)

CREDITS

Director, Philip Leacock. *Producer,* William Bloom.
Screenplay, Bernard C. Schoenfeld, Robert Presnell, Jr..
From the novel The Tiger Among us, *by* Leigh Brackett.
Photography, Charles Lawton, Jr. *Music,* George Duning.
Art Director, Walter Holscher. *Editor,* Al Clark. *Running
Time, 80 minutes.*

CAST

Walt Sherill, ALAN LADD; *Detective Sergeant Koleski,*
ROD STEIGER; *Chuck Landry,* MICHAEL CALLAN;
Tracey Sherill, DOLORES DORN; *Paul Logan,* KEN-
NETH McKENNA; *Mrs. Landry,* MARGARET HAYES;
Finney, STANLEY ADAMS; *Everett,* CHRIS ROBIN-
SON; *Mrs. Quinn,* JEANNE COOPER; *Bill,* ARNOLD
MERRITT; *Tommy,* MARK SLADE; *Joe Bradford,*
HENRY BECKMAN; *Noddy,* CLEGG HOYT; *Jack,*
JORDAN GERLER; *Doctor,* ROBERT CLEAVES; *Ne-
gro,* BERNIE HAMILTON; *Mexican,* PEPE HERN; *Mr.
Johnson,* FRANK GERSTLE; *Baldwin,* TED KNIGHT

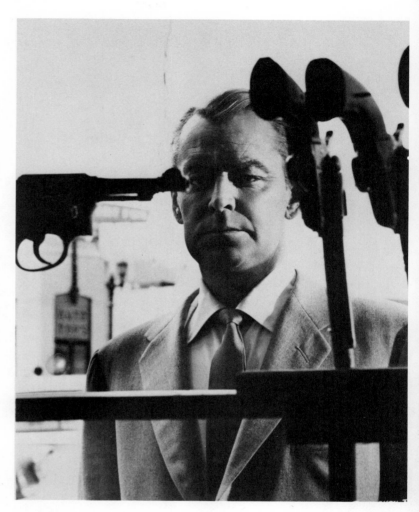

For his last starring vehicle, Alan Ladd returned to his
home field—both geographically and cinematically. *13
West Street* is set in the modern world of dark city streets
and sudden violence where Ladd made his first mark
twenty years earlier.

Ladd plays Walt Sherill, a comfortably middle-class
citizen with a happy marriage, a good job, and a quiet
suburban home life. Heading for home after an unusually
long day at the office, Sherill finds himself out of gas
and resigns himself to a hike to the nearest station. But
he never reaches it. His orderly world is shattered when,
alone on the dark street, he becomes the target for a
brutal beating by a group of teenaged boys he has never
seen before.

Walt's physical wounds heal quickly, but the deeper
scars left by his ordeal refuse to fade. He finds that every
youth is now a potential threat and every waking hour
a painful reminder of the constant danger lurking in the
apparently placid environment. For Walt Sherill there
can be no rest until his assailants are caught and punished.

Sergeant Koleski (Steiger), the Juvenile Division detective assigned to the case, soon discovers an extra problem on his hands: Sherill has no intention of waiting for

Detective Sergeant Koleski (Steiger) asks Walt to lay off the case.

Walt Sherill (Ladd) is waylaid by a group of young hoods (Chris Robinson, Mark Slade, and Michael Callan).

results from an official investigation and has begun so reckless detecting on his own.

Neither the authorities nor the victim is able to tu up a concrete lead. But word of the inquiries has reach the teens' leader. Chuck Landry (Callan), the spoiled s of a rich socialite, is more upset by the threat to power and prestige than by any fear of arrest.

The war of nerves that develops between Landry a Sherill escalates until it has claimed two lives. The m galomaniac Chuck finally decides on a murderous inv sion of his adversary's home, but when he arrives Wa is out; ironically, he is out trailing Chuck. But o person is at home—Walt's wife (Dorn). Chuck is pr paring to amuse himself with his prey's beautiful, te rified spouse, when he is surprised by the opportu arrival of the incensed Sherill. On the verge of killir the boy with his bare hands, Walt realizes that he h become as consumed by hatred as the young hoodlum had been the night they left him bleeding in the stree Contritely, Walt turns Chuck over to Koleski, leavin the law to deal with him.

13 West Street's tightly knit eighty minutes punctuat its mounting suspense with brief but savage scenes. Th screenplay avoids belaboring the point that the juveni offenders are obviously from the "right" section of s ciety. Instead it aims at its wider theme: that later violence is inherent in us all.

Ladd had one of his better roles in *13 West Street*, bu it came too late in his waning career. His performanc does show more effort than had been evident in any his recent work, but the sharp, no-nonsense voice gone, replaced by a weary, muddled reading. The "tight lipped violence" that had for so long been second natur to Ladd is the very element necessary to, yet missin, from, this final starring performance.

Whatever the reason, with its failure to stir up eithe business or attention, *13 West Street* became the addres at which Alan Ladd threw in the towel.

The Carpetbaggers

Embassy/Paramount   (1964)
Technicolor
Panavision

CREDITS

Director, Edward Dmytryk. *Producer*, Joseph E. Levine. *Screenplay*, John Michael Hayes, *based on the novel by* Harold Robbins. *Photography*, Joseph MacDonald. *Music*, Elmer Bernstein. *Art Directors*, Hal Pereira, Walter Tyler. *Process Photography*, Farciot Edouart. *Special effects*, Paul K. Lerpae. *Editor*, Frank Bracht. *Costume Designer*, Edith Head. *Running time, 150 minutes.*

CAST

Jonas Cord, Jr., GEORGE PEPPARD; *Nevada Smith*, ALAN LADD; *Dan Pierce*, ROBERT CUMMINGS; *Jennie Denton*, MARTHA HYER; *Monica Winthrop*, ELIZABETH ASHLEY; *Bernard B. Norman*, MARTIN BALSAM; *McAllister*, LEW AYRES; *Rina Marlowe*, CARROLL BAKER; *Buzz Dalton*, RALPH TAEGER; *Jedediah*, ARCHIE MOORE; *Jonas Cord, Sr.*, LEIF ERICKSON; *David Woolf*, TOM LOWELL; *Morrissey*, ARTHUR FRANZ; *Amos Winthrop*, TOM TULLY; *Prostitute*, AUDREY TOTTER; *Moroni*, ANTHONY WARDE; *Ed Ellis*, JOHN CONTE; *Denby*, CHARLES LANE; *Gambler*, DONALD DIAMOND; *Doctor*, VAUGHN TAYLOR; *Cynthia Randall*, FRANCESCA BELLINI; *Starlet*, LYNN BORDEN; *JoAnn Cord*, VICTORIA JEAN; *Moroni's secretary*, LISA SEAGRAM; *Woman reporter*, ANN DORAN; *French nurse*, GLADYS HOLLAND; *Theater manager*, TONY REGAN; *Sound man*, DONALD BARRY; *Assistant director*, PETER DURYEA; *Bellhop*, FRANKIE DARRO

Jonas Cord, the central character in Harold Robbins's *The Carpetbaggers,* is a multi-millionaire with interests in aircraft, women, movie production, international finance, women, and more women, who eventually becomes a recluse. Obviously, any resemblance between Robbins's Cord and any famous real-life personality was more than coincidental.

Nevada Smith (Ladd) was a former outlaw, now an aging confidant to the dynamic young tycoon Jonas Cord, Jr.—not a bad part, really, though Ladd was playing a supporting role for the first time since *This Gun for Hire.* It had been more than a year since Ladd had made a picture and much longer than that since he had been in a hit. Yet despite this, Ladd was able to secure second billing.

With Carroll Baker

Jonas Cord, Jr. (Peppard), gives old friend Nevada Smith (Ladd) a damaging dossier.

The *Carpetbaggers* opens in 1925, with an introductory narration to fill you in about the "fictional and fabulous" Jonas Cord, Jr. Cord's disposition is quickly established. Told of his father's death, Jonas wastes little time planning the expansion of his inherited explosives factory and making a play for his departed dad's young blond widow, Rina (Baker).

And so it goes throughout the film, as Jonas Cord bulldozes his way to a fortune, buying up a movie studio, turning his curvy blond former stepmother into a sex symbol and his middle-aged mentor Nevada Smith (Ladd) into a Tom Mix–like cowboy star, then picking up with a blond call girl (Hyer) who reminds him of Rina, who wouldn't have him, and replacing Rina with the call girl as the hottest sex symbol. And he meets and marries the daughter (Ashley) of an old business employee and later dumps her in favor of freedom and power. Jonas is callously insensitive to the effects his insatiable financial and sexual appetites have on others. At one point, Baker sums up the Cord personality: "You dirty, filthy, perverted monster! You're the meanest, cruelest, most loathsome thing I've ever met!"

Peppard sneered his way through the part with equal subtlety. Actually, nothing is subtle—partly because of some flamboyant directing by Edward Dmytryk (who had directed Ladd in *Her First Romance* in 1940) and partly because of the lurid material. Carroll Baker (even

Nevada checks in at Central Casting.

Dan Pierce (Cummings) and Nevada look at the rushes.

Nevada and Rina are married as Pierce and Jonas look on.

247

Jonas makes a movie of Nevada's past—starring Nevada. With Francesca Bellini.

without the nude scene, which was shown only in Europe) is the most prominent of Cord's victims. Baker seems to have difficulty making sense of her Rina character, and as the reviewer for *Time* noted, she "seems uncertain about which actress, living or dead, she's not supposed to resemble."

Alan Ladd's farewell movie appearance cannot be called an unqualified personal triumph, but neither is it the embarrassment of some of his more recent vehicles. He had lost some weight and seemed more in shape than he had recently, but time had taken a heavy toll.

Whatever his appearance, Ladd manages to create a reasonably convincing portrait of a square dealer among a pack of cutthroats and his natural tranquility worked well against the surrounding hysteria. He is the only character you can truly admire. He also has the honor of deflating the power-mad Cord, in one of the most viciously realistic fights in Ladd's long tally of screen brawls. These final scenes are his strongest in the picture and allow Ladd a dignified last bow.

Alan Ladd might conceivably have gone on to a successful second career as a character lead; possibly, with the responsibility of maintaining a star image removed, he could have found parts that would have gained him the critical approval so long denied him.

But this was not to be. By the time *The Carpetbaggers* reached theaters, Alan Ladd was dead.

With Carroll Baker

OTHER LADD APPEARANCES

The brochure that accompanied the short commercial-informational film Meat and Romance, *in which Ladd played a young husband, Bill, who learns to carve a good roast.*

SHORTS, COMMERCIAL FILMS

Blame It On Love, a commercial short for the Hotpoint company. Ladd had a small role in this commercial musical promotion. 1940

Unfinished Rainbows, the story of Charles Martin Hall, the scientist who learned how to produce aluminum. Ladd played Hall, and Janet Shaw played his sister. Aluminum Company of America. 1940

American Portrait, a short film concerning insurance. Ladd played a youth and a senior citizen, complete with white hair and moustache. Mary Brodel (Joan Leslie's sister) was his co-star. 1940

Meat and Romance, an instructive short on how to buy, cook, and carve meat. Ladd played a young newlywed, Bill. National Live Stock and Meat Board and The Bureau of Home Economics. 1940

Soundie #1125, I Look At You, a Juke Box musical short in which Ladd sang the title song accompanied by Rita Rio (Dona Drake) and her all-girl orchestra. (Sound and visual, 10¢.) 1941

GOVERNMENT SHORTS

Letter From A Friend, an army morale-booster short. 1943

Hollywood In Uniform, an army morale-booster short. 1943

Skirmish On The Homefront, an army morale-booster short. 1944

THEATER SHORT

Eyes of Hollywood, an all-star short. 1949

MOVIE GUEST APPEARANCES

y **Favorite Brunette,** an unbilled cameo in this Bob
Hope comedy film. 1947

A Cry In the Night, a brief voice-over as narrator of
this Ladd-Jaguar Production, which starred Natalie
Wood, Edmond O'Brien, Brian Donlevy, and Raymond Burr. 1956

Radio

In the late thirties, Alan Ladd worked on local Los
Angeles radio shows and some network radio shows,
but these were not starring roles and have been lost
into the airwaves. After his rise to stardom with
This Gun for Hire, however, he was a popular guest
on those programs which dramatized current films,
such as *Lux Radio Theatre* and *Screen Guild Players.*
He also did starring roles on *Suspense,* several guest
appearances, and in 1948 he starred in his own
syndicated show, *Box 13.* Though this list cannot
be complete, here are the shows he was known to
have done.

Ladd and Bob Hope in My Favorite Brunette.

LUX RADIO THEATRE

This Gun for Hire (January 25, 1943, CBS) with
Joan Blondell
China (November 22, 1943, CBS) with Loretta
Young and Bill Bendix
Casablanca (January 24, 1944, CBS) with Hedy
Lamarr and John Loder
Coney Island (April 17, 1944, CBS) with Dorothy
Lamour
Disputed Passage (March 5, 1945, CBS) with
Dorothy Lamour
And Now Tomorrow (May 21, 1945, CBS) with
Loretta Young
Salty O'Rourke (November 26, 1945, CBS) with
Marjorie Reynolds and William Demarest
Whistle Stop (April 15, 1946, CBS) with Evelyn
Keyes
O.S.S. (November 18, 1946, CBS) with Veronica
Lake

Two Years before the Mast (September 22, 1947,
CBS) with Howard da Silva, Macdonald Carey, and
Wanda Hendrix
Shane (February 22, 1955, CBS) with Van Heflin

LADY ESTHER SCREEN GUILD
PLAYERS

Lucky Jordan (January 31, 1944, CBS) with Helen
Walker, Marjorie Main
This Gun for Hire (April 2, 1945, CBS) with
Veronica Lake
The Glass Key (July 22, 1946, CBS)
The Blue Dahlia (April 21, 1949, CBS) with Ve-
ronica Lake

SCREEN DIRECTORS PLAYHOUSE

Saigon (July 29, 1949, NBC) with Veronica Lake
Whispering Smith (September 16, 1949, NBC)
Chicago Deadline (March 24, 1950, NBC)
Take a Letter, Darling (February 1, 1951, NBC)
with Rosalind Russell and Bob Hope
Lucky Jordan (February 8, 1951, NBC)
Beyond Glory (May 31, 1951, NBC)

SUSPENSE

The Defense Rests
A Killing in Abilene (December 14, 1950, CBS)
Motive for Murder
One Way Ride to Nowhere

BOX 13

(Syndicated by Alan Ladd Productions 1948/49.)
Ladd played Dan Halliday, a writer who advertises
for trouble.

GUEST APPEARANCES

Alan Ladd appeared as a guest on a number of shows
including *The Kate Smith Hour* (1942), *The Bob Hope
Show* (1943), *The Rudy Vallee Show* (1946), *The Milton
Berle Show*, and *The Abbott and Costello Show*. He was
also interviewed several times by such columnists
as Louella Parsons.

...ica Lake and Ladd doing a Lux ... Theatre broadcast on CBS.

TELEVISION APPEARANCES

...an Ladd did just three television performances, ... on *General Electric Theatre*, a half hour anthology ...w.

...E GENERAL ELECTRIC THEATRE

...mmitted (December 5, 1954)

...dd plays a writer in search of ideas who runs into ...venture and exciting action when he advertises for ...uble.

...rewell to Kennedy (November 12, 1955)

...dd plays a young policeman wbo sees his superior ...cer (and father of his fiancée) take a bribe and ...own moral dilemma leads to an investigation for ...rder.

...ent Ambush (January 26, 1958)

...dd plays a frontier sheriff who is losing his hear-...

Opposite: With Marjorie Reynolds, Cecil B. De Mille, Red Skelton, Jack Benny. (Bottom) Two Years Before the Mast on radio with Macdonald Carey, Howard Da Silva and Wanda Hendrix.